A Mother's Steps

Family Tree of My Mother: Ruth S. Lessler

Michael Aaron Lessler
(1848-1912)
married
Sarah Marsh
(1848-1920)

Louis Kurland
(1845-1917)
married
Sivia Ruchel Gamzon
(1843-1910)

Isaac Joseph (later Joseph)
Lessler (1872–1933)

Channah* (Annie)
Kurland (1875–1925)

[Married in 1895]

Surviving Lessler Children (birth dates)**

Celia (March 10, 1896)
Simon (April 2 or June 18, 1897)
Betty (June 14, 1898)
Hyman (High) (September 15, 1899)
Esther (March 3, 1901)
Robert (Bob) (March 7, 1902)
David (Davey) (February 24, 1904)
Dorothy (Dotty) (April 17, 1906)
Jules (December 12, 1908)

Miriam (Mim) (June 29, 1910)
Ruth (April 4, 1912)
Mildred (June 20, 1914)

My First Cousins

Celia's Children
Mitchell

Shirley

Elaine

Simon's Children
Abby

Arlene (Cissy)

Carol

Betty's Children
Frances

Muriel

Doris

Ann

Margerie (Margie)

Hyman's (High) Children
Richard

Kenneth

James

Ronald David

Rhett

Esther's Children
Jerome (Jerry)

Arthur

Robert's (Bob) Children

Alan

Gloria

David's (Davey) Children
Adrienne
Stanley

Dorothy's (Dotty) Children
Anne Lee
Joel
Judith

Jules' Children
Ruth
Paul

Miriam's (Mim) Children
Michael
Robert
Richard

Ruth's Children
Mark
Deanna (Didi)

Mildred's Children
Martin

---

* Also referred to as Hannah.
** I have given an exact date of birth when I had this information.

It will be obvious from its very first pages that this book is dedicated to the person it is about, my mother, Ruth.

It would not have been possible however, without the help of her granddaughter, Ruth Syvia Mirsky. My daughter was tireless in checking this text. I also leaned on my son, Israel, who encouraged me to begin my ventures in book publishing. My wife, Inger Grytting, scanned all the photographs and constantly advised me, taking time away from her own career. I can't remember when I first started collecting materials—the dreams about my mother began after her death in 1968. A family meeting at a hotel in Westchester at the end of the 1980s organized by my two cousins, Robert Pozen and Stanley Lessler, and my sister, Deanna, brought together my Lessler cousins, the surviving aunts, and other branches of the Lesslers, Kurlands, and Gamzons. Many photographs were put on display and I was able to see beyond my mother's albums and my own memories.

I owe a debt as well to the three aunts who were willing to contribute their memories, honest and unflinching in the frank manner of Mother's brothers and sisters, namely Aunt Dorothy, Aunt Miriam, and my uncle Hyman's first wife, Celia. My older cousin Alan Lessler, the son of my uncle Robert, compiled the chart of family births that gave me a sense of where to begin. My cousin Shirley, the daughter of Mother's oldest sister, Celia, contributed endless anecdotes. Uncle Simon's daughter Abby sent valuable materials. Three of Aunt Betty's daughters, Margie, Doris, and Muriel, also shared memories, as did Aunt Esther's son, Harold. My mother's cousin Milton Kurland had an extraordinary recall of facts. He made the Eastern European world of "Annie Kurland," who married my grandfather, Joseph, clearer to me and spent hours recalling my grandfather and my grandmother, whom he observed from the unique perspective of a nephew whose father worked in Annie's silk business.

My mother's silence with regard to herself during her lifetime, I like to think, posed a mystery that she knew I would someday try and decipher; she hovers over me, teasing me to find her and unriddle her taciturnity.

Contents

A MOTHER'S STEPS

A Meditation on Silence

MARK JAY MIRSKY

Mark!

"Mark!"

The voice, sharp, staccato, like the ring of an old alarm clock, set on a bureau across from my bed, echoes in the loft.

I start upright from the sheet and blanket.

It's my mother's voice, I know it better than my own, and for almost twenty-nine years, even before I spoke words of my own, like it or not, I respond as I do now, jumping with a shiver down my back.

I didn't have to write down this moment, as I might a dream, so as not to forget it.

I heard her voice speak my name in the first light of morning a few months before my seventy-fifth birthday.

I can still hear it.

What does she summon me to, for?

I don't ask that—it is enough to chase the echo of that voice through the rest of the day and subsequent ones, to know that I did hear her speak to me, a crack in the spheres of time, uncanny, but in her voice all the reassurance and direction a child might seek.

"Mark!"

"What do you want?"

In her peremptory summons, to get up, get ready, hurry, come to the table, comb my hair, stop dreaming, pay attention, there was something more, something I did not understand, something secret I felt until just before I lost her, a demand that she carefully kept concealed.

I hear it, though, now, as I did months ago, and its echo lingers, tells me that I heard right, my name less a command than an assertion of her presence.

"Mark!"

A Mother's Voice

Mother's voice always echoed out of her habitual silence. She told no stories in contrast to my father. When I was little he talked about his childhood and recalled it in much greater detail when, at Harvard College, I asked him to let me write down his memories of Pinsk, the town in Belarus where he grew up. Dad was always telling stories, anecdotes of his law practice full of characters like himself, and bitter, but often comic, moments from his career in the Massachusetts Legislature. Of course, the story that was perhaps the most important in his life, he did not speak about until very late, though details of it could not help but escape at moments, particularly when his fiery, younger sister, Hilda, was at the table.

Like many children, I never questioned my mother's reticence about her own childhood and adolescence. As number eleven in a family of twelve brothers and sisters, her older siblings, my aunts and uncles, often seemed like grandparents. Some of my cousins whom we met at family meetings, weddings, bar mitzvahs were more like young aunts and uncles. She was particularly close to three or four of them in whose houses we were regular visitors, and who sometimes came to ours, though we were in Boston and most of them lived in New York or Connecticut. Her brothers and sisters, however, did not speak about their childhood—at least not in front of me.

When my mother did mention her family it was to speak with pride about several of her nieces and nephews, and to urge my sister and me to be more like them—these were not stories, but rather moral injunctions. They signified her disappointment in us.

As a novelist, my mother presents a challenge to me, since, in reconstructing her for you, and for myself, I seem to have so little to work from.

One of my close friends, a talented writer, asked when she looked at my first draft of this manuscript, "What did you call your mother?"

Was she ever the all-American, "Mom"?

I can't recall ever speaking that name to her, or calling out "Mom."

The truth is I can't recall the exact cry with which I called out in pain from a skinned knee, or burst through the front door to report something that I hoped would earn a rare smile of appreciation. In the wake of her death the formal, "Mother," now seems appropriate to signal the powerful and uncanny love with which I try to summon her presence again. Did I ever call her "Mother" to her face? It sounds far too cold, restrained, and her own restraint provoked a need to somehow break down hers, to draw her towards me, from the ironic distance with which she habitually regarded or listened to me; but she was never a comfortable, friendly, "Momma."

I called my father, "Dad" to his face, and my mother referred to him as "Dad," when she wasn't angry with him. He was "your father," when she was warning me that my father was going to enforce a discipline or administer a rebuke—something that was more awful than what she, as the gentler, more merciful of my parents, could bring herself to impose. Sometimes, when the affection toward my father bubbled up in her, he was "Wilfred," his first name, and I think he called her "Ruth," as a matter of course, but when speaking of her to us, he never used her first name. He never addressed her as "Mother," though like my mother, when we were both being scolded for some common offense against her sense of propriety, he would refer to her as "your mother," as she in warning us would say that "your father" will really be upset by this.

Dad bought me a BB gun when I was five or six years old. It was an incredible present for a little boy in a Jewish neighborhood of narrow backyards where not a single one of my playmates had a real gun, a gun that could shatter a glass window or take out an eye. I remember the excitement of going with him to the store without my mother's knowledge and his mischievous appreciation for the wild joy in my eyes. He was open to forbidden dreams like this and conspiracies between us, but my mother met us at the front door, saw the box, demanded an explanation and told us to go around by the back door. The gun was unpacked there and banished to the ignominy of the back staircase down to the house's cellar, never to be allowed inside our first floor apartment. It was of course stolen within days as word of it trickled out to the neighborhood kids and a boy from one of the desperately poor families on the next street facing the railroad tracks crept in through the unlocked door to our backyard and grabbed it. My mother insisted when I found out who had taken it that I go back and retrieve the gun but it would be stolen again and never found. It was at moments like this that my father would explain with a note of fellow-feeling, "Your mother doesn't want it in the house." Would I have protested to her, "Mom," or "Momma"? My sister called her "Momma," but my sister was the baby in the family, and had a nickname, "Deedee." I was always, except for my grandfather Israel's affectionate "Maishe" (he passed away when I was four and a half), just "Mark."

I mulled over how I normally addressed my mother as a boy, and sent a note to my sister asking what she called our parent, but before her answer came, another word rang in my head, "Mommy." And I seem to recall that as a child I did call her "Mommy" and that the habit may well have persisted into adolescence and beyond, with its strange echo of my infancy, as if only in that stage did I have the privilege of intimacy and a call upon her physical closeness. My sister too, when she replied, found the same word, "Mommy." My mother could reduce me to a screaming infant and often did until our final months together, and I have no doubt that in my frantic response to her cool, only too accurate, critical remarks, "Mommy!" was coupled with the cry for her to desist.

Among my earliest memories, however, is not her voice, her sarcastic, cool, often wounding assessment of me, her scolding that went on into a kind of cruel teasing, but the way she communicated when she refused to speak. Her footsteps in shoes with sharp heels across the linoleum of the kitchen, the wooden floor of the bedroom, the bathroom, which even the living room rug did not muffle, spoke to me as a little boy of the anger locked up between lips that remained compressed as she refused to speak to my father, me, and even my baby sister, when the latter was able to speak. That staccato drumbeat still echoes and no appeal to "Mommy," could break into its angry march.

Images and Text

She was "Mommy," but most of the time she was someone else, always at a slight distance. When I look back and call her "Mother" to be next to her again, it is to hear her deep and thrilling voice, her proud step when she wasn't angry; the gait of the princesses I admired since childhood on the silver screens of Hollywood.

Left solely to words, I would be forced into fiction, weaving the memories I recorded from aunts and cousins into a fantasy. Like the fairy godmother of children's tales, my mother left me a crumbling trail in the underbrush of an attic in our summer cottage. Did she want me to find her there? She threw out, or gave away, all of my first toys, the playthings of adolescence; there were no objects preserved from her own childhood. (When we sighed as children over the beautiful gown she had been married in and asked to see it, we were told she gave it away to a bride who could not afford one.) Buried, however, in the midden heap stuffed into the cottage's attic, bed frames, ashtrays of old bottle caps, stacks of law books, massive black-bound volumes of legislative records, hat boxes, broken valises stuffed with sheets, pillowcases, rugs, mothballs packed between their layers, and abandoned appliances, she had left clues. In the boxes from all the places my parents had lived I found her albums, their photographs and handwriting that had not dissolved yet on the flaking pages. A path back was still there.

Each time I stared at her handwriting; her neat, sharp hand, which threatened to crumble into fragments as I turned the fragile page on which it was written, or stared at the image beside it (if the photograph had not slipped out of its tiny black holders, or come loose of paste that fastened it beside her notation, orphaned in the process of examination, its context lost), I saw a different young woman.

Who was she?

The girl on the sands of Nantasket Beach, a photograph probably snapped in the summer of 1932 is twenty, already cuddling with Wilfred, my father.

Would I have fallen in love with her?

At this point I am many years away from the last of her clues. At times they meet my memories, more often I step into moments of Mother's life when I did not exist, or was too young to recall. It is a shock to discover myself in the last books and albums in which she recorded herself, since they belong to a time before I am present to myself in my thoughts.

Will her images, her thoughts, interest you? I recall the tongue-in-cheek remark of Robert Creeley in his story "Mr. Blue," "I suspect that you have troubles of your own, and since you have, why bother you with more? Mine against yours? That seems a waste of time. But perhaps mine are yours."

As I completed a first draft of this manuscript I happened upon Tolstoy's book, *Childhood* and marveled at the recall of moments when he left his mother, a home in the country, to go to Moscow and adolescence. Later I learned that he had no such memories. Tolstoy's mother died when he was two years old. His sense of her was a collage drawn from her letters, diaries, and the recollections of family members. When I read *Childhood*, though, I sensed that it was provoked by Tolstoy's sense of loss not just for his mother but for the child's life left behind, and every word, color, smell he could recover was a way of touching it again, though imagining her in the midst of it. I was tempted to try to write in a similar vein, though I was close to thirty when I lost my mother, and so many more years of memories and complex transitions would crowd my pages. There are, however, more interesting differences. Tolstoy's own sense of his mother as he records it is idealized:

> *My mother I do not at all remember. I was a year and a half old when she died. Owing to some strange chance no portrait whatever of her has been preserved, so that, as a real physical being, I cannot represent her to myself. I am in a sense glad of this, for in my conception of her there is only her spiritual figure, and all that I know about her is beautiful, and I think this is so, not only because all who spoke to me of my mother tried to say*

only what was good, but because there was actually very much of this good in her.

Happily, the mother of *Childhood* is not entirely "idealized" and so she lives, dealing with a feckless husband, on the page. What is striking in Tolstoy's attempt to recover childhood is the need to feel that his mother loved him. He mentions this twice:

> *I have been told that my mother loved me very much, and called me 'Mon petit Benjamin.' ... The fourth strong feeling, which did perhaps exist, as my aunts told me — I earnestly hope that it did exist — was her love for me, which took the place of her love for Koko* [his older brother], *who at the time of my birth had already detached himself from his mother and been transferred into male hands. It was a necessity for her to love what was not herself, and one love took the place of another. Such was the figure of my mother in my imagination. She appeared to me a creature so elevated, pure, and spiritual that often in the middle period of my life, during my struggle with overwhelming temptations, I prayed to her soul, begging her to aid me, and this prayer always helped me much.*

"Her love for me"—if what follow in my pages has any coherence, it is the search for that and trying to mediate with "the figure of my mother in my imagination."

Thinking about Tolstoy's *Childhood*, words rather than images are his sole resource. The shock of a loss before he can remember provokes not only Tolstoy's fictional memoir, but the convention of keeping to convention in regard to time, ordering the events leading up to her death in chronological order. Tolstoy's memoir associates in my mind with lines of Isaac Babel's, written when Babel's mother was alive. Babel chose to put them in the mouth of one of his characters, Gedali, an old man who is taking the young war correspondent, Isaac, riding with the Cossacks in 1920, to a ruined synagogue and its rabbi. Gedali declaims:

All is mortal. Only the Mother is destined to immortality. And when the mother is no longer among the living, she leaves a memory which none yet has dared to sully. The memory of the mother nourishes in us a compassion that is like the ocean, and the measureless ocean feeds the rivers that dissect the universe.

The words are tinged with irony since the character is reminding Babel of his identity as a Jew, stamped by his descent from a Jewish mother, and in a sense also asking for the Soviet soldier's protection. Babel wrote in the iron grip of the Bolshevik censorship, and it is clear that the sad, helpless Gedali, characterized as a parrot, is speaking for the author. If the rhetoric is exaggerated, at the edge of parody, it also conveys Babel's sense of a mystery that does not square with an atheist's universe.

Tolstoy in the 19th century inhabits a world that is still under the spell of Sir Isaac Newton's logic, and the canvas of Tolstoy's narrative, though full of puzzles and contradictions, is meant to create the illusion of a world on the page that is as lifelike as the world we see when look up to observe a room in which we are reading. In the second and third decades of the 20th century Babel has already felt the disruptions of a science that questions the obvious reality of what we observe. Babel's generalizations about "the Mother" do not echo with the tender sentimentality of Tolstoy, but they pose her as a force in nature who influences us from a source beyond our comprehension. In the 21st century, the sense of coherent narrative is even more elusive. Still I am tempted for a few pages to emulate Tolstoy.

I began trying to assemble the facts about both sides of my mother's family leaving Europe, coming to America. I kept going back and forward though, as I tried to understand, not just my mother, but myself. Tolstoy's *Childhood* despite its sense of the elegiac in regard to his mother, centers on the boy. We know little or nothing of the mother in girlhood, though Tolstoy's reminiscences preserve a fascinating story of a lost love of hers. As I wrote the second and third drafts of my book, I returned to the Baby Book my mother kept to check my first memories against her impressions. I had always imagined that my first vivid memory was the moment I struck my head against a tool chest by the entry to our kitchen, at three and a half, while Mother was away in December of 1942 giving birth to my sister. My grandfather rushed to the house to comfort me when I woke up, as I had been knocked unconscious. I had dashed from my bedroom to the kitchen excited and blacked out in a moment from which I awoke with a sharp sensation of pain, adults crowded around me in my bedroom, then suddenly the five or six adults hovering over me where I lay on the pillows, a faint stinging in my temples, parted. Grandpa! He had come from the synagogue, handsome in his frock coat, and striped pants, like the President, or mayor, a prince before whom everyone seemed to bow with respect. All pain vanished. His pockets always contained a lollipop or a Tootsie Roll for me—he never came without a present. He bent down and I felt his nose rubbing mine as he laughed over the big queen-size bed that had been moved into my room, the tickle of his silver moustache, a glint in his icy blue eyes when I smiled back. All the sailboats in the wallpaper began to move.

I do retain a moment, possibly my earliest, when I am dragged from under a crib, but staring at the dates in the Baby Book, I can construct a narrative of childhood before that knock against the carpenter's wooden tool chest since the day remains so sharp. My mother has entered the date, June 1942, in her book. I know therefore that I am two years and ten months old. Her notation records that the surgeon was a Doctor Wolfson, but I seem to recall our family physician at the bedside as well.

I am to have my tonsils out, a procedure that no one has explained. It is early morning and the sun is shining through the windows of my mother and father's bedroom, a room that served as a dining room when the two-story house was a middle-class home in a rural district of Boston at the end of the 19th century. The French doors to the living room, whose glass panes are hung with partly transparent pink curtains, disguise and reveal the space's original purpose. Now, the former dining room houses two beds, as well as my mother's dresser and the pillows of a window seat. The adults urge me to lie down on the twin bed where my father sleeps, the one closest to the tiny hallway into the kitchen. From it Dad can slip away at five in the morning, when he invariably awakes, leaving my mother in the bed by the windows to slumber on until seven or eight o'clock. I imagine that our family physician, Doctor Ingalls, whose hoarse voice conveys assurance, is there. My father and mother have talked about this operation to me, my tonsils will be taken out. Ingall's presence, which I am accustomed to when I have had a fever, and in whose wake I always seem to feel better, works its spell. I watch the light playing on the perfume bottles on Mother's dresser of blond rock maple, a part of their set of twin beds, the colored photograph of Mother's favorite sister, Miriam, her brother Bob, a frame of her mother Annie's smiling face and dream myself into the world of a tin box full of sewing needles and buttons, painted with men and women in the costumes of the mid-19th century, high silk hats, billowing skirts, horses and buggies, walking and riding round its oval shape. Someone gently puts a cloth over my nose and mouth. Afterwards they tell me it is ether, but I drift off so quickly that when I wake it seems that time has slipped away and unexpectedly, it is almost afternoon.

"What happened?" I ask my mother, who is watching me, as I get up out of bed. The doctors, my father, several other people who were crowded around me earlier, have left.

"They took out your tonsils."

"Where are they?" I ask.

She laughs. "Why, do you want to see them?"

"Yes." She waits as I get up from the bed and walk through the tiny foyer that opens on my parents' bedroom, my bedroom, the bathroom, and the kitchen. Passing the successive doors into the kitchen, by the opening to a narrow pantry, we come to a locked door for the back stairs and walk down one flight to the backyard through the smell of old, stale linoleum. The odor of coal ash wafts up from the cellar where the furnace lies. We unlock the back entrance to the yard and my mother points to one of a row of tall metal trashcans to our left. "In there," she remarks, her expression amused, but tinged with sarcasm.

I am not going to root in the deep trash barrel for my tonsils, but I feel cheated. I don't know if I express it. I should have had a look at them before they were just tossed out. Recalling my mother's amused look, the inference that they would be smelly, and not very interesting, I remain silent.

Looking away from the barrels, I see the two tall Seckel pear trees that are the glory of our yard. Those slender trees, their grey bark marking the world of the house's former owners from the world of a genteel 19th-century Boston, are still giving fruit and fill the kitchen with their sweetness. My mother halves them, boiling and bottling their plump shapes in sugar water. There is a war raging, its echo at the edge of the adult's talk, fear that is registered, if not entirely understood. Canned fruit is hard to come by. That smell of the sugary steam summons a lost happiness and these trees are shapes of my mother's form in my mind, graceful, fruitful in my mind, as present as the stone wall at the back of the yard, which in a few years I will be able to scale and walk on; the concrete blocks of the garage that abuts the yard just beyond the trashcans, and defines our property line with the next house as you go up Warner Street toward the cross street, Harvard. My mother next to me repeats that my tonsils are now in the trash. I am growing up, she seems to imply, and this does not entirely please me as if I am bound to lose more than tonsils.

I think the image of me below was taken when a small shack sat in the middle of our yard. It was torn down between the time I was two and three. Of course I grieved at its loss, for it would have been a perfect playhouse and ever after, the flagstones that led out to what was

now just a barely discernible outline in the grass, seemed to signal a permanent hole in my life. Until this moment, November 2012, looking hard at the photograph, I had forgotten about that shack.

But I am putting myself, as Tolstoy does, at the center of the narrative, not my mother. This is a search for my mother. There are chapters to follow in which I am not present. I hope to pursue her even beyond the boundary of death, since she has drawn me there. I will try to recall Mother at the moment when in my consciousness, she left me, us, our family, or the long prelude to it in her final six months that changed the way she and I looked, spoke, touched each other. Not yet, because that would bring me to the end of my narrative, though not the end of our story.

Chapter One

Where do I begin?

"*In medias res,* into the middle of things?" It's my mother I wish to please. My father like me educated at Boston Public Latin would be tickled by the Latin from Horace, but not "Mommy." An offer to shovel snow might draw her appreciation. The photograph above in front of our apartment in Mattapan, Massachusetts, on Hazelton Street, is probably from January of 1957, my senior year of high school. I am seventeen, Mother, forty-five, holds on to her youthful beauty, not yet cajoled into taking a position as a commissioner on the Industrial Accident Board of the commonwealth.

My mother's expression above is cheerful. Was I talked into shoveling the stairs and sidewalk or helping clear snow from our car? In many of the photographs that follow you will find that look on her face, though the more characteristic one I recall, slightly amused, suspicious, wary, she rarely shows to the camera.

My father world appears in the background of several of my novels but I have written about his life as well in short essays finding their most appreciative audience in Boston's newspapers. My father was not just a good storyteller. He offered himself as a subject when I began to write; his career in politics, the dramatic events of his childhood in Eastern Europe, the passage to America, early years at the demanding Boston Public Latin School, Harvard College; the eight years he spent in the Massachusetts Legislature. "Say whatever you want about me," he laughed, patting my knee. I was headed for the Masters Program in Creative Writing at Stanford. He would have cause to rue that permission later. Even in the relatively simple lens of newspaper articles the forbidden always teases my thoughts.

Until her final moments my mother gave me no such permission. Her unhappiness in childhood, enthusiasms, she never talked about. She did talk *about* me and *to* me. Her frustration with my character was a constant topic. My father almost never spoke his dissatisfaction to my face. He spoke through Mother, but he had a habit of vaunting his early achievements, which spoke volumes. He had achieved this and that, and already at eight, nine, ten, I was falling so far behind, that his usual manner of speaking at the table was, "Tell your son ..."

When I began to show some promise, at fourteen, fifteen, Dad and I came to an understanding. He would, in general, let me go my own way. Later, when I achieved some honor that had eluded him (although his achievements far outrank mine), I noted even a touch of jealousy. I never doubted that he was fiercely attached to me and even his lapses in judgment did not diminish my sense of his authority. There were a number of subjects we never talked about. The young women I dated, for instance; several disasters that brought me close to a breakdown, and cost the family budget more than my parents could afford. I like to think that our conversation was always direct and that my conversation with my mother was indirect, but when I review what really went on, I face a riddle. My mother knew much more about me than my father. She knew several secrets related to my sexual life, from adolescence on. When I collapsed in the wake of breakups it was to my mother that I went in tears, right through college and graduate school. At times her practical advice infuriated me. "You should get a haircut," was not, I felt, going to improve my character or solve my problems with a departing girlfriend. Even when I abused Mother, in a way I would never dream of doing with my father, making sarcastic and demeaning observations about the way her mind worked, it was to Mother that I went with my troubles.

Why, then, was I under the illusion that there was no exchange between us? My father boasted that when he came to America at fourteen, he had gone through six grades of public school in a single year. My mother never mentioned that she had skipped two grades in the public school system. My father, in fact, was older than most of his classmates. My mother was younger. She told my sister, three and a half years younger than me, secrets that Mother withheld from me. She remained hidden and it was characteristic of her to disparage the bond between us. "I love you," she would snap at me as a teenager, "but I don't like you." The remark stuck with me because it was only one of dozens of similar remarks, which seemed to deliberately put me at a distance, and confirm her sense that I was a mistake that she somehow had to bear. It was only when it was almost too late, when the time we had with each other was rapidly coming to an end that everything changed.

It was my father whose shadow flitted through my novels, stories, for in the one instance when I did reference not her but her family in a play I wrote, she burst out, "Don't you dare." (I had used some of her sisters and brother-in-laws' names, etc., for the outrageous cartoons of a demented family in the Jewish suburbs.) I think of my father's answer to me, when we talked about his father's response when Dad and his sisters tried to talk to my grandfather, Israel Mirsky, about the way Gertrude, their stepmother, was behaving. The patriarch waved to them to be silent. "*Iz pasht nisht,*" "It's not befitting." To twist my mother into my fiction, though I tried, did not seem to work. After her death, however, she became my principal guide to what I called "the uncanny." It was Mother who hovered over me as a writer of fiction.

I have to write about her directly, but she is also a fiction. It's painful to do so, as if I am violating her privacy but something tells me that she wants this.

A year or so ago, my cousin Margie, the youngest daughter of Aunt Betty, my mother's second oldest sister, mailed back to me a valentine I had sent her as a child. It set me thinking, though I was not surprised. Margie was the sweetest of my older cousins to me. (My uncle Simon's daughter, Cissy, closer at hand, only a few years older than me, was more an affable tomboy and friend.) The date on the envelope is February 1945. I was about five and a half, in kindergarten, but evidently able to print out my name. Margie was very special for many years to me, and the card set me thinking not only about her, but my mother and the family.

I began to gather materials for a book about Mother shortly after her death when some of her sisters were still alive. I interviewed, taped them, took notes, collected facts about my grandmother, Annie Kurland, and my grandfather, Isaac Joseph Lessler. About four years ago, I started to put these materials into chapters, and re-examine photographs and documents, but I was puzzled. What exactly was my mother's story? To a novelist, plot is uppermost, and that is the thread of a story I find most interesting. Constructing a novel the simplest way is to start at the protagonist's birth and go on to a happy marriage, a disastrous ruin or a balance of the two. What I wrote seemed to be organized in response to my own curiosity, not chronology. My first chapter sifted some of the family materials and my memories. I called it "Who is she?" and began with a photograph from her albums that always thrilled me, my mother at about twenty, just after she met my father, bouncing happily in the sand on Nantasket Beach, a popular bathing resort during the summer just south of Boston. Only after wrestling for a chapter with the question of who the young woman on the beach was, did I try to understand the world of her parents and grandparents, their roots in Eastern Europe, their passage as immigrants to New York City.

Now, some years later, I realize that before I ask the question, "Who is she?" even at twenty, I have to put in place the fact of her characteristic silence.

Before I go on to the chapters I have already written, the card Margie sent me begins to tease me. It turns me back to a document I will mention frequently, a silk-covered Baby Book with flowers in blue thread and a pink and orange infant, blue eyed and blond haired on the cover. My mother recorded in it my progress from birth through the first three years of my life. Several sentences that slipped by me, previously, now catch my attention. Mother in her meticulous way, noted my first words, my gestures in the crib, the birth of my consciousness. I am three and a half, when she makes this entry, just before the birth of my sister, Deanna.

Dec. 1942 Mark is an omnivorous reader. The first pet story was 3 bears thumbed and re-thumbed given by Aunt Sunny [Sonia]. Next was Black Sambo-the Raggedy Andy Books and the Camel with the Wrinkled Knees. Noah's Ark comes in for strong measure. As for poetry the nursery jingles & RL Stevenson Me & My Shadow

6 AM begins reading time for Mark. We can hear him telling himself the stories from our room.

Dec 19th Mark seems to have a good sense of rhythm and on hearing the radio or his records will improvise marches. He is always singing & humming improvising what he forgets. At 3 he could sing Of En Pripichuck but at 3 1/2 can only remember the words if he hears it first. He loves to imitate his grandpa and sing as [?] but with a yamekele & a taliss which he calls a "collar." He drapes the sheet around his toy box for an altar or one high end of his crib & chants away. His memory is prtty [sic]good. He can recall events of over a year. He likes to draw with the help of a penny a man's head tho [sic] his drawings are pretty unintelligible.

I must be about two and a half years old in the photograph above, taken in Boston's Public Gardens at the edge of the pond with the swan boats, a favorite place of mine at that age, with its sense of a mini-adventure. The card sent to Margie, however, dates from a moment in childhood when I am, relatively, much older.

Mother must have taught me to sign my name, though it is her handwriting that addresses the envelope into which the valentine was put. She would have noted that at four and five, I had a crush on my cousin, Margie. Valentine's Day had lost its Christian significance and become a secular holiday in Jewish America. It meant more, however, to my mother, like her siblings born in the United States, than my father. Despite his fluent, perfect English, learned at fourteen, Dad's first language was Yiddish, although he never spoke it in the house or to me. All his childhood memories lay back in Pinsk. My mother's brothers and sisters were Americans. She was the second youngest of her twelve brothers and sisters. Those who had been successful, lived in handsome houses, or mansions, drove expensive cars, and seemed in my childhood part of the dashing, happy life of an American upper class that unfolded in the pages of *LIFE Magazine*. Cousin Margie was slim and sylphlike, the daughter of a successful businessman, David Lesser and blossoming at eleven into a young woman. Her oldest sisters, Francis, Muriel, Doris, were already adults and on the verge of getting married. Margie was just six years older than me, almost twelve on Valentine's Day in 1945. Of those older cousins, she was the only one who seemed to notice and talk to me when our family drove down to Bridgeport. Margie had a special smile for me when I saw her. If it was the summer months, after a grueling five-hour drive from our home in Dorchester, we went directly to her mother Aunt Betty's beach house in Fairfield, Connecticut, to take a swim. Most of the family who lived in Bridgeport would be gathered there on a day of hot sunshine. There were a number of outdoor shower stalls in back and the front porch was square on the sand beach, which fronted Long Island Sound. Aunt Betty had married her first cousin, David Lesser. A prominent retailer in Bridgeport, Uncle Dave was always generous to his wife's sisters and brothers, throwing open his comfortable home in Bridgeport, and their beach cottage. I remember his wide smile, open arms, and genial hospitality whenever we showed up at his door. Dave Lesser's oldest child Francis had married in 1941, but there were two weddings in 1945, Muriel and Doris, the next oldest ones, and I can recall the men in their military uniforms, the banquets at the hotel in Bridgeport, the excitement of being part of what seemed to me a vast family. It was hard to imagine that these adults were just cousins. My mother treated them as brothers and sisters, not nieces and nephews. Margie, however, at the edge of adolescence in 1945 was poised just between these adults and another set of cousins closer to me in age or younger. Her cheerful face and graceful manners reminded me of Mother in a good mood. Even a few minutes of Margie's attention and smiles, made me feel as if I had brushed up against a princess from an American romance.

Her kindness was more striking, because her next oldest sister, Anne, eleven years older than me, was always strange. She seemed to belong to the younger cousins, of whom one could count Margie as one of the oldest. Later it would turn out that Anne had crippling mental problems. She asked me questions that could not be answered and shadows crossed her face when I approached, hoping for the same sympathetic attention I had just received from Margie.

Their mother, my aunt Betty, loomed over me as a boy. The first thing I remember Aunt Betty saying to me was (I must have been four or so) "You ruined my Oriental rug."

A sentence like that from the mouth of a matron bearing down on me with a glowering face was doom. It stripped me of the pretense of rapidly growing out of kindergarten, into the first grade or second. It returned me to a dark time.

For far back in memory, fixed by a photograph in which I am no more than three, there is a moment in my mother's albums where I appear in a neatly tailored black woolen sailor's suit, the replica in a child's size of an American sailor's outfit in World War Two. That suit was my pride—I can recall my excitement climbing into it, the white flap in back, having Mother button me into it as it seemed to fit skin tight. I beam from the picture and can almost touch the moment

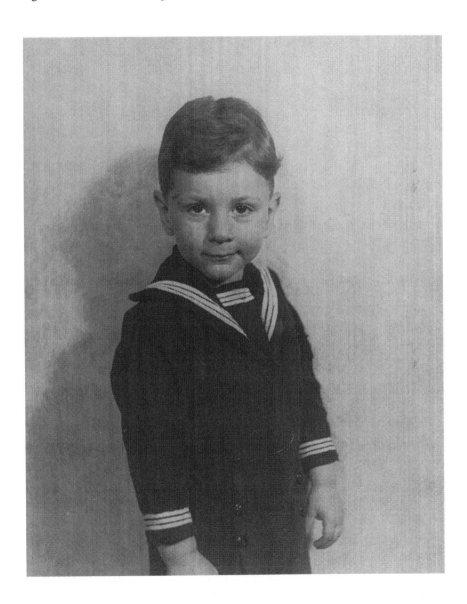

when I posed. When we set out for a family affair in Bridgeport with it, I could hardly contain myself because I knew I would be admired as I strutted before my mother's sisters, brothers, nephews and nieces, my cousins. My love of costumes somehow fixed on that sailor's suit. We went to my mother's youngest sister, Mildred's, to spend the night before a family affair where there would be a live orchestra, dancing, and all the foods which my mother, as a strict dietician, had forbidden me: the greasy knishes, which I could never get enough of, noodle and potato puddings, chopped chicken liver—best of all an endless processional of cookies, cakes and soda. Already experience had taught me that my mother would be distracted by her family and caught up in the circle of brothers and sisters. I would be free of supervision. I insisted that my sailor's suit be laid out on top of my blankets so I could feast my eyes on it. I went to sleep anticipating a Garden of Eden. In the morning when I woke, I was wet through and through, and so was the woolen suit. It smelled of urine and in an era before laundry machines came into the home was impossible to wash and dry before the looming event.

"You can't go," I was told. "You have no clothes to go in." I was inconsolable. That afternoon and early evening, confined to my aunt Mildred's house was possibly the first time I realized that one could be trapped in moments of such boredom that, to echo Hamlet, life seemed, "weary, stale, flat and unprofitable." I was also the laughing stock of my mother's sisters and brothers when they next laid eyes on me, and so Aunt Betty's additional charge, which referred to an act of incontinence I had no memory of, namely peeing so hard I ruined a priceless rug, rubbed salt into the lost wedding festival. (In retrospect, I imagine that with so many male cousins just a few years older, clothes could have been procured.) Happy to consign me to the care of a babysitter at Mildred's, Mother went off merrily, without having to worry about me being underfoot.

Aunt Betty, like Mother's two other oldest sisters, Celia and Esther, was more like a grandmother than an aunt. At least Aunt Betty took notice of me if only to scold me for past offenses. Aunt Celia, the oldest of my mothers' sisters, ignored me, although her husband Uncle Louie, who was always jolly with all his nieces and nephews, would ask what I most wanted in the world and promise electric trains, ponies, and encouraged my dreaming to go to limits that even I knew were outrageous. I was too young to understand that this was teasing, whether merry or threatening, but it was characteristic of my mother's siblings. Even when I was much older, nine, ten, this teasing went on. One of the most impressive of my mother's brothers, David, whose dark, handsome face evoked the movie actor, Cary Grant, was a distinguished lawyer. His summer house was more a mansion than beach cottage and I seem to recall that in their home, his son Stanley's elaborate electric trains took up half of an attic. Uncle Davey hardly ever spoke to me and his wife Aunt Claire's exterior seemed so aristocratic that it was daunting to approach her. (When I went to interview her at the end of her life, she revealed that her first language was Yiddish, like my father's, and I understood that I had entirely misconstrued her.) In the small space at my uncle Simon's lakeside cottage in Rhode Island (Simon was the oldest of the brothers), where the family had gathered for one of its reunions, we were all brought into closer proximity than usual and out of politeness when I passed my uncle Davey, leaning against a wall, I paused to say hello. He began to needle me about my "tail." He was a man of quiet dignity, who had barely nodded at me in the past, but now he went on and on about whether I knew I had a "tail." There was a lot of tension between my father and David, who had been one of my mother's protectors, but what it was all about I didn't find out until long after both had passed away. A letter of Uncle Davey's fell out of an old file of my father's that I was raking through to make sure there was nothing valuable inside. It was one of the many painful moments in the life of the Lesslers, but my mother was so discrete, so careful of the image she wanted to project of a happy, healthy family, that she never mentioned problems to me.

It was very rare for any of these aunts and uncles to speak directly to me a child. My older cousins in the main ignored me. Much later, after my mother's death, I would grow close to my aunt Dorothy. Even while my mother was alive, however, Miriam, the sister whom she was closest to in the family surveyed me with an affectionate eye. As I entered college and graduate school Miriam began to talk to me and listen. She and her husband Morris, and their three boys, would sometimes come and stay at the beach cottage my father bought for us in 1950, in Hull, Massachusetts. Miriam, however, like my mother, was discrete, often silent at family meetings and, like Mother, usually distant. In this world Margie's sweetness always touched me and so I am not surprised, that she alone in this large family, once upon a time, received a valentine.

Chapter Two

Silence was my mother's medium.

My mother never talked about herself, except in regard to fatigue, or her disappointment with me. She quoted a few sayings of her mother in Yiddish; that was all. Mother never mentioned her father. She rarely talked about her twelve sisters and brothers, though it was clear that she admired them. When she referred to her nephews and nieces, it was usually to point out how far I fell short in comparison. When I asked my mother about why she married my father, her cheek puckered with irony. She said that she found him amusing, but was well aware of his failings and that he was a lucky man. Now and then I guessed something more of what she thought, not from words but from her face.

She did smile though. Her smile had many shades, from cheerful to enigmatic. When she showed delight in something I had done, I entered a happier world.

What did I see the first time I looked in her albums? I was still a child. I recall just waves of faces, events, the youth of the woman who was everything to me, and a more genial version of the father who commanded the house as a mercurial giant, sometimes laughing, generous, then, for no reason, angry; with snapshots of uncles and aunts as younger versions of themselves, and a few glimpses of my father's father, who died when I was four and a half.

Here is a photograph that puzzles me. I don't know how old my mother is. I could place it at the time of her graduation in 1928, or when she began to work for the Red Cross in Bridgeport in 1929. I suspect, however, that it was taken in 1930 or early 1931 since it appears in a pamphlet from about that time. She could look like a girl of fifteen when she was leaning up against an oak in our backyard at Warner Street in Dorchester, though she was already in her thirties and had given birth to me, or appear as the opposite, a sophisticated professional woman. Except for photographs taken when she was a child before her mother Annie died, or the last photographs of Mother at the very end of her forties and early fifties, the camera catches her at the age she holds in the frame of her mind.

My mother and father were opposites, or that is how I regarded them as a child. Dad shouted, sang aloud, teased one into revolt, made the sounds of a mountain gorilla beating his chest when I had misbehaved and chased me into my bedroom. I fled, scurrying under the big queen-sized bed, bequeathed to me after the birth of my sister, afraid that only hiding would save me from his sudden, inexplicable burst of wrath and a pummeling. Only a moment before he had been smiling but now I faced an ogre. His mouth contorted, eyebrows raised; the water of anger was in his eyes. In such moments he could even toss a lamp; never directly at me, but at the wall in the opposite corner, to indicate what lay in store if he could lay his hands on me.

Until the moment when, at thirteen, I was strong enough to lift my father off the floor, the fear of his physical punishment was always with me even though it was always just a threat. He never did touch me in anger.

My mother's temper was slow but never just a threat. That staccato tap of her heels across the kitchen linoleum, speaking her rage, often went on for two or three days. If we crossed paths in the hallway, or at the table, her lips compressed, she re-fused at these times to meet my eager eyes, hoping for forgiveness. It was better when she took me firmly by the cheek in the moment if I was being awful or if I really provoked her, slapped me.

At those times she became the im-posing woman, whose elegance and disapproval went hand in hand. Some-thing of that is caught in this snapshot. She sits at her older sister Dotty's house in Brooklyn in the early or mid 1940s. From about the same time I have snap-shots where she looks like a teenager. The silent withdrawal from me was worse than any slap. Once started, she would not quickly stop. Since my father never did hit or slap me, and his fits were over within an hour or two, I learned to weather his anger. Mother burned with a silent, stubborn fury until she made me feel not just her anger but disgust, resignation. It took weeks, it seemed, before she would smile at me again.

My father was a hugger. When he was pleased with me, he would give me a crushing embrace that made me feel his delight. My mother never put her hands on me except when I was sick. Fevers were then treated with an alcohol rubdown and while the memory of the chills, nausea, cough, the painful colds and grippes of my childhood have faded away for the most part, the surprise of feeling my mother's hands moving over my arms, my legs, belly, with a cloth dipped in the cooling alcohol, remains with me.

Political life, its rounds of dinners, snacks, glad-handing at constituents' receptions, doomed my father's waistline. Dad began to sag at about the time of my birth; his belly prominent in suits with tightly buttoned vests, or in a bathing suit. My first impression of my father is of a portly man. Mother remained slim, tall, like an older sister, unlike many of the short, often dumpy ladies who were my friends' mothers. Even among her sisters, younger and older, she alone remained almost a "girl."

My father's stories—when I was a three, four, five, around 1945, before the understanding of the Holocaust drew a curtain over his birthplace—he talked about the world he had been born in and left when he was only thirteen. Three quarters of Pinsk, the town in Belarus he came from, was Jewish. Dad would tell tales of the wolves following my great-grandfather, Maishe Mirsky, a woodsman, through the forests, the oven my father slept on, the Germans marching in during the Great War. I seemed to have experienced what he did, and walked Pinsk's streets with him.

Did my mother tell me nothing of her girlhood? This morning, it struck me after responding to a letter from a friend whose father had divorced her mother, married again, so that my friend now felt "abandoned," that there were one or two anecdotes. My mother told me that when she was little she had found the branch of an evergreen with a girlfriend and they pretended it was a Christmas tree. Mother liked to sing a song when I was down in the dumps that began, "Nobody loves me / everybody hates me / I'm going to eat some worms …" More than once she repeated a story, which in the context of her silence now tells me a lot.

First, though, I have to tell a story about my mother a few years before the end of her life. It was in the spring of 1967 in California. It is a story I repeat in a manuscript about my father, but there I saw what happened from his point of view, not my mother's.

My father, my mother and I were visiting my father's sister, Aunt Hilda, in Pasadena. We were sitting with my aunt, two or three years younger than my father (ages in Pinsk, where he was born, were not necessarily exact) at her dining room table. Brother and sister began to reminisce about their childhood. One of the topics that always brought my father and his sister together was their stepmother. Their father, Israel Mirsky, had remarried in Boston. His wife, Devorah, had died as the boat bringing her and the children to America docked in New York harbor after a nine year separation from him. If Devorah was conscious of Israel, it was for just a few moments when he came onto the boat. Dad and Aunt Hilda were talking about how Gertrude, their stepmother, cut up their mother's fur coat for herself, locked the refrigerator on them, denounced them to their father, and tried to separate the youngest, Sonia, from the two oldest. Hilda, who was the firebrand of the three, took the brunt of the abuse. As a young woman she left Boston for California to join her fiancé, Joe Levy. Hilda had taken the family silver by force that her own mother had brought from Pinsk. "I beat her up!" Hilda cried, triumphant that day in Pasadena, thirty-five years or so after the event, but in tears.

My mother tried to intervene as Hilda grew more and more agitated. In the voice of the social worker, which had been Mother's profession before my sister was born, she tried to represent Gertrude's point of view. "Think of what it was like for her," Mother counseled, "Marrying your father with a child of her own, a child soon on the way from this second marriage, and three children who had lived through the years of the war, 1915-1919." The three children who came from Europe had starved. The two girls had never seen their father, and Dad, only four or five years old when Israel left Pinsk, had few memories of his father. With their mother dying moments after they met their new parent, the three hoped to hold on tightly to this new, loving father. "She can't have had an easy time of it," my mother interrupted Hilda. My aunt was in the midst of a soliloquy about sinks full of dirty dishes left for them to wash and wipe.

Aunt Hilda wheeled on Mother. Hilda rose from her seat, "Ruth, how can you be so *obtuse?*"

My father and I looked at each other in shock. My mother's face went white. She looked to us for support, but Hilda's grief was obvious. I was too stunned to know what to say and my father was caught between loyalty to his wife and the bond to his sister, the only person I ever saw him bow his head before and take abuse from. "But it was my life," my aunt cried, sinking back into her seat. "My life!" she screamed, banging the table, the tears flowing faster, "And I wouldn't take back a minute of it."

The narrative of my father and his sisters coming to America was an epic I hardly understood—my grandfather had fled from the in-laws' house in 1910. For a year no one in Devorah's family knew where her husband had gone. When they did, it was to learn that he was sending money to his father and sisters, but not to his wife. The children lived on the charity of Devorah's parents. When my grandfather sent tickets in 1914 or 1915, my great grandfather refused to let them go. From 1915 to 1919, Devorah waited in a city starving under shelling between the Russian and German armies. In 1919, Devorah's brother, who had served as the children's surrogate father, was shot by the Poles in a massacre. The old steamer that brought them across the Atlantic was battered in winter hurricanes and almost swamped. Their mother died as the boat came into New York harbor and docked. They found a loving father, but he quickly remarried and Devorah's children found an unsympathetic stepmother. Hilda lived through this again in recollection. Mother's calm perspective as a former social worker only upset Hilda.

I tried, when Aunt Hilda left the table, to come to my mother's side but although I could feel she wanted my support, she was silent, and too proud to say anything. I did not understand my mother, and only now, after gathering clues from her albums, and collecting the reminiscences of her sisters, my older cousins, does what she suffered at my aunt's table become clear; how "obtuse" my aunt, in her turn, had been to Mother.

My mother too had an "absent" father, and had lost a mother as a young girl. She had swallowed endless humiliations. She just didn't talk about it, or dramatize it.

Recently responding to a friend who wrote to me, upset after a visit from a father who had been absent for most of her life, having divorced her mother and devoted himself to his new family, that she felt suicidal, I began to understand what it means for a fourteen-year-old girl to feel abandoned.

My friend wrote that one day, while walking her dog, another dog without a leash ran over and jumped on hers. She started screaming at its owner about how he should keep his dog on the leash. He had the leash in his hand. When he hit his dog with it she pulled the leash out of his hands, threw it in his face, yelling, but the man spoke no English. "All my yelling was pointless," she sighed. "I guess I just needed to yell. I encounter a lot of angry girls who also have absent fathers. They're always looking for a fight. I guess this doesn't go away as you get older."

My mother's father I know now was largely absent by the time she was born, number eleven of his twelve surviving children.

Just how angry Mother must have been about what she felt was neglect, I only guessed after her death. When my aunt told her story, I suspect my mother's own grief was eating at her.

What was the "story" my mother had told me more than once?

It was about the Spartan boy who steals a wolf cub and conceals it under his sheepskin coat. He is standing at attention in a row of boys, and the wolf begins to gnaw at his stomach, but impassive, stoic, he bears the pain, until the cub eats his stomach away and the boy falls down dead.

He is a hero to his whole city.

This was my mother's moral tale, if my memory does not play tricks on me. And if it does, no matter, it was a story everything about her manner seemed to exemplify. Most of her deep feelings were concealed from me. The story of your guts being eaten out but remaining with an impassive face drawn up at attention was the credo by which she lived. And she died by it as well. She could admit to disappointment with me, my sister, but that grim face of disapproval, the angry tap across our apartment floors, was as far as she would go.

It is not, however, the whole story of my mother by any means. She could often summon up a mask of cheerful encouragement. Her sense of social poise was absolute. In her high school yearbook from Central High in Bridgeport, on the page listing the graduating class of June 1928, under the title, "Senior Characteristics," she is described not as "most popular," "best looking," but as the "class talker." I laughed reading that, because while I felt her silence, I often watched her pleasure in voluble chatter. She was a skillful actress, but it was a means of guarding her vulnerable self.

I felt the measure of her love, far more than her anger, and I still do. King Lear's youngest daughter, asked to put the bond between parent and child into words, whispers to herself. "What shall Cordelia speak? Love and be silent." I might well imagine the caution on my mother's lips.

Chapter Three

I enter the picture ...

IN PROFILE - 3 wks old.

"You were an accident."

Of all her sisters and brothers, my mother was closest to the sister born two years before her, Miriam, the next oldest to Mother of the twelve surviving siblings. I observed my mother and Miriam's mutual affection throughout Mother's life. They were also close in temperament. Miriam's grandchildren complain, I am told, that she said "mean things" to them when they were children. Aunt Miriam, however, was always the kindest of my aunts, always particularly sweet whenever I came to visit, and never disapproving. My mother, too, seemed to find it easier to delight in Miriam's boys than me. Mother's remark to me, when I think I was no more than six or seven, "You were an accident," I have never forgotten. At the time, I did not fully understand its sexual implications. I did feel the note of accusation, hostility and the implied threat. "I did not ask for you. Watch out." It seems in retrospect, as I travel through my seventies, not so much "mean" but a moment when "Mommy" was naked before me, forgetting all the rules of child psychology in her social worker's bag, exasperated, speaking a painful but curious truth. It was one of those times, when, instead of being concealed, she was startlingly revealed.

At this point, again, I have stepped out of her albums, her own chart of experience. I know now as I look at her photographs of me as a baby that she tied me tightly to her. There are lots of pictures focused on me; then, when my sister is born three and a half years later, on the two of us.

I see clearly that I am half my father in the photo—a squalling baby, who as an infant quickly grew a head of unruly curls. Remarkably, my birth did not ruin my mother's figure, but Mother told me I was a slow learner, incapable of coherent speech until I was past three. The baby book she kept, however, contradicts this oft-repeated assertion. Still, I was not the genius or worthy successor that my father had hoped to his own precocious childhood.

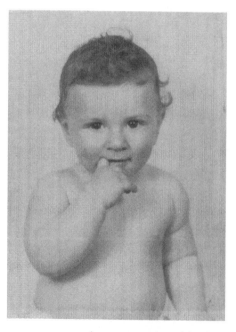

From at least two years and ten months old I have memories that stick fast. Before that, in the haze, I can only best decipher Mother and me through the album photographs.

In her book about me as a baby, abetted no doubt by my father's father, Israel Mirsky, she compiled a genealogy going back several generations on both sides of my father's family, the Mirskys, and his mother's, the Liebermans. It reaches to my great-great-grandfather, Reuben Mirsky, born in Slonim, a small town in Belarus to the north of Pinsk, and buried in his old age on Jerusalem's Mount of Olives. On my mother's side, she notes only her parents, and the grandmother, Syvia Ruchel, for whom she was obviously named. (So she knew that "Rachel" as my father told me after her death, not "Ruth," was her name in Hebrew and she preserved the "Syvia" as the "Sylvia" of her middle name.) It also records the gifts given to me at birth and increments of weight I gained.

I have no memory of the yellow brick apartment building at the corner of Blue Hill Avenue and Hazelton in Mattapan, where I was taken home after being born, nor my first few years, although there are photographs of me with my grandfather, Israel, in front of the building. Grandpa holds one of my hands; my other tightly clutches an ice cream cone. In another I am bundled into a snowsuit, at seventeen months, in front of the Blue Hill Avenue building. When I was about two years old we moved to a house nearby in Dorchester, within the same Jewish district. My father bought it and had an Irish-Catholic carpenter, his client and boon companion, Bill Daugherty, turn the second floor and the attic into apartments so that the rents could help subsidize our family budget. My grandfather officiated as the *shamus*, or sexton, at the Fowler Street Synagogue and our house at 46 Warner Street in Dorchester, a part of Boston just north of Mattapan, was close to the synagogue. My father, despite his distaste for his stepmother Gertrude, remained devoted to his father, and my mother was fond of her father-in-law. His aristocratic bearing, rabbinical learning, and beaming smile would echo for me as well in the pats on the head I received before and after his death as "Mirsky's *aynikel*"—the chosen grandchild. As Israel's first grandchild, a boy, I was the "*bocher*," the chosen one, and much fussed over in the Fowler Street Synagogue. Where, often deposited with Grandpa for the morning or afternoon, I had the run of the entire building, including the vast banquet hall where a long table was set with bits of herring, sugar-sprinkled cookies, orange soda, bottles of whiskey. Nothing was forbidden once my grandfather, who was in charge both of the building and the congregation, set me down inside its doors. I could climb up to the raised platform, the *bema*, in the midst of services, where I sat among the velvet-clad scrolls of the Torah, topped with silver crowns and tinkling bells. Along Blue Hill Avenue, the central artery of the Jewish district, I was a much-petted object, as Grandpa was one of the community leaders.

I could have begun this chapter with my father's half-sister's remark to me in the late 1970s as I began to research my father's family, the Mirskys. "You were such a happy child Mark." Certainly I was attached to "Mommy." I see now, as I did then, the slim reflection of an older sister, a girl posed by our backyard oak tree who was the mysterious companion of my first memories. She still takes away my breath.

I had to be dragged from beneath my crib in a corner to be taken off to nursery school. My mother had resumed her profession as a social worker. The Baby Book confirms that this scene took place a year and several months before my sister's birth, at 46 Warner Street, a home that I can recall in detail from the spring of 1942 starting with nursery school to the sixth grade until my father moved us back to Mattapan in 1950. (The Jewish streets were contiguous from Roxbury, south to Dorchester and then Mattapan. The Jewish district was known in Boston as "Blue Hill Avenue," its major thoroughfare.) One fragment of early childhood that I still retain is being taken to the swan boats in the Public Gardens by Aunt Sonia and before this by Mother.

I have a hazy sense of the nurseries where my mother parked me. The first, which I "hated" was the Jack & Jill. Hiding from being taken there, the removal of my tonsils, waking up in her absence after hitting my head on a large wooden carpenter's box left in the passageway between my bedroom and the kitchen as I ran from one to the other. There is some floating space, not anchored to a date, possibly before my sister's birth in December of 1942, when, as a child, I was expected to be toilet trained. I was not breastfed (according to my father, my mother had some problems producing milk) and without diapers, as a three-year-old, I was expected to know how to "go to the bathroom." My mother's withdrawal from my body in this respect was subtle. I must have been bribed with many attentions to wean myself into an independence of both bowel movements and bladder. I remember marching into the living room, while my parents were entertaining guests, and announcing to general and condescending laughter, as well as my mother's discomfort rather than the applause I was expecting, that I had just "made a doodie." The euphemism "bowel movement" was not in my vocabulary. I mentioned, as well, associated with the black woolen sailor suit, wetting a bed in Bridgeport. That I had not met the standard of my older cousins' achievements was a common refrain of Mother's, always magnified in the car ride home to Boston. My mother would suffer the same scolding from older siblings. She was still under the spell of her elder sisters Celia, Betty, and Esther. My father's two sisters, his cousins in Montreal, a large family to whom we made annual pilgrimages, never criticized us. This made the contrast between the two families, the Mirskys and Lesslers, even more striking.

My mother's stare was more painful than the disdain from my aunts. Again and again it established the barrier between her body and mine. My father, who was not afraid to throw lamps at me when provoked (though carefully aimed well out of range), make threats, or chase me until I scurried under my bed, was always ready to forgive and hug. The moist warmth of his embrace, his relative indifference to being seen in the bathtub, on the toilet seat, made me aware of our closeness. My mother did not usually touch me unless I was sick. Then her hands, like a nurse's, professional but more compassionate, healing, moved over my aching body. Fevers were treated in the 1940s with an alcohol rub. The smell stung my nose but left me cooler in the sheets, feeling the sensation of Mother's touch. (The rectal thermometer was more troubling. And at four, five, playing doctor, neighborhood boys and girls tried it with twigs). Fevers brought me back into unexpected intimacy with Mother. (And, yet, the photograph above taken at Nantasket Beach, probably when I was between five and six in the summer of 1945, contradicts this pervasive sense of her distance.)

In 1944 and 1945, we rented summer cottages in Hull Village, Massachusetts, at the tip of a peninsula, where trucks full of soldiers, and Italian prisoners of war, rattled past the front door. There were PT boats, their long, sleek hulls, anchored just two or three hundred yards off the beach on the other side of the road. The photographs reveal the glow of my mother holding me close in the surge of the tide, or posing with the family at the flagpole across the street.

Off to the first grade, I knew that something was lost. The sense of separation had begun earlier, with my grandfather Israel's death when I was four and a half. Handsome, silver-haired, with brilliant blue eyes, Grandpa would arrive at our house with an elegant fur- or velvet-collared overcoat, often wearing his Saturday costume as the presiding spirit at the synagogue, a swallowtail or frockcoat, striped pants, and a Homburg with a high crown.

Grandpa Israel sat next to the rabbi, the cantor, the reigning elected officials of Fowler Street, formally the Beth El synagogue, wearing, like the latter dignitaries, a high hat made of silk or beaver. That top hat, the presidential crown of past American inaugurations, still hangs in my closet. And until I was four and a half, I enjoyed Grandpa's undisputed attention since my sister was only a baby, and my cousins in California could only come for a single visit of a week or two each year. Grandpa's pockets were a cornucopia of candy. Traveling to Manhattan on business, I remember him asking to speak to me on the telephone and wanting to know what I wanted as a gift. "Tootsie Rolls," I replied, thinking immediately of a candy that I could not get enough of during the war years. Instead he brought a fancy pencil box, colored and regular black lead, for drawing and writing, a compass and ruler tucked in. At the moment I received the leather case, I was hoping for the chewy chocolate Tootsies, but after his death, the box became a magical object in my toy chest. My grandfather, not my father, was the reigning lord of our house, and I was regularly indulged, learning from Grandpa my first few words of Yiddish. I suspect, had he been there when I was five or six, he would have tutored me in Hebrew.

That disappearance, dramatically announced by the arrival of policemen at our front door, my father's anguished cry, "Why did they send him home from the hospital so soon after pneumonia?" was followed by the arrival of aunts, relatives, a bustling house. My mother withdrew as well in the next year, and I was no longer the "chosen one." That, I imagine, is what my father's sister Aunt Rochelle meant when she remarked to me in my forties, "You used to be such a happy child …" As a five-year-old in kindergarten I maintained the illusion of being special, possibly by being loud and obnoxious, but at six, in the first grade, it was over. There were much smarter children than me in the class. By the second grade I was put in the middle reading group, rather than the first, and listened angrily as they got the more complicated books, the favored *Dick and Jane*, whom I quickly learned to resent, with their perfect and normal American lives.

There was no doting grandfather. My grades in the first few years of elementary school announced to my parents the disaster. I was not that smart. My mother had skipped grades. My father had been an *illui*, a prodigy, at five, six, the talk of the Mirsky family in Pinsk and other towns. Coming to America at fourteen, Wilfred Mirsky zoomed through six grades in a year, won the classical prize during his first year at Boston Public Latin, "with an English dictionary stuffed in my back pocket." I limped through the Boston public schools as an average student but in Hebrew school I disgraced my father who had been a Hebrew teacher. As I reached ten, eleven, my mother began to sense the danger that I would go off the tracks and by twelve, thirteen was trying to repair it by insisting that it was enough for her if I was "happy." It was plain, however, that my father did not see it that way. He rarely spoke directly to me in those years. "Your son," was his preface at the table. He communicated his displeasure through my mother as she reported, "Your father ..."

My father's political career required that we, his family, go out into the neighborhoods of a political district, Ward Fourteen, which stretched from very poor streets in Roxbury, through decent, and lower-middle-class streets in Dorchester, to the relatively prosperous streets of twin-family homes, usually landlord and renter, in Mattapan. We had to carry Dad's nomination papers for state representative in the Massachusetts legislature, up first, second, third floors to strangers' front doors every two years. It made me queasy—knocking on doors and asking a favor of people I didn't know. My mother, over-stressed by all of Dad's demands on her managerial skills, was deaf to my protests. My father squelched objections with "Do you want to eat?" On the other hand, the drama of his political campaigns, the excitement of watching my father on the floor of the legislature making speeches, mocking his opponents, the fact that he often took me on his tours across the state, and welcomed me into the lobby of the House of Representatives, where access was restricted but where I had free rein, absorbing the atmosphere of American politics, cancelled out my humiliations. I experienced doors slammed in my face from families who were supporters of other candidates, but also met those who knew and loved my father. Later, as African-American families beginning to trickle into Roxbury, I talked to men and women clearly superior to me in manners and extraordinarily polite, others angry at all "whites," not afraid to show it, and who would gladly interrupt my spiel about my father and the Massachusetts "Fair Employment Law" he had written with their view of the world. I learned about "Black anger," when it was concealed from many others in New England at the time since there were relatively few African-Americans living there in the 1940s.

My mother was my father's conscience and she kept him almost unwaveringly honest in a fairly corrupt world. She was proud of his political career, his refusal to play by the rules of the game, his stubborn independence on the floor of the House of Representatives. In four two-year terms he left a remarkable record of legislative accomplishment. She glowed at family meetings, proud of what her husband was doing and had accomplished. We arrived in our pedestrian Dodge economy four-door as her brothers and sisters drove up in Cadillacs or at least a Buick gleaming with chrome. Some of their Connecticut and Long Island homes were opulent. My father had decided that it was unwise to be a landlord as a Democrat elected from a district of salesmen, small shopkeepers, taxi drivers and workers struggling to make a living. There were very few single homes in Ward Fourteen, so one either rented or lived with one's tenants in a two- or three-decker. Dad had sold our house after his first election. For several years we rented the first floor of the Warner Street house, then moved to Mattapan, where again we rented. Almost all of my uncles and aunts owned their houses. Some seemed to me like mansions with their wide lawns and many rooms. As I grew up they represented for me the world of F. Scott Fitzgerald's "Winter Dreams," an affluent social world of luxury, though I doubt that they cared for country or yacht clubs. My father, perhaps uneasy that he could not provide my mother with their cars and houses, made light of such things. With one exception, Aunt Celia's oldest son Mitchell, most of our extended family lived in that suburban world where much of what was specifically Jewish was slowly laundered out of their lives. Or so it seemed. Later, while reading Philip Roth and Harold Brodkey, I recognized that the Lesslers were part of a very specific American-Jewish culture. Ward Fourteen, my father's political district until its Jewish population fled, smelled of Eastern Europe and held on to something of that world's intense religious life. I also learned more of what drove the Lesslers to grasp at material things, and feel proud of them, and generous as they were to each other, recognized how strong the ties were that bound the twelve brothers and sisters together.

My mother's career as a social worker was over, but she worked tirelessly beside my father as his untitled campaign manager. For the next fifteen years or so, every second year, she was on the telephone calling twelve, thirteen, fourteen thousand numbers, everyone whose street address fell within my father's political district as a state representative to Ward Fourteen. When circulars had to be folded, envelopes addressed, stairs climbed so as to have voters personally sign my father's nomination papers, we were all drafted; my sister, me, but foremost—until she dropped exhausted into bed—my mother. What did this cost her? Our house was filled with the sad cases and hangers-on that attach like barnacles to political campaigns and she could barely disguise her distaste for them, lacking my father's relish in eccentrics. And there were the late night pinochle parties in the kitchen that filled our Dorchester house with cigar smoke and the shouts of Dad's cronies at his card tactics, "Jesus, Mirsky!" She was cranky enough to be known among this circle as "Lady Macbeth." On the other hand, she was proud of my father's accomplishments in the legislature and she took an active role in the discussions that preceded his votes and committee work there. The photograph above is from the campaign brochure of spring 1948.

My mother, though, had a secret. I learned from my sister that in the summer of 1948 my mother had a miscarriage while I was away at summer camp. She was 36 years old. It must have shaken her but she was still a girl in those first Julys and Augusts at our beach cottage, the older sister who skipped ahead of me as we explored the empty lots across the street. My father bought the cottage soon after he gave up ownership of Warner Street. It was only three quarters of an hour's drive from our rented apartment in Mattapan, at the bottom of a street surrounded by cemetery green space. Climbing up the cliff in a sandpit opposite our house, bending down the barbed wire on an old fence, we gained entry to an abandoned military fort. I remember Mother vaulting over that fence to lead us in exploring acres of pasture and buried military installations. The fort had housed cannons to command the southern entrance to Boston Harbor. Across its fields rose a concrete tower where during World War Two they had scanned the waves for German U-boats. Even four years later, when I was fourteen or fifteen, it was thrilling to see Mother's slim, handsome figure dive beside my father into the ocean at the foot of our hill, while Dad's body showed the bulge of too many political banquets and irregular meals.

I was a boy when I first came out to the beach cottage. Dirty words were something I heard in Dorchester and my mother had explained sex to me when I was eight years old or so, but I first heard "fuck" on the playground in Hull, where the village kids were bored, nasty, and sophisticated in such matters. My mother had to explain sex in more graphic terms all over again and warn me about what language was permissible and what was not. She was very good at this, no doubt the gift of her professional training as a social worker, but in a few years, thirteen, fourteen, I was beyond her training.

I was an unhappy adolescent, ill at ease with myself, scratching my face, trembling with sexual need, doing mediocre work at school and increasingly desperate as I came up against my limits in mathematics and languages. In subjects that I loved like English, I was weighed down by the rigidity of uninspired teachers. Girls at that age sprang ahead of most boys. At fourteen, fifteen, my friends and I were often forced to date girls one or two years younger. By fifteen, sixteen, at the all-boys school Boston Public Latin, where graduation could guarantee you admission to a good college, there was no chance to meet girls. In junior high school, where classes were mixed, the attractive girls in Dorchester-Mattapan had already begun dating older boys. My next-door neighbor, a year younger, who had blossomed into womanhood at twelve, was a professional model at fourteen, and soon going out with Red Sox baseball players. At thirteen and a half, when she looked like a Hollywood starlet she briefly taught me on her front steps how to "French kiss." Or perhaps it was one of her compassionate friends at a back porch gathering down the street, a girl not so developed, but already far out of reach.

My mother tried to help but I was an awkward adolescent. I was beginning to define my sense of who I might be by retreating into books, playing the part of an intellectual rebel. My love of theater might have brought us closer together (in fact she encouraged me one summer to join the troupe of the Boston Children's Theatre that traveled from playground to playground putting on dramatic sketches) but we did not talk about books or theater in a way that I found interesting. Even later on, when we went to see dramas or musicals together, there was little or no conversation in the aftermath of the performance about what we had seen. My father's Harvard education, his memories of teas with Alfred North Whitehead, his reminiscences of the foibles of great scholars like Harry Austryn Wolfson began to draw my attention. My mother either could not or would not follow the conversation. And I was cruel to her, happy to have something with which I could tease her. I proposed that she read Plato. My father professed enthusiasm for philosophy; he gave me Will Durant's *The Story of Philosophy* and talked about his fascination in college with Spinoza. My mother shrugged off the challenge and remarked that she didn't understand Plato; neither did I in any real sense. When I finally read Plato formally as a college freshman, I was lost and dropped the idea of being a philosophy major.

The last book we shared enthusiasm over was Thomas Wolfe's *Look Homeward, Angel*, which she had read as a young woman, one of the few books I took from her shelf in the house. But apart from her recommending that I read it, we never discussed what drew her into Wolfe's story.

Her attempts to give me a social life were embarrassing. When she dragged me off to introductory lessons at the Arthur Murray Dance Studios (for which there was no charge), those evenings were humiliating. Almost everyone in my age group who showed up was a "loser." The dance steps demonstrated were so basic that I knew them already from the community centers, where the club I was part of showed up on Saturday nights for dances. (The local Jewish community center tried to guarantee that every preteen and teen would be cajoled into a club under its supervision.) My father was a good dancer but despite my agility as an actor at school, I could not master the formal steps of the waltz, the foxtrot, the polka. My initiation into dance was influenced by the African-American world, "rhythm and blues," which in Jewish Dorchester was called "the dirty Guinea." Later, at Harvard, I watched African-Americans from Roxbury dance in the back of the Palace on Washington Street and something in me responded as I tried to follow their steps. (I would be surprised to see, in my last pass through her albums that at twenty Mother danced in Harlem at *Small's Paradise* to jazz, and exclaimed in a note beside a pasted-in menu at the same wild energy.) Her role, however, when I was thirteen, fourteen, fifteen, was that of my mother, not of a fellow free spirit. Her mantra for all my misery in trying to find a girlfriend was, "Cut your hair."

And she could be cruel. "Am I good looking?" I asked her when I was thirteen, in a state of perpetual anxiety, tearing at my face, turning a normal curse of adolescence into patches of bleeding sores. I was afraid to go out on Saturday night after staring in front of the bathroom mirror, dissatisfied with my blemishes and perversely making it worse until I gave up, appalled at my appearance.

"Am I good looking?" I bleated.

"Not particularly," she answered.

"Who do you think is good looking?" I grumbled.

"David O."

David O. had become a friend that summer, a Catholic boy, German-Irish from the cottages a few streets over with all-American good looks, a square jaw, snub nose, and creamy complexion. He was undeniably handsome at fourteen. My own face, when I look at photographs, was in confusion at that age but I smoldered with resentment. I knew only too well what she was saying. "I don't find 'you' attractive." My uncle Morris, Aunt Miriam's husband had a square jaw and muscular frame, like David O., maintaining it into middle age, the look of a fit training sergeant in the army. He was also handy with tools, something that eluded my father, who by now was portly and I saw my mother's face of appreciation when Morris and Miriam came to visit as she watched her brother-in-law repair our screen doors. Morris looked a bit like Mother's adored older brother Davey, who had been as handsome as the Hollywood matinee idols as a young man and in middle age was still good looking, had gone to Columbia, had an important career as a lawyer leaving his mark on Connecticut state law and was much more successful, financially, than my father. Under my mother's efforts to make me feel less depressed, her ideological campaign for me to be a happy, normal young man, I felt her distrust of me, even her distaste. "I love you, but I don't like you," even if uttered only once, was echoed in her expression over and over, furious at adventures, which she felt were taking me beyond the border of the ethical. I felt her judgment.

My mother had been forced to take care of herself at thirteen and a half, and show the face of a mature young woman at fifteen to her high school classmates. I was so obviously immature at fourteen, fifteen and continuing on into my twenties that I suspect she felt I was someone who might never "grow up."

One initiative of hers, however, did help. Frugal, ever on the prowl for free tickets, she signed me up for the American Legion's Boys State.

I was just two months shy of sixteen when I went out to the University of Massachusetts, a campus for which my father, as chairman of the House Committee on Education in his second term in the legislature, had secured a fifty-million-dollar building program; a place previously known as a farm training school, "Mass Aggy," his legislation began the process of developing it into its present status as a major university. That spring of 1955 I was cocky, feeling superior to the farce that the legion staged with regards to elections at the week-long encampment on the university's grounds for governor, lieutenant governor, attorney general, etc. My junior year would bring me into the class of a young English teacher who assigned us texts like Dostoyevsky's *Crime and Punishment* and Tolstoy's *War and Peace*. Rather than requiring mindless plot summaries, the standard fare of other instructors, he asked what we thought of the books and I leapt at the opportunity, though it puzzled some of the school "geniuses" whose gift was rote memory. The previous year I was so bored by the requirement of writing plot summaries of the minor classics we were reading, *Silas Marner, The Tale of Two Cities,* summaries that were rarely read aloud and infrequently graded, that I stopped doing them. The ploy I developed (not alone) was to lean over the desk and read the summary of the student who sat there, one of the "good" boys in the class, who unfailingly did the assignments. I was confident that the Master, who had no real interest in teaching, would not be paying attention. (He only quickened when telling stories of his professors at Harvard, the legendary George Lyman Kittredge and Charles Copeland.) In the middle of my recitation, however, stymied by the handwriting of my classmate, I burst out, "Sir, I can't read K's writing."

What was I thinking? I should have failed the semester, or been expelled. Before the next report card there was a parent-teacher conference. The teacher brought up my case with my mother, who promptly replied, "That's awful. Fail him." According to her, he was so impressed by her forthright denunciation of my conduct that he spared me with a C for the semester.

In the spring of 1956, however, despite desolate grades in French and mathematics, I was soaring in English with an A, had won the gold medal in declamation (a signal achievement for a junior) and was looking forward to resuming history in my senior year. The friendship of several older boys who were science majors going on to M.I.T. and Harvard, but like me curious about texts of philosophy and the new "existentialism," had buoyed my confidence. In the picture taken of our family for my father's re-election campaign in 1956, as he ran for a fourth term in the Massachusetts legislature, I have been ordered to cut my hair and smile, but I almost smirk while my sister seems to be equally removed from the occasion. And I am already taller than my father.

So I go off to the legionnaires' carnival, where they marched with chests full of self-awarded medals, ready for mischief. It was obvious from the beginning that there was nothing "fair" about the elections. A circle of boys from the Catholic parochial schools and youth organizations, had already decided on the candidates and the outcome. (Curiously, I would meet several winning candidates later: Daniel Sullivan at Harvard; George Higgins, the detective novelist, at Stanford.) I opted to write a column for the newspaper. Just as my father had the gumption to stand up in the legislature and be the single "Nay" vote, when the other 240-odd votes were "Yea," I also had the *chutzpah* to stand up on a chair in the middle of the choreographed proceedings, shouting out that I was running as an independent candidate for governor. With a voice trained in declamation, I needed no microphone in the huge hall as I intoned that I was running "in the great American tradition of Henry Wallace and Aaron Burr." That caused an immediate uproar and a posse of twenty or thirty boys shouting, "Communist!" chased me from the convention hall. I had to run back to the newspaper office and barricade myself behind the door. The grizzled old gentleman, in charge of our mimeographed sheet, who had been a reporter and an editor for a number of newspapers in Massachusetts over the years, was amused rather than offended by my prank and let me write a scathing column on the official candidates' speeches.

One of the remarks I made was about the candidate for attorney general who, I wrote, displayed his Boy Scout Eagle Badges as his qualification for the Commonwealth of Massachusetts' highest judicial post.

The next day, six-foot-two Ted Kelley came knocking furiously on the door of the newspaper office. He had been elected president of his senior class for the coming year at Wellesley High, and I believe was also one of the star athletes and was strikingly handsome. Somehow I diffused his anger, tickled that he cared about what I wrote, and we became friends. It made all the difference. Wellesley was a wealthy suburb of Boston where Jews were excluded in the 1950s, by an unspoken understanding among the realtors, from buying property. As Ted's friend though, I was welcomed into his circle. Wellesley High was coed, unlike Boston Public Latin, and its social mores very different from the ones that operated in Dorchester, Mattapan and Roxbury. Boys dated girls of the same age through high school. Ted's girlfriend looked like a model of twenty or twenty-one with a full figure. Ted was also the center of an adoring circle of other young women and he was eager to "fix me up" with one of them. I must have seemed exotic since none of them had dated "Jewish" boys and perhaps I was attractive since their parents usually shared the prejudices that had shut Jews out of the housing market. At one point one of the fathers of a girl I took out on several dates, was so angry that she was speaking to me on the telephone that he pulled the line out of the wall. It didn't really upset me. The girl was still enthusiastic about talking to me. She and her friends, in contrast to those willing to go out on dates with me in Dorchester, were interested in books and ideas. Their conversation, Ted's warm friendship, the glow that it cast over my presence at the parties I was invited to for the seniors at Wellesley High and which subsequently also brought some of his friends close to me, drew me out of my fantasies that I was a pariah. It was an introduction to an America that had existed for me only in the pages of *LIFE* magazine. At the end of my senior year in high school I went along on a four-day hike with Ted and four or five other young men up Mount Katahdin, high in northwestern Maine. I was woefully unprepared, wearing the wrong shoes, bringing the wrong food (I had volunteered to make salmon croquettes, but forgot that you needed to add eggs to flour to make croquettes stick together) but it introduced me to the American wilderness. That hike begat a lifelong love of forests, and my grappling with Henry David Thoreau. We swam naked in cold lakes, hiked almost up to the mountain peak, finding the trail up above the tree line. At one point I fell behind the others, and pausing by a stream rushing down saw to my amazement an otter twisting through the tumbling water. On the final day, driving out from Baxter State Park, we saw moose suddenly by the side of the road, a herd of them rising out of a muddy pond and like elephants of the north, ghostly in the fog of the morning, ambling in front of our automobile, in no hurry to cross and go down the bank on the other side. My parents had never taken me camping. Summer camp as a boy was a world of wooden dormitories, baseball games, music, crafts, but no experience of moving in the solitude of the forest, climbing to high peaks, swimming behind beaver dams, sleeping in the open.

What was my mother's reaction to these new friendships in Wellesley? She liked Ted Kelley, but the non-Jewish girls I was dating made her nervous. When I brought them by the house, she withheld her approval, though my acquaintance with them was short lived.

I was making my own way in the world though. At Harvard the next year, teachers, upperclassmen were finding me interesting. My skills as an actor were projecting me into new social circles. The young women I dated were rarely Jewish. Mother was confused, wanting to be hospitable to all of them, yet afraid that I was leaving the world that she was attached to. My father, by contrast, was curious, even delighted by some of the friends who floated through our house. Young painters came who lacked a bed for the night in Cambridge. I entertained the future Duke of Bedford at a party at our beach cottage. Abby Rockefeller came by with her canoe one afternoon. Mother was unimpressed by this. She wanted me to marry a Jewish girl.

Did she recognize that in the same years in which I was reaching out to other worlds, Scottish, Irish, English, Yankee New England, the Cambridge academic aristocracy, I was also becoming more and more interested in my identity as a Jew? This, however, did not bring us together. It was my father who held the stories of an Eastern European childhood in his head and could unroll a magic carpet of details from his childhood to transport me to that world. When I met the new rabbi at Harvard Hillel, a man who had gone through the death camps of World War Two and had grown up in the Poland of the late thirties and forties, I found someone who began to give me the texts to understand my father's stories. The world of his town, Pinsk, and its rabbinical traditions became more and more romantic. It had all been destroyed in the Holocaust, and that made what had survived in memory, or in the streets of Dorchester, more precious. My father was flattered by my sudden curiosity. My mother felt excluded.

• • •

This is only part of the story. There is a narrative, which might show my mother as coming closer to me during my adolescence and college years; moments of direct looks at each other.

Somewhere in those painful years, when I was fourteen, fifteen, as my mother was on my "case," in a manner that Aunt Miriam would describe as her father's, nudging, nudging, not letting go of an argument or an issue until I was screaming, I simply shut down. In the middle of her incessant monologue that was suffocating me, I withdrew and smiled back. No matter what ammunition she fired, I refused to engage, or let her draw me into a response.

She stopped, suddenly, looked at me curiously, and stared for a long time. "You're on to me, aren't you?" she asked. I didn't answer, but she got up and left the room.

I hadn't planned it. She would certainly send me into screaming again and again, when in a weak moment my defenses would crumble, but we had changed. This was the first time I had seen her looking at herself in regard to me, seeing me as a person, who faced her with his independence. It was an admission on her part that I was someone separate.

In another moment at this age she caught me trying to smoke—perhaps I had raided one of her packs. Both my parents were addicted to tobacco and my mother in particular was a chain smoker. (I have no doubt that it contributed to her early death.) My sister and I were often shut in our parents' car for long trips down to Bridgeport or Long Island from Boston for family meetings. In the winter the windows were closed as they drove and we breathed the air of countless cigarettes stubbed out in the ashtray, growing cranky in the back seats, poisoned by secondary smoke. Discovering me with her cigarettes, instead of scolding me, she talked about it calmly, asking me to put off the decision to smoke for three or four years until I was an adult. I did. By the time I reached college I wasn't interested in smoking any more as there was no social prestige attached to it. The direct, understanding side of my mother always touched me, and often guided my behavior.

She was indeed intimate, even though to my regret I did not manage, or try hard enough to include her in my intellectual life. Again and again she stepped in at critical moments in my life to help or to steer me toward something she felt I ought to have. Despite the gold medal in declamation, the As in History and English, during my senior year, the SAT scores that were so high that they surprised the Boston Public Latin School, my record there over four years was not particularly distinguished. Dartmouth and Bowdoin had accepted me unconditionally but Harvard would not allow me to live in the dormitories. I was admitted, but only if I would commute. It left me in tears, since I had come so close to a dream that I had not dared to have, following my father's footsteps into a college that was a religion to him. He stormed into my bedroom, "You want to be a big fish in a little sea?" he shouted. I angrily went into the dean's office and accused them of offering me a "yellow passport," the fruit of my reading in American history, the notorious second-class citizenship that the United States had let its Chinese workers come into the country with at the turn of the century. "No, no," the young assistant dean insisted, "We think you can even make the dean's list here. There just isn't enough room." My father bought me an old Buick convertible as a consolation prize and I sped off to Harvard Square where I slept in the back seat, trying to join the intellectual life of the college at the cafeterias where students and professors met in May and June, staying late as well through September and October, furious that I was assigned to the commuter's hall, Dudley, and not one of the freshman dormitories. Theater, in a sense, made up for it since I was immediately cast in several of the major productions at the Harvard Dramatic Club, acting with seniors and juniors, even directing the Radcliffe musical (badly) in my freshman year. My mother, though, sensed my frustration, and quietly determined that there were a number of empty freshman dormitory places in the second semester, due to students who had dropped out. She wrote a letter implying that it was unhealthy for me to go on living at home, and they ought to admit me to one of the dormitories as a full-fledged member of the Harvard Class of 1961, and it worked. I got a place in Matthews, even a tiny room of my own, in a double suite. The larger of the two rooms with the fireplace was occupied by a Jewish boy from Arizona, who seemed to tower above me, half a foot taller, the future translator of Mishima and Oe, John Nathan. He was an intimidating individual, not only because of his height and powerful build, and that he was already studying Japanese (from scratch), but he also had a girlfriend who was a professional model back in Arizona, whose handsome figure and face adorned the back of a national magazine. I recall the first time I laid eyes on him and the room, however, because my mother accompanied me with a large laundry bag full of clean sheets and pillowcases, as well as my clothes. John had not changed his sheets since his first day at Harvard. It was black with sweat. My mother took one look at it, and stripped it from his bed, throwing it in the laundry bag to take it home, and putting our own fresh linen on his narrow cot. At the time I was a bit embarrassed, but now I admire her forthright concern for another boy whom she saw needed a bit of maternal care. Her arrival through my four years with that laundry bag embarrassed me. At that point Mother was a commissioner of industrial accidents in Massachusetts, taking a position meant for my father when he left the legislature.

It was almost humorous; the tall, commanding woman, whose face reflected her new judicial authority, with laundry, knocking peremptorily at my door, to make sure I had fresh sheets. I ought to have grown beyond this, but secretly the fact that nothing could change her attitude toward me was reassuring.

It was in my sexual life that my mother was most included. She was privy to some of my most painful secrets, though it was rarely my choice that she should know. She was a skillful detective and from my infancy could follow a trail of cookie crumbs, discarded wrappers to come to an unerring conclusion. She understood the language of sheets and underwear, though she was discrete in this regard. Still, she had an uncanny habit of opening my bedroom door at an inopportune moment if a girlfriend I was wrestling with was in the house.

At the end of my sophomore year at Harvard, teased by a roommate who was much older and had dozens of tales to tell of his exploits with the opposite sex, I crossed a sexual boundary with a young woman that I ought not to have. Despite my grappling and wrestling with girls through adolescence and my first years at college, I was still uninitiated into the mystery of intercourse. Raised in my mother's house, with her strict sense of propriety in front of me, I was a puritan, though I did not suspect it. I seethed with sexual desire but the consequences of making fantasy real without a partner whom I had truly committed myself to were something I had not anticipated. My body reacted violently with guilt, terror and physical consequences. The latter took several weeks to manifest itself and I had already left Cambridge, Massachusetts, and gone out to the tip of Cape Cod, where I had been selected for the repertory company at the Provincetown Playhouse. I found myself in the hands of a small-town doctor who misdiagnosed what would be identified later as a nonspecific urinary infection. Anything suspicious to do with the male organ was gonorrhea in his eyes. His treatment was not just wrong—it was brutal and left me with permanent damage. He was ready to proceed to even more radical procedures that might have crippled me further when my mother intervened. I had to confide my behavior and its consequences since the medical bills passed through the house. Mother was upset with me but taking a calm look at the situation, ordered me into Boston to see a family doctor, a urologist, who counter-ordered all of the Provincetown practitioner's procedures and cured me with an ointment within a week.

I have no idea what my parents' sexual life was all about. I know that at the moment of her death, my father's physical presence was important for my mother. As long as she could stay out of the hospital she did, and she needed him to be close to her. We observed this with bitter humor just a few weeks before her death, when we gathered for the Passover family meal that she managed to come home for, but had to leave, to be taken back to the hospital. One of my cousins attended. He was put in my parents' bedroom, in the twin bed my mother usually occupied, for the night. Dad forgot that Mother wasn't there, and in the middle of the night we heard an outraged shout from my cousin, as Dad tried to climb in beside the body he thought was his wife's. Throughout the whole of childhood, adolescence, adulthood, I saw, heard nothing. It never occurred to me to be curious.

I entered my junior year at Harvard in that strange twilight moment as the 1960s were about to begin, diaphragms and then birth control pills began altering attitudes toward premarital sex. It was still, however, a time when classmates took trips to Puerto Rico when the women they were making love to became pregnant and needed an abortion that was illegal in the United States. There were only too many cases of friends whose procedures were not just dangerous but left women sterile. There were months when I lived in terror that I was going to have to assume the responsibilities of marriage and fatherhood. My mother looked at me sternly, again and again. As I graduated Harvard, Mother met me for breakfast, just the two of us. I was in love with a Radcliffe freshman with more experience than I had and my mother was concerned. There was no such thing as "fool-proof" birth control she warned me as we had an unusually frank conversation.

Something was altering in her attitude toward me, though I was not aware of it at the time. I had a sudden flush moment as I graduated Harvard, almost received a Fulbright to study theater in London. I did in fact receive it from the New York Theatre Committee, but since it was to work with the left-wing director Joan Littlewood, the State Department intervened and cancelled it. I was also awarded a Wilson Fellowship, as well as admission into the Stanford University graduate program in English. Unexpectedly, at the last moment, probably in recognition of my work in the Harvard Dramatic Society (I had directed the third production on the main stage of the Loeb Drama Society), I was inducted into Phi Beta Kappa. I expected my father to proudly show up for the ceremony. He loved such triumphal moments of pomp. He did not. Was he a bit chagrined that at the last moment I had graduated Harvard College with a degree that was a step up from his *cum laude*? (In fairness, Mother did come and reported that Dad had a court appearance, which he could not shift—and the Phi Beta Kappa announcement was made at the last moment.) Was that my mother's moment? She came to see me march in the Phi Beta procession, now a commissioner of industrial accidents, the glow of her authority not just in the family but in the commonwealth surrounding her. She took on the role that my father had backed her into, and never quite surrendered its authority.

How had this happened? In 1958, my father decided not to run in the Democratic primary for reelection in Ward Fourteen. He explained to me that he couldn't serve another term in the House under the Democratic Speaker of the House of Representatives. The man, a towering giant, was a bully and according to Dad, loved nothing better than to knock an opponent down in a fistfight. (I had a personal taste when the Speaker exploded in front of me, a sixteen-year-old, in a string of obscenities as my father pleaded for a favor from him at the entrance of the House's lobby.) Dad didn't have the money or connections to run for the state senate, nor the warm friendship with the new Democratic governor that he had with Governor Dever or Tip O'Neill, who as House Speaker, had landed Dad a committee chairmanship after only two years in the legislature. Dad made a deal with the sitting governor to rewrite the latter's proposal for a statewide sales tax, a tax my father loathed as an unfair imposition on the poor and the lower-middle class. Dad had helped bottle it up so it could not reach the floor of the House, as clerk of the Committee on Taxation. The rewritten bill offered some additional protection to the poor and credits for parents who had to foot the bill for their children's education. The governor, according to my father, promised him a judgeship, a position my father had long coveted. It was a prize that he had hoped for through several administrations. "The Republicans," he complained to me, naming a prominent Yankee who had recently been seated, "just contribute regularly to the Party each year, and when they want to sit, only have to mention it to the state's Party. The Democrats don't have that mechanism." And when push came to shove, the governor wanted to be paid for the judgeship he offered. It was a seat on the Superior Court, according to my father, and in a single year he would have recouped the sum asked and gone on through the rest of his life at a handsome salary. I asked my father, mischievously, why he had refused.

"You're not your own man," he replied. "Everyone knows that you paid. You can't make your own decisions on the bench. You are always subject to be shaken down or told what to do." (David Nyhan who became one of *The Boston Globe*'s top reporters, told me that as young man working for the Democratic Party he was given a list of judges' telephone numbers during a subsequent Massachusetts gubernatorial campaign and told to "shake them down" for contributions.) Dad added in an angry whisper, "If I sit, I want to sit as a judge, making decisions on the merit of the case." When my father refused to pay, the governor offered him a seat on the Industrial Accident Board as a commissioner.

"I've been a commissioner," my father complained. After his defeat in the ward's Democratic primary of 1951, Dad had briefly served as a commissioner of the Metropolitan Transit Authority until Governor Herter abolished the sitting board. He turned to my mother, "You take the position."

Mother was reluctant. Everyone understood that the post of commissioner was being given to my father. A seat on the Industrial Accident Board did not require its members to be lawyers, but its decisions were appealed directly to one of the highest courts in the commonwealth. (I believe it was the Superior Court.) The law relating to industrial accidents was complex and some of the best lawyers in the state argued before the board. My mother had been in the background of Dad's career, coming in to clean up my father's desk in the law office twice a year, acting as the unofficial and tireless campaign manager through all his political runs for office, successful and unsuccessful. As his aide de camp in the ward, she had taken on the leadership of the local junior high school PTA, served without salary under Governor Dever as chairman of a commission on immigration to the commonwealth. And of course there was her degree in training from Simmons College in social work, her work as a supervisor of girls at a Rhode Island orphanage, the fact that in the middle and late 1930s, as a young woman, she had been responsible for a district job of retraining centers from Connecticut through Rhode Island and Massachusetts as a professional employee of the federal government. She was hardly removed from the plight of exploited workers. She told Dad she preferred to remain in the role of a housewife and mother. He was insistent. He had agreed not to run for state representative in exchange for a job. He had expected to be a judge, but he saw some wriggle room for himself if she became the commissioner. It might be possible to break the ethnic barrier in Boston that kept the city council, which after an electoral change a few years before led to citywide rather than district elections, all Irish, except for a lone Italian seat. My mother probably sensed that she would be thrust into a double role; sitting as a commissioner and yet expected to continue as Dad's backseat campaign manager. Still, it was hard to resist my father when he was charging at you. My sister and I had the option of fleeing the house, but not Mother. She pleaded that she knew nothing about law, let alone industrial accident law. My father, however, was a brilliant teacher. I had seen that when he tutored me, a balky, untalented student in Hebrew school for my bar mitzvah; training me in the trope for the lengthy portion from *Isaiah* that I was expected to sing from the stage during the Sabbath service, giving me a sense of its poetry. (He invited no less than two thousand people, not only all of his supporters in addition to my mother's family and his own, but members of the legislature. His political opponents showed up too, though I never found out whether they were invited). In just a few months he prepared my mother so well in both the general law and the specifics of industrial accident law, that she never had a single decision in the four years and some odd months she served as commissioner, overturned. (Just the other day, a neighbor from our summer town, noticing one of the old campaign badges we have pinned to a board on the wall, mentioned that he knew the McGuire whose pin announced a candidacy for lieutenant governor. Our neighbor asked McGuire, when they met in a Worcester restaurant if he remembered the Mirskys in Massachusetts politics. "Ruth Mirsky?" McGuire replied, mentioning my mother not my father, "She was the most compassionate person I ever met. I argued some of my first cases in front of her."

My father loved to repeat the story of former Governor Endicott Peabody approaching him when the latter had a case about to come up in front of my mother at the accident board. "Could you put a word in on my behalf?" Peabody asked my father. "Governor," Dad replied, "The only possible influence it could have would be prejudicial to your case." We, my father, my sister and I knew that was true. She was incorruptible, although it did not help her cause when her term was over and Dad tried to get it renewed.

After the first few months, my mother began to enjoy her new role. She was now the major breadwinner in the family. She enjoyed the prerogatives. The commissioners decided to attend a convention in Hawaii with members of industrial accident boards from other states. My father balked at the expense. "I'm going," my mother announced. "You can stay behind if you want to." My father quickly decided to go along. In her mid-forties, still slim and handsome, glowing with her newly acquired authority, my mother was a striking figure. Dad began to become apprehensive about her traveling all over Massachusetts to hear cases. The commonwealth paid for her hotel room and transportation when the board met in the center and in the west of the state. There were young, attractive lawyers waiting to plead before her, and Dad was suddenly jealous. He insisted on accompanying her when she went out of town. It was a demand that amused my mother no end, not used to such attention. I don't know how she communicated this to me, but it tickled us both. (Dad had been the one who was always late to the house, who lit out every two years or so to see his sister Hilda in California, often on his own, who traveled regularly to Montreal by himself to see his two aunts' extended family there and his half-sister, Rochelle.) In fact, the hearings before the commissioners could get quite rough. One anecdote that she enjoyed was her strategy when two lawyers were arguing before her, lost their sense of propriety and began to berate each other with obscenities.

"Gentlemen," she said, rising from the bench to leave the room, "When you can behave as gentlemen, I will listen to the case. Until then I will be in the corridor, where you can find me, if you decide to."

The commissionership, however, had not been for a full term. It was over in four and a half years. And as my mother had feared, Dad began to run for office, leaning on her. One of the letters I received from her in the fall of 1961 tucks those grim details in between advice about linen, towels, laundry (everything she made sure I had while I was at college and graduate school in California) and boxes of my books that I had requested my parents send.

"This is three days post-primary. The results were disastrous—but Dad's vote in Ward 14 was excellent & Ward 18 rallied [wards that still had a large majority of Jewish voters]. *He now has dreams of Senatorship."* There follows questions about the difference between classes in the East and the West, names of people to look up, and then a personal voice that I missed entirely at the time but hear clearly now with a pang in my chest. *"The night is still and lonely—Your father is out consoling himself with pinochle ... So many things to do mopping up after a campaign—it has sort of got to be done—but everything eventually will get straightened out—it always does—at the moment however, it seems overwhelming—in any event that's the reason we couldn't get your shipments out sooner—.*

"Let us know whether the books have arrived safely—and how you are faring now that you have settled down—We miss you—we miss you—so keep the letters flying.

"Love

"Mother"

Dad's campaigns, taxing her strength, would go on and on, more and more out of touch with reality. When her term as a commissioner was over, their income was severely reduced. I was out of college already, happily, so my bills were over for my parents, but my father's best efforts could not get my mother reappointed and when I briefly touched base with them again, after completing my Air Force Reserve duty in the late spring of 1963, the atmosphere in our Mattapan apartment was tense. Without the business that came in as a result of his political office, my father's law practice was going downhill. They had hoped that he and my mother could develop a business based on her experience with industrial accident law, but it did not happen. Dad's campaigns for a seat on the city council were equally futile. My mother confided in my sister that she was worried about my father's state of mental health. When not running for offices that given limited resources there was little likelihood of his being elected to—city council or state senate—he was depressed. I fled to Manhattan at the end of the summer of 1963, and my sister got married. I spent several months trying to break into the New York theater and worked on a draft of the manuscript that, abridged as a collection of short stories, earned my master's at Stanford and in its original form became my first published novel *Thou Worm Jacob*. I found a job at American Heritage writing copy.

My father had advised me that I was eligible for a small dole of unemployment insurance, as a result of my military duty, and my membership in the acting union, Equity. With this, some twenty-two dollars a week, I was able to pay my rent on the Lower East Side and eat for at least five of seven days in the week at its inexpensive Polish restaurants. It was a relief to my mother when I was hired in December at American Heritage. This enabled me to put a few dollars in the bank. I began to develop a career as a director as well. I received a fellowship at the Breadloaf Writer's Conference in the summer of 1964 and started seeing a young woman whom I had met several years before when she was just sixteen and visiting Woodstock, New York, where I acted at the playhouse with a professional company that included Estelle Parsons. In 1965, I began to teach at The City College of New York, inheriting a position from a fellow writer, Jerome Charyn, whom I had met at Breadloaf. I had recommended Jerome for a job at Stanford to my former professor, the American critic, Albert J. Guerard. When my novel was accepted at Macmillan in 1965, Guerard invited me to join the Voice Project at Stanford, headed by the novelist John Hawkes.

Now, in 1966, when I went out to Palo Alto to teach, both my mother and father were dreaming of leaving Boston behind them.

Did I betray them by coming back to New York City?

Some years after my mother's death, my aunt Sonia, would remark in an odd moment, "You know Mark, when you first came to New York City, your mother told me, 'Don't be too nice to Mark.'"

"Why?" I asked, dumbfounded.

"She said, 'We want him to come back to Boston.'"

"If she had told me that," I said, surprised, "I would have gone back in an instant."

Was it true? Did Mother really say that to my aunt? Was my response, hearing it, after my mother's death, honest?

Why had she kept repeating that refrain through my childhood, adolescence, "Twenty-one, you're out of the house."

Why did she conceal just how much she wanted me near her?

Would I have stayed in Boston if I knew that she wanted, possibly needed, me a few doors away, or no more than a half-hour's drive?

Certainly my first response on hearing this was to cry, "Yes." One night on a mindless TV talk show, the host asked the actress Goldie Hawn what she wanted most in the world. Without a pause, the actress replied, "To please my mother." *Yes*, I nodded in front of the screen.

In Boston, I was still my father's son, in the shadow of his brilliant childhood in Eastern Europe, his early achievements in school, linguistic abilities, and his political accomplishments during eight years in the Massachusetts House of Representatives. My mother's eye still saw me as a reckless adolescent. She hid her pride in me almost to the last moments of her life. Others told me that she went up and down the corridors at the Shattuck Hospital as long as she could get out of bed, smiling, suggesting to patients that they might like to read her son's first novel. When it was published I only remember her scolding me for including the name of a real person from the streets of Dorchester in the book, exposing myself to a suit for slander. In those six years between 1961 when I graduated Harvard College, and 1967 when she went to the hospital, the first indications of a change in the way she allowed me to see her were in her letters and our brief times together at the house. But I was too full of myself, too apprehensive of her grip over me. If I had noticed, it would have been hard to resist the tug of her curiosity, her love.

New York City was full of possibilities for me. Harvard University had no MA program in creative writing. Its doctoral program in English was forbidding for a person who had demonstrated incompetence mastering foreign languages. None of my professors at Harvard had encouraged me to go into such a program. At Stanford, when the department chairman generously offered me full support to become a doctoral candidate, and a year's travel in Europe, the man I had come to Stanford University to study with, Albert J. Guerard, didn't just discourage me from seeking a doctorate, he basically ordered me to leave. Harvard Law, where, my father kept hinting I ought to apply, required a course in statistics and my eye still swam at the sight of graphs, mathematical signs, number problems. Teaching in a public school seemed like a dead-end and the Boston world of theater was small with few opportunities. No one was offering anything in Massachusetts. It was in California and New York City that there were opportunities.

Why didn't my mother tell me that she wanted me back in Boston? She was herself probably unsure of how a mother should show her feelings to a young man growing into his middle, then late twenties. She had no experience of a mother after the age of thirteen.

She needed me and I needed to know that.

It took her dying to let us both see this.

Chapter Four

As a little boy, this photograph of Mother's mother, Hannah or "Annie," hung on our living room wall. I saw Grandmother as much older than she was when it was taken. Here, at the turn of the century, Annie is twenty-five, twenty-six, possibly as old as twenty-seven, no longer a girl but a young woman, an image that my mother never saw but that she clung to.

Now as I study the progression of photographs: Annie, at twenty with a beautiful, wasp-like waist and delicate face, then her marriage photograph followed by succeeding ones in which, after bearing child after child, she became heavy and thick through her torso, cheeks, chins, I read part of my family's story. It is revealed in a photograph from 1911, the year before my mother is born, where Annie, with Miriam (the baby born that year), sits in the midst of ten children. After the birth of Mildred, the last of the twelve that survived in 1914, Annie resumes something of her former face and form. In the photograph above, taken after the first few children, a trace of the girl still lingers in her eyes though I see it only now, staring from my own parapet of seventy-five years. This photograph of Annie, a competent business-woman and mother of a growing family, is one of two images that my mother, Ruth, prized and modeled herself upon. The other was taken from one in Mother's album, a few years before Annie's death. The shadow of her illness almost dissipates in her smile. I remember seeing it in Mother's most private, devoted place—by the mirror on her bureau.

The larger photograph of Hannah "Annie" Lessler hung next to that of my father's mother, Devorah. Annie's mild, thoughtful look was always reassuring when I stared up at the wall, By contrast, my grandmother Devorah glowered, though my father was silent about why. The set of his mother's jaw presaged her death a few months after it was taken. My father's father, Israel Mirsky, joined his wife Devorah and Annie Lessler on our wall after his death when I was four and a half. He was the only grandparent I had ever actually met. Whenever we moved, these three portraits took up their stations of prominence in the dining or the living room.

I know so little about my mother.

Her story, as I understand it, is partly based on photographs. Like fragments of a language, a text dug up on tablets, scrolls found in jars far back in a cave, already crumbling, this narrative has an editor, a person who not only assembles but whose own experience dictates his interpretation. My mother's birth certificate is stamped: April 15, 1912. Her parents, Annie and Joseph, the former thirty-eight, the latter forty, their address as 234 West 121st Street, but gives her name as "Sylvia." She did retain that as a middle initial, but who first nick-named her "Ruth"? No one can tell me that.

I am a scavenger, and so I hold on to every scrap that my cousins or aunts have given me, envelopes full of photographs, albums, and documents. Unfortunately, like archeological digs, the circumstances of a bowl, a scroll or jar's recovery, the place, the level, the neighboring evidence, is almost as important as the artifact itself. I can't always tell whether she carefully pushed a photograph into the little black corners that held her most precious pictures, glued firmly into place on a page where it was surrounded by expressions of happy times; or whether it was simply stuffed in as an afterthought. I can, however, report one strange fact that did not register until after my mother's death. There was not a single photograph of her father in any of her albums though many existed in the collections of other family members. Even more telling is the fact that my father's father and mother hung on the living room wall, but only my mother's mother was there.

As a little boy I sometimes traipsed through Mother's albums when I came upon them in my relentless search of the house's closets for secrets. They were kept in a box, hidden away deep in the recesses of hanging coats, boxes of shoes, hats, at the very back of the deepest closet in our apartment. They were stacked on a shelf, which required me to drag a stepladder from the kitchen, and it was an expedition that could not be embarked on while my parents were in the house, or a babysitter on watch.

A copy of a photograph of Annie from the last years her life is pasted into the front of Mother's first album, on the back of the cover. It might well have come first in this book because it was the image that my mother fastened on to the back side of the cover as the beginning of the two albums when she began to record her life at thirteen. This was a death album. The photograph was probably taken the year before Annie died in 1925 and the album started just after Ruth lost her mother. Four grandchildren surround Annie. I recognize "Buddy" or Mitchell Greenbaum, son of my mother's oldest sister, Aunt Celia, and her baby, Shirley; Mother's second oldest sister Betty's daughter, Muriel; Annie's youngest, Mildred, who clings to her skirts only three years older than Annie's first grandchild. The photograph was intended to hold the position of honor, the first word.

Above it, my mother, Ruth Sylvia Lessler, making light of what was to follow, wrote: "just a scrap or two / that would not mean much to you." It is the verse of a fourteen year old. There are no photographs in my mother's albums, or in any of my cousins' that I am aware of, which show my mother with her mother, Annie Lessler.

Why?

Were none taken?

In pasting the photograph of her mother with her grandchildren, was my mother speaking to the strongest image she had of Annie Lessler?

Did my mother acquire the album immediately after Annie's death to paste pictures, theater tickets, corsages, and newspaper clippings into it?

There are no photographs or mementos of Mom's (did I ever call her that—"Mom"?) from 1925 or any moment that took place before the photographs featured in her albums. All the images from 1912 until 1925 that appear in this book were borrowed from the albums of older cousins or given to me by my aunts and uncles. Only in 1926 does Ruth Sylvia Lessler, my mother, paste in a photograph of her drama group at Central High School in Bridgeport from a newspaper. Was it a way of recovering from the shock of her mother's death in the fall of 1925 that set my mother to recording her life? Or, since it is a photograph of her in costume as a character, does it speak to her search for a persona?

Again, I am bewildered by the silence that she left behind her.

My mother was the twelfth child in a family of thirteen siblings, five brothers and seven sisters who survived their first year. (One, Benjamin, died within a few months of birth.) My cousin, Abby, my uncle Simon's oldest daughter, recalls hearing that this Benjamin was the first child.

This, however, opens up some conjecture about the circumstances of the marriage—for Celia, the oldest was born on March 10, 1896, and Isaac Joseph Lessler and Hannah ("Annie") Kurland were married the previous year on March 29, 1895. My aunt Dorothy says that Benjamin died of summer sickness, but if the child was conceived before the marriage there was barely nine months between a death in June and Celia's 's birth. Annie is slim and petite in her wedding photograph. It seems that Aunt Dorothy's memory is correct and that Benjamin was born between Dorothy and her older brother, David.

The boys were all older than my mother: Simon, the oldest, born in 1897, Hyman or "High," born in 1899, Robert or "Bob," in 1902,

Davey in 1904, and Jules in 1908. Jules was four years older than my mother and evidently a terrible tease—I heard this from her many times—and his picture has "pest-beloved brother" written beside it in the album. Celia, my mother's oldest sister, born in 1896, was followed by Betty in 1898, Esther in 1901, Dorothy or "Dotty" in 1906. The sister my mother would be closest to was Miriam or "Mim," who was two years older than her, born on June 29, 1910. The only one younger than my mother, Mildred, the last of the siblings, was born in 1914.

Mother was born on April 4, 1912, when the family still lived in Manhattan and almost certainly named for her maternal grandmother, Tsivia Rochel Kurland. "Sivia Ruchel" Mother wrote in my baby book, the one great grandparent she recorded on her side of the family tree. Tsivia or Sivia had died the previous year. (Mother's name is listed as Sylvia on her birth certificate.) My mother was known in her family as "Ruth Sylvia," preserving the "Tsivia" as "Sylvia." (After her death, my father told me to recite Kaddish for her as "Rochel," which is Yiddish for "Rachel," not "Ruth.") My mother lost her mother, Annie, when she was thirteen and a half in October of 1925.

As I mentioned previously, I have no pictures of my mother with Annie, though my mother did talk about Annie with admiration and peppered conversation with her Yiddish or Yiddish-English expressions. "My big spoon, *mein grosse lapin*," (Mother translating it for me probably misunderstood *lefin*, the Yiddish for "hand," thinking it meant spoon, though the import of the rebuke is the same) when I ladled more onto my plate than she thought appropriate, "Don't mix *kashe* with borscht," (two conflicting foods for an observant household— *kasha*, or kasha, usually has a meat sauce, while borscht is served with a dollop of sour cream—meat and milk are always served separately in a kosher household), and "*Iz nisht gefilte fish*," (Which meant that it was something but not the real thing—it lacked the subtle taste of the elusive homemade fish pudding or gefilte fish.) I have mentioned that hazy, sepia photograph of Annie a few years before her death, when illness had worn her down to the slimmer figure she had once enjoyed when she first married. This image sat on Mother's dresser, taking pride of place among the perfume bottles; it perches now above my writing desk.

You will find that photograph in the chapter, "Who Was My Mother"—a photo of Annie surrounded by her grandchildren—but Mother's dresser copy cut out all the grandchildren and her younger sister, Mildred, preserving just Annie's face.

The amused smile and regal bearing of Annie shines through. An astute businesswoman, in contrast to her husband Joseph, I recognize in Annie's tightly compressed lips, bending upward in good humor, dimpling her plump cheeks, a familiar look with which my mother regarded me, not entirely devoid of suspicion.

Another picture joined Annie's on my mother's bureau, namely Miriam's. Miriam was the sister Mother was closest to. She would marry a handsome salesman, Morris Pozen, whose bark and bearing suggested his World War Two service as an army sergeant. Miriam would be the most forthright with me of all the family members I encountered. My mother had suffered, Miriam told me, from being born between herself, whose bouts of illness brought her the constant attention of her mother, and the youngest, Mildred, who was coddled as the "baby." There is a photograph that wandered into my possession long after my mother's albums had been closed by her, of an infant in a baby carriage in which the name of another sister has been crossed out and "Ruthie" written in.

My wife says that she can discern the determined look of my mother in the baby's face—laughing but direct. Was it taken before her younger sister, Mildred, was born? My mother obviously resented losing her position as the "baby." She resented Mildred and I noted that Mother was never particularly friendly

to Mildred, my youngest aunt, at family events. (Mildred's husband according to my older cousins was an inveterate gambler, and though others in the family found this attractive and cousins have boasted to me of their trips to Las Vegas with him, Mother and Dad obviously did not.) My mother was closer to Miriam than to any of her other sisters or brothers. Throughout our childhood, Miriam, her husband Morris and her children were the Lesslers that we saw the most, and most frequently entertained at our beach house.

The first photographs I have where I can clearly identify my mother, she must be four, since according to the notes they were taken in Flatbush in 1916.

My mother, Ruth, at four is looking warily to the side while her older sister, Miriam, smiles into the camera's eye and her brother Jules, at eight, looks serious but a bit befuddled, his arm around Miriam. "The Pore Kid" [sic.] has been written across the bottom of the photograph, as if it was always Jules' fate to be in the company of the younger rather than the older children and condescended to. My mother's scribble next to another picture of Jules, "my pest-beloved brother," is just one of many moments. At family meetings, his older, often more successful siblings still looked on Jules as "the pore kid." Two of the younger ones, my mother and Miriam, skipped grades in school and he suffered by comparison. Of all my uncles, however, Jules was the most fun to be with. He remained a kid at heart, sometimes joined my games in our backyard and his teasing was light hearted and affectionate. Apart from Simon, however, whose home in Providence meant that we saw him frequently, Jules, a salesman, was the one who often showed up at our house.

Above is a picture of Annie in Flatbush around the same time of the photograph of Ruth with Miriam and Jules, posing in front of their house. Is Annie distracted, amused, faintly ironic?

Two years later in 1918, Ruth at six years old is smiling in the photograph but there is no sweetness in her expression. I read a fierce determination in her eyes as she squeezes into a photograph with the oldest, Betty and Celia, already cradling their own babies. Ruth intends to be noticed, to get her share of attention. Her lips are again compressed. In the backyard of their Bridgeport home in 1918, my mother peers from on top of the group beside Bob, who together with Davey, was her favorite brother, but ten years older than her. Like Celia, Betty, Esther, Bob is in another world. My mother is up there, making sure she is not obscured, and when the group switches to the front yard, on the same day I suspect, but certainly the same year, my mother places herself at the very bottom in the center of attention, next to Dorothy, and Ruth has the same extravagant ribbon in her hair

as her sister, six years older.

Here is Ruth, dancing in front of a Bridgeport house with her sister Dorothy.

Though six years younger, she obviously intends to imitate Dorothy, copying the gestures of her adolescent sibling, competing. Taking a train back to Manhattan from the hospital in Boston with Aunt Dorothy who has come to see my dying mother, her older sister reminisces about how particular Ruth was as a girl. "Everything had to be just so, her dresses, her hair. She was meticulous. All that changed when she married your father. He didn't care about it, and so she let it go." I remembered how my uncles, her brothers would tease her at family weddings. "Ruth, the same old dress?" And they let my father know that he wasn't doing right by their sister. On the drive returning to Boston from Bridgeport or Long Island, Dad often fumed.

Now on the train, Aunt Dorothy, trying to lighten the gloom we both feel at my mother's condition, remembers her little sister Ruth, in a fit of jealousy, envying her older sister Dorothy's beautiful underwear, and tells me, "She took a scissors and cut up my silk panties." There is a pause and my aunt adds, "I smacked her."

My mother will not be ignored. To get her fair share is something I observed in my own daughter named after Mother, Ruth, as she watched portions doled out on her brother's plate. When my son was four I went to buy him a three-wheeler

and his two-and-half-year-old sister, who was just beginning to talk and walk around in the world, climbed onto it at the store and claimed it as her own. She could barely reach the pedals, but no matter. We had to buy a second tricycle.

In a photograph titled "Our Gang, That[']s Only Part One" and dated 1919, the youngest girls and the brother closest to them in age, sit on the steps of a Brooklyn stoop. My mother smiles, six or seven, nestled in among her sisters. Jules, four years older than Ruth, is at the top, then Miriam, Mother, and Mildred. This must be the four-story house on Hooper Street in Williamsburg that Miriam and others recall. My mother's hair is cut differently, and the face is not a child's, but the expression is my own as it was stamped into my face by Mother, staring back at me, the mixture of amusement and curiosity, in marked contrast to the sweetness of Miriam, Mildred, the laughing baby, and the squint of Jules into the camera. Jules is obviously still the "kid" he was in 1916 despite the advantage of his seniority to the girls ranked under him. His ears stick out. He seems rankled at having been photographed with the three girls who are younger as there is

another photograph with the older siblings on the same stoop, both of them labeled in the album. (That used to happen at family weddings too, when some older, unmarried cousins and all the younger ones would be grouped at the same "kiddie" table. Twenty-two, twenty-three years separated the oldest from me. Miriam and Mildred's children were even younger. Only Dorothy's youngest daughter, Judy; Paul, Jules's son; and Davey's son, Stanley, were my contemporaries.)

In my mother's smiling curiosity there is also wariness and a hint of the slow anger that used to burn in her for days. I have a single photograph of my mother between 1919 and 1927 standing with a brother, two sisters, and a niece. It is the last image in this chapter. Her brother Bob has his arms around Ruth and Miriam. I see on Mother's face the same expression and shadow of frustration I saw so often in childhood and adolescence. I could hear when she was angry in the staccato tap of her heels across our apartment floors, loud enough to penetrate the closed door of my bedroom. The tale of "Ruthie" in a fit of jealousy cutting up Dorothy's fancy underwear, as her sister, six years older, streaked into adolescence, suggests that Mother's anger was not always in control. I suspect there is a streak of madness in the Lesslers. At our final family reunion in the 1980s, which brought together many of its branches, not just Lesslers, but Annie's family, the Kurlands and others, I heard it whispered by those who had married into Isaac Joseph Lessler's clan, "There was something not quite right about the Lesslers."

Don't all families have their secrets?

"Don't talk to Mark Mirsky!" my aunt Esther cried to her sisters after Mother's death when I asked them about the family. She was the older sister my mother looked to for guidance, the angry censor of its secrets, guardian of its respectability. My mother felt that it was in Esther's house that she had been raised after her mother's death. Esther's children, Jerry and Arthur, were like younger brothers to her when I was growing up. It was Esther alone from my mother's family, who came up in the year of my father's death to stand in a freezing January cold in the wind buffeted graveyard for the burial. I loved my aunt, even though she was embittered by the premature death of her brilliant elder son, Jerry. It was painful to set myself in opposition to a woman whom my mother had looked to as a surrogate parent, but I had to know. Who was she, my mother? What was her family like during her childhood?

When I began to search for answers I pursued Mother's two older sisters, Dorothy and Miriam, with tape recorders, notebooks, video-tape. I began to sift through birth and death certificates, street addresses listed for her father, Isaac Joseph, and his business in the New York City archives. I interrogated my older cousins who remembered their grandmother, Annie, and grandfather, Isaac Joseph.

Of course, there was one piece of gossip that I knew was fact, since I had heard it when I was very young from my older cousins. And when I went down with my mother for the funerals of her siblings, who were buried in the same Bridgeport cemetery where their mother lay, I observed it myself. Annie Lessler's husband, Joseph, was not buried beside her.

That alone belied the smiles in the photograph below. I know my mother. She is cradled in arm of a favorite brother, Bob (whose early, questionable death would haunt her). Her favorite sister, Miriam, is smiling beside her, and her baby sister, Mildred, only a few years older

than Mother's niece, Muriel, Betty's second child, who is also in the picture. Ruth's expression in the photograph (taken, I suspect, three years before her mother's death) I interpret as wary. Her mother has just moved to Bridgeport, but in the past Ruth has been farmed out to her older sisters' houses. Her mother, as the reigning matriarch, having pushed Joseph Lessler out of the picture, rules over a quickly growing clan in addition to the family's stores. Ruth must be wondering exactly where she can elbow in.

Chapter Five

What did Ruth Lessler see at three, four, and five? What did she hear?

As the next to last child born to Annie and Joseph, my mother grew up among brothers and sisters old enough to be her parents. What did she know about her family's origins? She never talked to me about it. When Dad teased her about coming from a town near Warsaw, being a "Polish" Jew, she was silent. In my baby book, my father's family is traced back three generations in her hand; on the page for hers, after her father and mother, only her mother's mother, "Sivia Ruchel," is named.

"Who was my mother?" As this book developed from a few pages, it kept circling that question, spinning back from her death to her birth and what family history I could gather from her surviving sisters, my older cousins, and records of immigration, business addresses, the U.S. census, births and deaths. I will never know if my mother knew anything of this.

"Who were the Lesslers?" Since the family my mother grew up in turned into a matriarchy, dominated by my grandmother Annie (and her daughters would, to varying degrees, dominate in their own families), I want to know as well, "Who were my maternal grandmother's family, the Kurlands?"

The families of both my mother's and father's great-grandparents came to America from Eastern Europe, from within what was then the Russian czar's empire. When I was growing up there were a few stories about the Lesslers' origins—and even fanciful tales about their aristocratic origin in France. My father, as mentioned above, used to tease my mother about her ties to the Polish-Jewish world. One descendant of my great-grandfather, Michael Aaron Lessler, was told by his father Zelig (my grandfather Isaac Joseph's brother) that the family emigrated from Nashelsk [Nasielsk], a small town a short distance to the northwest of Warsaw. The manifest of the ship *Bohemia Le Treile* out of the port of Hamburg lists one of Isaac Joseph Lessler's brothers, Abraham, as a passenger in 1889 and mentions Nashelsk as his birthplace. None of my mother's twelve sisters or brothers seem to have retained a memory of their father's place of birth. Most of the Lesslers wanted to assimilate into American culture. My grandfather would eventually drop the "Isaac," from "Isaac Joseph" and become just "Joseph" or "Joe," as he got older. The passport application that my grandfather filled out in 1913 would seem to be the most reliable source of information. He lists his birthplace as Nashelsk, and the fifteenth of August, 1872 as his birthdate. He reports that he came to America in 1888, from "London, England" and was naturalized in 1894. Joseph Lessler was living at 86 113th Street at the time of the petition. By 1913 he had dropped the "Isaac" since his passport lists his first name as simply "Joseph."

The Kurlands proudly recalled that they came from Szczuczyn, maintaining ties to its burial society and other immigrant institutions. Szczuczyn is in Poland today, far to the northeast of Warsaw but west of Białystock. My father was inordinately proud of his status as a "Litvak," the world of Lithuanian Jewish customs. He spoke Yiddish with its accent. My mother never mentioned where her family had come from. When I asked Dad, he said with condescension, "Somewhere near Warsaw." Pinsk, where he was born (now situated in present day Belarus), retained its sense of belonging to Lithuanian-Jewish rabbinic learning with strong links to Vilna, Brest-Litovsk, and Grodno. My father, proud of his father and grandfather's Talmudic skills, had faithfully retained much of the family history back to his great-grandfather Reuben Mirsky's generation on his father's side. On his mother's side, the Liebermans, he knew both his great-grandfather Baruch Lieberman and his great-grandmother Sulia, and her maiden name, Feldman. His retention of family history was, of course, influenced by the fact that Dad grew up in the house of his great-grandfather and great-grandmother on the Lieberman side and saw his father's father, Maishe Mirsky, regularly before he came to America in 1920.

Dad's condescension was unfair. My mother's mother, Annie, came from a much smaller town than Pinsk, but Szczuczyn, while clearly Polish, was not that far from the district of Grodno and the Lithuanian sphere of influence. Szczuczyn was a small place compared to Pinsk, but had a similar Jewish majority of citizens through the late 19th century, with an estimated population of 2,268 Jews out of a population of 2,996 in 1857. The town grew to 5,043 by 1897. The migration to the United States of Jews in the years since 1857, however, had reduced their percentage of the population from 76 percent to 66 percent.

While Szuzuczyn could not boast, as Pinsk could, a long history of famous rabbis (though one would head the Mir Yeshiva in Jerusalem) the Kurlands, like the Mirskys, held on to their ties to synagogues and Orthodox observance in the United States.

Annie's mother, Sivia Rochel Kurland, died in 1910 while living with her daughter Annie and her son-in-law, Isaac Joseph, at 234 W. 121st Street in Manhattan.

According to her death certificate, Sivia Rochel had been born in 1843 to Louis Gamzon and Ida Groshtein. Sivia's husband, my great-grandfather Louis Kurland, according to his death certificate was born in March of 1856 to Hyman Lazar Kurland and his wife, Rebecca, whose maiden name was Gamzon. (It seems as if Sivia and Louis Kurland were cousins.)

I no longer believe the dates on Louis Kurland's death certificate. Sivia would have been thirteen years older than her husband. The Federal Census of 1910 recorded them living with their daughter and her husband and reports Louis (spelled "Lewis" on the census rolls) as 65 years old and lists his date of birth as "about 1845."

The death certificate of a son of Louis and Sivia Kurland, Jacob, a carpenter, seems to confirm Louis's date of birth as 1845. Jacob's death certificate lists his father as "Louis," and his mother as "Sylvia" though spelling her maiden name as Goldstein. (Jacob was born in 1862, as his death certificate records, so if his own death certificate's birthdate were actually correct than Louis would have had to sire him at six years old, rather than seventeen, which seems more plausible.) My great-grandmother was, it seems, only two years older than her husband Louis. Jacob was born in Lomza, Poland, so Louis and Sivia Kurland were on the move early in their married life. Lomza was a much larger town, 27.9 miles southwest of Szuzuczyn, with a Catholic majority, but a substantial Jewish population. If Jacob, Annie Kurland's older brother, was born in Lomza that may have been Annie's birthplace as well.

On the Kurland side, the Gamzon name recurs, and the family memory is that Sivia was a cousin on her father's side of her husband Louis. The tie to the Gamzon branch would continue in the United States. Isaac Joseph Lessler visited the Gamzon family in Chicago, where they sold leather goods when my aunt Dorothy was a little girl. My father and mother stopped at the Gamzons in 1936 on a honeymoon trip to the West.

Sivia Rochel only came to America in 1897 or 1898. On his death certificate in April of 1917 Louis Kurland is listed as having been in the United States for twenty years, which means that he came in 1897, some ten years after Michael Lessler.

Annie's young brother, Hyman Kurland, probably came at the same time as his parents if he was born in 1880. Milton Kurland, Hyman's son, says his father was sixteen years of age when he immigrated. According to Aunt Dorothy, after the death of his wife Louis Kurland spent most of his time in his daughter Annie's house. Dorothy said he died from a cold he caught while visiting his children in Manhattan. Milton recalls that Louis Kurland spent the last six months or year of his life at his father Hyman's house at 57 East 110th Street and Louis's death certificate lists that same address.

Michael Lessler, my great-grandfather, came to America in 1886 or 1887 when he was thirty-eight, according to his death certificate. Michael's wife, Sara Marsh, immigrated at forty-five according to her death certificate but the census lists her coming at forty or forty-one in 1889, which makes more sense. (Michael's 1912 death certificate records that he had been in the United States for twenty-five years. The 1900 census lists him as coming in 1886 and Sara as arriving in 1889.) Sara's death certificate in 1920 lists her as being in the United States for thirty years, which seems to confirm that she came three years after Michael. According to the census of 1900, Sara did not speak English or work, although the Manhattan Street Directory in 1893 lists their business in trimmings and clothing at One Orchard Street in her name. At his death in 1912, Michael would be described as "a merchant in silks." Born in 1872, his son, my mother's father, Isaac Joseph Lessler (named after his grandfather), was probably brought as a boy of sixteen by way of England. Aunt Dorothy thought he was eighteen when he emigrated. Sarah was either a year older than her husband, or a few years younger, but she died eight years after him. My mother would have had many opportunities to see her father's mother before she died, but neither she nor most of her sisters or brother spoke much about Sarah. Aunt Dorothy, six years older than my mother, tells an anecdote she heard from her older sisters, Celia and Betty, about spilled soup they poured back into a pot at Sarah's. Aunt Dorothy had vivid stories about her grandfather Louis, who died in 1917, since Louis lived with his daughter Annie until shortly before his death. While my father had dozens of stories about his great-grandmother and great-grandfather, as well as his grandmother and grandfather, figures he remembered from the age of five onward, my mother never mentioned Louis Kurland

or Sarah Lessler to me. Only her mother's mother "Sivia Ruchel" is listed after Mother's parents in that baby book, an indication that she knew whom she had been named for and was proud of it.

Although my aunts Dorothy and Miriam had dozens of anecdotes about their mother, apart from her Yiddish sarcasms, Mother never told me a single one.

Annie or "Channah" (Hannah) Kurland, born in 1875, came to New York City in 1891, before her own parents, five years after her father-in-law and two years after her mother-in-law. Aunt Dorothy thinks she was sixteen when she arrived. Above is the only photograph of Annie Kurland that I have from before she wed. She was twenty when she married. Though there may have been family in New York, Annie was on her own for four years. A talented seamstress, whom daughters and nieces recall being able to whip up a perfect copy of some fashionable dress just by eyeing the original, Annie may have met her husband in the world of fabric and sewing supplies, possibly at the Lesslers shop in "trimmings" at One Orchard Street on the Lower East Side. It is clear, however, that Annie Kurland didn't wait for her parents to arrive for her wedding. Why?

I puzzled over this until, re-examining the wedding certificate and a list of birth dates for the family that was compiled by a cousin, Alan Lessler, I suddenly noticed two things. Annie's brother, Jacob Kurland, was older than her. Jacob is listed as being born in 1861 in my cousin's list of family birth dates though Jacob's death certificate lists his birth as June 19, 1862. Beryl Kurland, another brother, was born in 1871.

Jacob was working as a carpenter in 1894, according to the Manhattan Street Directory for that year. Jacob's death certificate, which records his dying on March 21, 1935, says that he had been in the United States and New York for forty-three years. If he arrived in 1892, did he come soon after his sister? The marriage certificate for Annie and Isaac Joseph lists their residence in 1895 at 135 Monroe Street. In the New York City street directory for 1894, Jacob Kurland, a carpenter, is listed as residing at that address. When Annie married Isaac Joseph Lessler in New York City her parents had yet to lay eyes on him. It speaks to the kind of independence that Annie's first years in the United States must have fostered that she married before her father and mother came over, though she was obviously being looked after by her older brother, Jacob. Isaac Joseph Lessler would prove a difficult husband, and Annie would need all her pluck and independence to keep the family afloat.

Was it an arranged marriage? I doubt it, but Jacob Kurland was in Manhattan and close to the bride since his house was listed as her residence and that of her new husband's. Several hand-colored, framed images of their wedding portraits were passed down in the family. In 1895, Annie at twenty and Isaac Joseph at twenty-two look like a handsome couple.

Isaac Joseph quickly set up shop in the family business. In 1895, the year of his marriage, he had a trimming store at 3 Orchard Street, a few doors up the street from his parents. By 1897, he had crept further up Orchard Street to number 187. He and Annie must have been living over or in the back of the store, as their oldest son Simon's birth certificate in 1897 lists that address.

By 1900, Joseph and Annie had moved their trimming business to 38 Bond Street. Michael and his son Leo were still at One Orchard Street also in "trimmings" and they would remain there at least through 1906.

By 1905, ten years after their marriage, Annie had given birth to seven children (eight if we count a boy, Benjamin, who was born in that year but lived only a few months). She is shown below in a picture dated about 1905 with her oldest child, Celia, born in 1896, and High (Hyman) born in 1899. In 1910, Isaac Joseph (or "Joe"), and his wife, Annie, are listed as owners of a trimmings store at 47 East Eighth Street and of a silk store at the same address in 1912, the year of my mother's birth. They were no longer living on Eighth Street in the "Village" but on 121st Street in "Harlem" just above where Columbia University sprawls today.

My cousin Shirley, Celia's daughter, recalls finding a wig, or *sheital*, in her mother's trunk that belonged to her grandmother Annie. Did she, like most Orthodox-Jewish women, shave her head at marriage?

Annie did live an Orthodox-Jewish life. Celia's oldest daughter, Shirley, recalls her mother trying to emulate Annie's traditional practices, *niddur*, the separation of man and woman during the latter's menstrual period. ("Mom told me the story of her early days of marriage—when she had her period, she had to sleep in a small bed alongside the marriage bed. She did so for a few months, till my Dad said, 'The hell with that bed—throw it out and come back and sleep with me.' ")

By 1910–11, the strain of bearing ten children one after another in rapid succession, nine of whom survived, and not just helping her husband run a business, but slowly taking it over, fighting with him over the shop and her children's education, took its toll on Annie.

The family portrait was posed with ten children; Miriam, her baby, on Annie's knee. It is just before my mother Ruth's birth. Annie has lost her figure, though her husband, Joseph (who had by now dropped the "Isaac" in his name), still looks slim and dashing, not yet gaining the weight that will swell his face and middle in the next ten to fifteen years.

Despite the smiles, a lot of tension is boiling under the surface. Annie has taken over the business, and Joseph is trying to assert control by disciplining his children, particularly his sons. In 1910, the family business at 47 West Eighth Street was listed in the Manhattan Street Directory as "Joe's Trimmings." In the 1911–1912 New York Street Directory, the business at the same address is called "Anne Silks." The family is recorded in the directory as living in 1912–13 at 86 W. 113th Street and Joseph lists that address on his passport application in May of 1913.

Joseph Kurland, a younger brother of Annie, was now working in her store on Eighth Avenue. His son, Milton Kurland, Mother's cousin, recalls "an iron staircase leading up to the door. It was called the German Silk Company, but later during World War One, the name was changed to the Freeport Silk Company, and my father used to work for her there. And I remember at the time we lived in the building in which I was born, 70 East Seventh Street, and my father had to work on Saturday sometimes and I remember my mother carrying a pot of hot soup for my father's lunch, from the house where we were born and lived on Seventh Street then, between First and Second Avenue to Aunt Hannah's store on Eighth Street …

"This was on Saturday … she used to carry a white enamel pot with a white towel over it, and would take me and my sister in a stroller, or a baby carriage. In 1915, I was six years old … My father was still working for his sister Hannah until July or August of 1917 when he decided to leave his sister's employ and go into business for himself."

Obviously, like many American Jews, the Lesslers did business on Saturday, accommodating the society in which they had to earn money. From Aunt Miriam, "Mim," to everyone in the family, I gleaned some sense of the life in the houses my mother grew up in. Mim, two years older than Mother, was born like my mother in Harlem at 234 West 121st Street, but since Mim did not remember that place, I doubt that my mother did. (Aunt Dorothy, six years older, proudly recalled being born on Eighth Street near Wanamaker's.) The Lesslers would lose this next house on W. 121st, then move to 86 W. 113th Street near Lexington (Dorothy remembers moving from 125th, but street records do not tally with Dorothy's memory.) "We moved from the house on 125th [121st] street [and] my father was very angry. He had bought this house at a very high price. He was very angry because nothing worked out right. So we left the house. I remember about this house—my older brothers used to show movies in the basement. We used to make the basement dark … We were there until I was four years old. I went to kindergarten with some gentile children on the street. There were no other Jewish families. We never lived amongst Jewish families because we were a very large family. We had to have a lot of rooms and we had to live in a big house. Then we moved to 113th Street near Lexington Avenue in a two-family house. [Lexington is on the east side of Manhattan so Dorothy was mistaken.] And I remember we had the whole floor, there were only like, two families, we had the first floor and someone else had the second floor. And I remember my sister Betty had a sweet sixteen party there. And she had so many admirers there that we had to put all the flowers, the baskets of flowers in the bathroom." (The family was about to move to Brooklyn when Betty was sixteen.) My mother would have been two years old at that event in 1914. Dotty recalled, "I used to take care of Ruthie because she was younger than I was, and I remember sitting on the stoop there, and once holding her and she wet me all over and I got so mad I brought her back up to the house ...

"We moved from 113ᵗʰ Street and it was very annoying to keep changing schools all the time. My father bought a house in Flatbush, 3503 Avenue I in Flatbush. It was a lovely house and in back of the house were all empty lots and they had a dump there about two streets back, in the lots ... And I used to go there with another girlfriend to look around ... to find things. I don't remember what we found but it was fun anyways, scavenging. There was another house next to us, where people called Leek lived; they were gentiles.

"My grandfather [Kurland] went with us wherever we went. And in Flatbush there were no *shuls*. And he was very upset about it because the *shul* was very far away. And people were very anti-Semitic there. I remember one Halloween, my grandfather coming home all disheveled. It was Halloween and the kids had taken rocks and put them in stockings and were hitting him with the rocks, because he was a Jew, because he had a beard. Today it's nothing to have a beard but then it was unusual. If you had a beard they knew you were a Jew. So after that my mother said he better not go anymore by himself for *shul*.

"My brother Davey and my brother Bob were very bright. They went to a school there. And even though they were Jewish, the kids liked them because they were smart, and they were able to help them with their homework. My sister Betty was working already and I think Esther was working too. Esther was very smart. She went to Hunter. She was selected from her school to go to Hunter, because she was one of the brightest in the school. And in that time to go to Hunter, you had to be very bright."

It's in Flatbush to which they moved in 1914, where Miriam has her first memories. "It was a great big house, and then we moved to Williamsburg. In Williamsburg on Hooper Street, we lived in a town house. It was four stories. Four stories high! One of the things I remember, after the first story, the second story was where the living room was. It was a double ceiling. And in the back of the living room was a music room. We always had music, a piano, Jules played the banjo; Davey played the mandolin."

In 1981, I flew down to Florida and sat with Miriam, taking notes. "The first memory of my mother was her sewing machine … I went to Mount Clemens, Michigan. [Mount Clemens through the 19th and early 20th centuries was famous for its mineral baths, hosting celebrities such as Babe Ruth, the Vanderbilts, William Randolph Hearst.] I had an attack of appendicitis. I had to go to the hospital there. When you took the train to Michigan in those days, you took your meals with you. Your mother said that I was the favorite. She felt that she never had any clothes of her own, [and] would always inherit mine …

"I slept with my mother. Everyone slept two in the bed. Since she didn't sleep with my father. He slept in the same room. I don't know if he slept alone."

I asked, "Did she talk about having twelve kids?"

"People didn't talk to their children in those days, about their ambitions, you cooked, cleaned …

"When we moved to Bridgeport [years later] we bought new furniture; it was supposed to be a new beginning.

"We moved to a new apartment. We had always lived in [a] house. We moved from Flatbush to Williamsburg. Originally we lived in the whole house. Then she turned half the house into apartments. There was always a live-in maid from Europe, some foreign people who helped her. I only remember her active in real estate. Never confined to one business …

"She bought one house that was a catastrophe. On Penn Street. They couldn't rent it …

"In Williamsburg, my father bought a store in an area of stores, bought some stock, got disgusted with the business. She had to step in.

"My mother used to read a book of stories about women, sad stories, in Yiddish. She was involved in the YMHA or something like that. [She] helped start the Conservative Jewish movement on Bedford Avenue in Brooklyn. We never felt poverty. She did the business. She worked it. He [Joseph] resented her ability. She would sit in the synagogue all day. We brought flowers to her. I remember the [Passover] seders in Bridgeport. We had twenty people. Only she, High and

Simon, would sit out the balance. My father was in Israel that year. [Joseph Lessler, in fact, did not leave for Israel until June of that year—and Passover falls in late March or April.]

"We were all sent to Hebrew school. I hated it. Used to get migraine headaches—I had them from childhood. As a result I could get out of anything.

"I remember a tug of war with your mother. We were both supposed to do the dishes. We were tugging on a dish-wiper. I let go and she fell down. She had *some* swollen nose.

"David [Davey] used to help us with our English. My mother spoke English but couldn't read it. In the backyard he would help us, teach us the broad jumps and high jumps. I had a great affection for my brother David."

Aunt Miriam showed me a book of mysteries in ten volumes. "David gave me [these] when I graduated high school. [Inscribed]

> *From David R. Lessler*
> *to*
> *his darling*
> *Sis Miriam."*

Whatever jealousies my mother felt were subsumed in her affection for Miriam. All through my mother's adolescence, there are pictures in her album next to this sister, two years older. It continued after Mother's graduation from high school. "Your mother and I were very close … We went to Bermuda together. She was very popular on board the boat."

Channah Kurland, known affectionately as "Annie," was already a matriarch at the time of my mother's birth, controlling her husband's business. Aunt Miriam recalls, "They were very orthodox. The holidays were observed. One of the fondest memories I have of my mother. On the high holidays … You know, she sewed. And she had this beautiful black velvet hat with a bird of paradise feather. And then she would always wear white. And she had an ermine scarf, which Celia had in her trunk for a very long time. And she had always a white silk suit. And grey suede high-laced shoes and on the sides of these suede shoes there were not beads, but sequins; on the sides there was like studs, a design. My mother was always … she would take that outfit out or a similar one but [with] a large velvet hat. And all the boys would be trailing her." Dotty and Miriam went to Hebrew school, but it was clear that the Lesslers were not as religious as Annie's family, the Kurlands, who "laid *t'fillin* every morning" according to Miriam. (Together with reciting the morning prayers, this generally takes three quarters of an hour.)

While Esther, the third-oldest girl, was the reigning authority for my mother in her family, Miriam was the one Ruth was closest to. I asked Miriam about that.

"What made you so close to my mother?"

"Because we were close in age, we were the only two … Mildred [the last child] … us two, and Dotty and Davey was the most of family that I remember. By that time everyone else had moved out, just the five of us were really at home." (Curiously, Jules who was younger than Davey is omitted from Miriam's list.)

"But you and my mother seemed to have had a particularly close … "

"Yes, because we had the same, the same, uh … we did the same things. We'd take a book out of the library. We'd read it together … because we both wanted to read the same book at one time. The one thing I remember about your mother and myself, your mother used to be upset. She thought that I was being favored … Some of our friends were the same, too, because she was only one grade behind me, actually, because she had gone, skipped a couple, you know, in those days. I had skipped once or twice, but she had skipped even more, so that we were practically in the same [grade]."

Miriam's husband, my uncle Morris, remarks as my aunt and I speak: "I think Miriam was close to Ruth and Davey; that was the only two I remember."

Miriam interjects, "And Dotty [Dorothy], a little bit too."

Dorothy was the "artistic" one, and independent enough to defy her mother when it came to choosing a beau, Willy Cohen, defending him from the family's disapproval, when they were dating in Brooklyn as childhood sweethearts. Willy remained faithful when she moved to Bridgeport, despite the fact that he was not welcome in the house.

Dorothy was sent away on trips to keep her out of his reach. Annie had made a sweet sixteen party for Dorothy in order to distract her, and had deliberately not invited Willy. Annie's sons and her husband were intent on keeping Willy away from Dorothy. What that meant was made clear to me during an interview with my two older cousins, Shirley and Elaine, Celia's daughters. They told me that "Grandpa Joe" had kicked their father, Louis Greenbaum, down the stairs when he came courting. He was "poor" unlike Betty's beau, David Lesser, and Joseph Lessler did not regard him as a desirable groom, although Louis had been dating Celia since she was fourteen. Aunt Dorothy remembers the conflict vividly. "My sister Betty was seventeen and a half. She was going to marry Dave Lesser, when my sister Celia was up in the country; Celia was my mother's favorite because she was always sick; she always had a headache … She was the oldest in the family and when everyone else had *flanken* soup, she had chicken soup, because she was always professing to be sick. She always had a cold rag on her head. When Celia heard that Betty was getting married, she got very angry, because she was going steady with Lou [Louis]. And my mother was very discouraged with Lou, because Lou … He was Hungarian. He was a tall, blond man, very likable, full of jokes, we all liked him but he didn't have anything. And my mother said, 'Celia is a sick girl, and she needs someone to support her. What are you going to do?' But anyways, she [Celia] heard Betty was getting married. [Celia protested. There is] no way Betty [is] getting married before her. She is the oldest in the family. So they had a double wedding [catered by] Trotzky's at The Broadway Central Hotel." [Celia lovingly preserved the menu of July 4, 1916. Matzo ball soup is listed as *Vermicelli avec Marrow Balls.*]

What did my mother see of this? She was three years old the year before Celia was married, then just four when Celia, at age twenty, left the Lessler house. Betty was seventeen and a half (married, according to her daughter, Margie, "Just to get out of the house.") Betty's house in Bridgeport quickly became a refuge for Annie's children, though Betty was encumbered by her own babies; one following another in rapid succession.

At the last family meeting in the late eighties, I brought up some of the family memories about our grandfather, Joseph. Aunt Dorothy protested at the bitter talk about her father. Even she, however, understood that the house was a battleground. "My father was a good-natured person but he couldn't take all the kids. When we moved to Williamsburg, the silk business ... there was a depression, right after World War One ... The silk merchants were throwing themselves out of the windows things were so bad. Everyone lost everything. Where silk was two dollars a yard wholesale, it turned out to ten cents a yard ... My brothers were in the silk business with [my parents]—High and Simon and Bob. So my mother, who had a terrific business sense, and I think

that was her trouble with my father, they were always tiffing. Whatever she did turned to gold, whatever he did turned to crap. My father was a very handsome man and he loved the children and everything but too much of the fighting with the children and everything made a lot of discrepancies. I remember sitting on his lap and he'd say, 'Give me a kiss, and I'll give you a nickel.' And I remember going to Coney Island with him. My father was a very big man and he [would] put two of us on his back and swim like a whale with the wide circular thing and we'd get so scared, you know.

"And I remember we took the trolley cars to Coney Island and he had a leather pocketbook that he kept all his change in ... But I don't think my father was too happy a man ..."

"Why?" I ask her.

"Well, there was always so much going on in the house and my mother was always too bright for him, I think. Not that he wasn't a bright man, but she overpowered him in her business manipulations ...

"After the depression [at the end of World War One], he tried very hard … They opened a little retail silk store so that my brothers would have something to do, on Segal Street, somewhere, that was the slum area and the market area of Brooklyn, and my father thought he'd found a big buy, someone had a sale of *brent* georgettes, georgette is a fabric, a silk fabric. ['Silk Georgette' is described as having a grainy texture and a sheer feel, like silk crepe, but not as soft or lustrous as crepe. The term *brent*, or 'burned out,' is a process in which the material, particularly silk is 'sheared' to show a pattern, the 'burned out-portions' more sheer than the other fabric.] And he paid a few hundred dollars for it and he brought all the georgettes home to the house and my mother said, 'What did you do?'

"He said, 'Don't worry. We'll sell. We'll get rid of it, it'll sell.' Meanwhile the house stank from the georgette and finally my mother threw [out] the whole goddamn thing … Oh, I think that's when she opened the store. She opened this little store and she said to Simon to take care of the store there, and she threw all that *crapiola* in there … [Joseph], his business sense wasn't as good as my mother's. She saw … People were losing their houses one after the other and she went to the bank—they were foreclosing a whole street of houses on Clymer Street between Lee and Bedford that was about five streets away from us and she bought up the whole row of houses for the mortgage. And she hired carpenters and contractors and redid all the three-story houses into three-family houses and she sold them individually, one by one, and that's how she recouped and made a lot of money on it."

My aunt Esther understood where any discussion would go when she warned her sisters. "Don't talk to Mark Mirsky!" Dorothy and Miriam, her younger sisters, were still, to an extent, under her thumb.

"Don't tell Esther that," Dorothy whispered to me when we talked, as one indiscretion after another slipped out, in particular a sarcastic comment of Annie's about Esther's not dating as a young woman. Miriam, whose quiet self-confidence often struck me as very close to my mother's was reported to often say with a raised eyebrow, "What will Esther think?"

According to Dorothy, from her childhood Esther was the power in the house after Annie. She was the first of the girls in the family to go to work and bring home an income. "Esther was working and she was the big boss. I used to fight with her a lot because I was never neat enough for her [and] I used to steal a lot of her things. [Only] her shoes—she liked me to wear, 'I am testing them out for my sister.' At night she used to give me fifty cents, [for] ice cream and Peter's chocolate, fifty cents for the both of us. I got it and she got it.

"My girlfriend Charlotte and I, we used to run upstairs, Esther slept in the upstairs bedroom, and look at her underwear, and we used to steal her scarves. So she used to say, 'At least if you take my things, put them back where you took them from.' And Sunday mornings, after all she worked [and] wanted to sleep, she used to pay me fifty cents to iron her chemises or whatever she wore, because she didn't want to [do] it."

· · ·

I return to the photograph of my mother, Ruth, and her father. What did my mother know?

What did she hear?

It seems as if my grandfather, Joseph, was briefly institutionalized, either for mental problems or alcoholism. No one wanted to talk about it while Esther was alive, since it tainted the family's image of itself. On a slip of paper I have written down King's Hospital in Queens, but I doubt that medical records go back that far and it's not a subject I really wanted to research. One of my older cousins, Shirley Winnick, Celia's eldest daughter recalled her grandfather being institutionalized during his years in Bridgeport.

My mother's cousin Milton Kurland, his father Hyman, Annie's younger brother, was a playmate of the children. Milton confirmed the rumors that Joseph Lessler had been put in an institution for problems, either for alcoholism or bizarre behavior. "So far as your grandfather Jake, [evidently a nickname for Joseph] I think you know about his reputation ... A strange one, yes, I know that very frequently he was a patient in Pilgrim's State Hospital. Then he would come out for a few months or a year or two, then go in for a few months or a year a two, and then go back again."

I asked Milton, "When did this begin?"

"In my childhood," Milton answered. "I was about five or six years old. Now whether it started before that or not, I don't know.

"The story that I heard was that he was an alcoholic. Don't forget I was only a child at the time, five, six, seven years old. And I didn't really ... I wasn't really a confidante as to just what was going on in my aunt Hannah's family. I do know that I liked my aunt Hannah and her children, my cousins very much."

"What was Joseph Lessler like?" I asked Aunt Miriam in 1981 (as I revise in 2012 Miriam at 102 years old, passes away on July 13, and though difficult to communicate with for the last few years, the loss stuns me).

"He was a very nervous person, would start things and not finish them ... not loving to my mother. It was a torment. There was nothing he could do with himself. She would be sitting, sewing and he would complain that he was ill-used ... He was always '*mutchkying*' about it."

Aunt Miriam enacted a nervous, aggressive, teasing, gesture. "The children came between him and her. He resented them."

That trait of Joseph Lessler—to tease or rag one, not letting go of it until you screamed, was one I recognized immediately. It was my mother's most dangerous characteristic. At twenty-eight, despite my degrees from Harvard, Stanford, my professorship at The City College of New York, already on my way to tenure, she could reduce me to a frenzied, shouting child, a wreck, in a matter of minutes over the telephone. And I had inherited the trait, an insane streak of bitter sardonic teasing that would not let up until it had the satisfaction of hearing someone else shouting in helpless fury under its lash.

Still there was something more than just teasing. Joseph Lessler's temper was not only out of bounds. It was dangerous. My cousin Abby, the oldest daughter of my uncle Simon (the first son born to Annie and Joseph), told me: "My dad always wanted to learn to play the violin. His mother bought him one but his father broke it over his knee. Joseph took Dad out of school at thirteen (the eighth grade) to work in a sweatshop. He studied at night school secretly to get his high school diploma. *Shlepping* heavy bolts of fabric in the sweatshop before his bones were through growing left him with one shoulder lower than the other."

Simon stares out happily in all the photographs, but like Bob's good-natured expression it is deceptive. Aunt Dorothy recalls, "Bob was going to Boy's High School. He was very bright. But all of a sudden my father decided that he needed him in the business. And he disrupted his high school, which we thought was terrible ... I don't think Bob was ever able to finish ... He was in his senior year. It was very, very sad because Bob was very bright."

My uncle Bob would take his revenge on the family store. The full measure of Bob's bitterness would register at the moment of his mother's death and it would go on. I don't think Robert Lessler ever forgave his father and it is hard to square his unhappiness with the genial uncle I recall before his tragic, premature death.

My mother growing up, four, five, six, seven years old, standing beside her smiling older brothers, must have heard these stories. Several of these older brothers, Simon, Bob, Davey, would become surrogate fathers, looking after and encouraging her. Joseph Lessler must have felt something special for Dorothy. She alone had good memories. When Dorothy was seven or eight years old he brought her a lavish doll from Chicago. She was still lamenting its breaking in her eighties. "The doll was about three feet tall ... And I stood it in front of a big chiffonier. It had a very large mirror, and room for two umbrella stands and I stood the doll up there and [the] next morning when I had woken up, the doll had fallen down, and the china face was broken. And I never got over that because it was the first doll that I really ever had. And I remembered it for many years to come. My mother got another head for the doll but it was never the same."

The boys seem to have borne the brunt of the abuse. Annie was able to protect Davey, the second youngest, from her husband's interference in his studies. She was in control of the family by the time he entered high school. Davey is also the one boy who seems to have retained affection for his father. (Muriel, Betty's daughter, remembers her grandfather having a heart attack. She and her older sister Francis were alone in their house when it happened, and Davey rushing over there, scolded them for not taking better care of Joseph.) The Lessler women seemed to have inherited a lethal streak of sarcasm and I often felt it. Simon and Jules, the two brothers of my mother whom I saw frequently, never spoke this way. Simon was rather austere in my presence; Jules a bit nervous when he came to visit, but affable, his teasing good-natured. Still, something of the childhood antagonism between my mother and Jules hung in the air, my mother was always reserved with him, never relaxed. Several of my mother's sisters were astute at business like their mother and all but the youngest, Mildred, dominating presences in their marriages. Did Annie elbow her husband, Isaac Joseph Lessler, whose store dated back to 1895, out of his business in silk? When hard times struck he proved incompetent in the family trade of silks, but the shift in the name of the business presages this. Annie Lessler and her sons would branch into real estate and retail stores in Bridgeport, Connecticut, and Portland, Maine, recovering from the ruin of the wholesale American silk business after World War One, but Annie's husband was excluded. During my childhood I heard something of the family's dissatisfaction with their father. It must have been a bitter pill for my grandfather, since the matriarch of the Lesslers, his mother, Sarah, was alive as it happened.

As my mother grew up, her own mother, Annie, had little time for Ruth. At two years old, in 1914, her father seated beside his second youngest son, Hyman, was still a relatively slim patriarch, but he would quickly grow portly. My mother, four years old in 1916, when the older children began to leave, must have felt the tremors. Her second oldest sister, Betty, left for Bridgeport, where her husband had a prosperous store. Celia, her oldest sister, and Louis Greenbaum went to live in the Bronx. Aunt Dorothy recalls the double wedding: "Coming home from the wedding … my grandfather [Louis Kurland] was in the car with us and he kept saying, 'Cholem, Cholem, dis gantzen leben is a cholem,' meaning the whole world is a dream—coming over the Williamsburg Bridge." Annie had brought her family, the Kurlands, into the trimming and silk business to help, obviously with an eye on her husband's problems. In 1917 (1916 in the photograph), the house suffered an outright desertion. Hyman ("High") ran off to the Navy. His mother tugged him home by the ear, and got a family friend, a judge, to force High's release. A few weeks later, High joined the Army and Annie threw up her hands and stopped trying to dissuade him. Dorothy remembered that "High came home one Passover night in the middle of the night and he said, 'Don't tell anybody, I went AWOL just to come home to say goodbye to everybody.' They weren't allowed to say that they were being shipped out—that morning. And he went AWOL and came home to say goodbye … He ran to everybody's bed and said goodbye to my mother, my father, and all of us. He went to all the beds … And he ran right back to New Jersey at Camp Dix … When he came back, he was shell shocked. Many times we'd have visitors, I told you, he was there for four years, who would come and bring regards from him. Because he was on the watch on the Rhine, that's what they called it, for two years. And he was so shell shocked that many times he would be sleeping and he would get up in the middle of the night with a nightmare because he would hear the bombs and everything going …

He was sick for quite a while after he came home." Celia, High's wife, told me that he was left for dead on the battlefield after being gassed. His recovery was considered a miracle. (The photograph of High in

France has the date 1917, though here he seems older.) High was reunited with his family by August 1920, when a photograph exists with his older brother Simon.) My mother was five when High left, eight when he returned.

Happily, Simon, the eldest, seems to have been a steady presence though he had to sneak off to night school to finish his high school degree. Davey, first at Columbia College, then Columbia Law School, slowly became his mother's right hand. By 1918, at six years old, my mother was obviously a regular visitor to Bridgeport and the home of her married sister, Betty. According to Miriam, both she and Ruth were

sent to schools in Bridgeport staying at their older sister's home, which explains the photographs of my mother both on the steps of Hooper Street in Brooklyn and in the front and backyards in Bridgeport, Connecticut. Miriam remembers Ruth crying bitterly at Betty's house and the latter scolding her for making noise that would wake the baby. Throughout those years, on the Upper East Side, then in Flatbush and Williamsburg, it seems as if Joseph Lessler increasingly became a ghost. When I pressed Milton Kurland for his sense of my grandfather, he replied, "Whatever knowledge I have of him is just my childhood impression because I very rarely had face-to-face contact with him."

Celia Zlot, who married High Lessler shortly after he returned from France, and was in and out of Annie Lessler's house, both in Williamsburg and later in Bridgeport, told me, "I didn't see the father much. The children would come and go. But the father, the children more or less ignored him. They didn't think very much of him ... It was the mother they idolized."

Annie had wisely diversified into real estate as well as silk. According to Dorothy, the family made one more move to Lee Street before Annie left Brooklyn in 1923 and joined her daughters in Bridgeport, living in a house on Savoy Street. Her daughter Betty had already moved to Bridgeport in 1918, and her other daughter Celia followed

Betty in 1923 as her husband, Lou, opened up a children's clothing store there called "The Kiddie Shop." Annie's sons High, Simon, and Bob were already there. Annie had set them up selling fabrics from a shop in a hotel in Bridgeport. Esther was there too, and would soon marry Harold Nishball in Bridgeport, whom she met on a double date with a friend. Over the years Annie had been sending Ruth and Miriam there to live with her older daughter, Betty. Annie, managing real estate with the help of her son Davey as he went through Columbia Law School, now created several stores with her other sons called "The Chain Silk Shops." The notice in the Bridgeport paper at Annie's death states that Simon, David and Jules Lessler were "associated with the store in this city," and that Robert and Hyman were in charge of the store in Portland, Maine. Annie's husband, Joseph, frozen out of the family businesses had been "sent off" on a trip to Palestine just to get him out of Annie's hair in June of 1925. He was abroad when she died. Annie had not only shielded Davey from her husband and helped shepherd Davey through Columbia and then Columbia Law. Miriam told me that Annie had also kept in bed beside her the youngest, Mildred, born in 1914, for longer than usual, just to keep Joseph, her husband, out of it. After thirteen children and a husband growing more unstable, she evidently had had enough. (Miriam later denied saying this but her remark is on tape.)

Even more shocking, Aunt Dorothy let slip a detail that sheds a macabre light both on Annie's childbearing and her death. "After Mildred was born, I think she was pregnant again, and she had an abortion. And I think it was probably a bad job and her kidneys were infected. And I think that led to her early death. Because when we moved to Bridgeport, she got very sick. She was in the hospital."

In May of 1913 Joseph Lessler applied for a passport. He lists only his wife Annie and one child, Celia, his oldest, who might accompany him. Was he thinking of visiting Nashelsk, his birthplace in Poland? Was the idea of traveling to Palestine, which he would do some twelve years later, in his mind? Did he feel at that moment, a year after my mother's birth, that he was irrelevant in the family silk business now being run by his wife and her relatives? In this year he would conceive the last of his children, but the strain, according to Miriam, was showing. In 1913, Celia would have been seventeen years old—could he have taken his wife and oldest daughter on a trip out of the United States and left my mother at one year old and Miriam, at three, not to mention the other younger children in the care of his mother, or a brother or brother-in-law? In any case, the birth of Mildred in 1914, and then World War One, seems to have put off any travel plans.

Joseph Lessler died in 1933, but again, there is no indication of his death or picture of him in any of my mother's copious album entries for that year. He was buried in the same cemetery in Bridgeport, but not next to Annie.

• • •

That fact echoed at the gravesites of his children in that tense year before my mother's own death. She asked me to go down to their funerals as Betty and then Jules passed away. Mother didn't talk about where her parents were buried in Bridgeport, either on the train down or coming back. Her eyes met me with a cold stare when I tried to ask, although not quite as awful a stare as the one she returned once, when, as a teenager, I saw her breasts exposed when her door was open by accident and as she sat on the edge of her bed, dressing.

The forbidden was strong in the presence of my mother. Only a childhood fever could relax the taboo about touching me. At Harvard, discovering Freud, whose books and theories I had brushed against in high school. Ahead of my ability to assimilate their radical suggestions, I could still make no sense of his Oedipus complex. Had I desired my mother? No dream, no fantasy, occurred to me. She had been beautiful all through my childhood and I often experienced puppy love for the tall girls, who, like my mother, towered above me. But short girls were attractive too. And when I started dating seriously, the women who exerted their hypnotism were often the very opposite of my mother: physically, emotionally, and from backgrounds very different from hers and mine. My father, Wilfred, inspired awe in me, some fear, but also a lot of affection and from the age of my bar mitzvah, when he began to actually teach and talk to me, we had a growing friendship and appreciation for each other, despite our differences. Like me he often teased with indiscretions, sharing information that he might well have kept confidential; not so much about himself but about the world of politics and the family. When he spoke about his childhood, he had the storyteller's gift of disappearing into the details, even when they were embarrassing. His first memory, as a child in Eastern Europe, he told me while unbuttoning the vest of his lawyer's pinstriped suit, leaning back against the slats of a hardback Harvard chair in my rooms at college, ended in his wetting his pants at three or four years old, in his father's arms at the Great Synagogue and and having to be rushed home. It was impossible to wring any compromising moments or disclosures of her girlhood out of my mother. This meant that much of the time she cast herself in the role of a disapproving elder. She also held the financial keys in our family. It was to her one went first for necessities: shirts, socks, underwear, shoes, the weekly allowance. (My father did take pleasure in draping me, as I passed into adolescence, in suits and coats, either at the Harvard Coop, bantering with a favorite salesman, or using his contacts in the wholesale clothing district to bargain.) Dad, however, was the one you went to when appealing for impractical items, or luxuries to which he showed a whimsical appreciation. There was no visible romance between my mother and me. She *loved* me. Her advice was often maddening. Still, I felt some sympathy at the edge of her exasperated frown and could stay at the house for a few days, knowing that she did care and in some silent way appreciated that I had come home to moon and whimper. The Oedipus complex, desiring a mother, seemed like Freud's unique problem. I didn't see it in my house.

Then, at the age of fifty-six in 1968, she was grappled by death. I didn't know it until it was almost too late, although the signs were there to be interpreted.

I had gone out from Manhattan to California, where I was invited by Stanford University to teach for a year. My mother and father visited me there and talked about moving to Palo Alto, if I decided to continue there. During the visit, I felt my mother's attention focused on me more directly than I could ever remember. Her attitude of indifference, exasperation, had seemed perpetual from childhood. "I want you out of the house, once you are twenty-one," was an oft-repeated line. I recalled the first, and perhaps most striking, of these rejections for an article I wrote for *The Boston Globe* on Mattapan, the particular suburb of Boston where I was born, and to which my family returned when I was ten. It is a section of the city that borders the Neponset River on its southern edge, and sucks up some of the sadness of its marshes.

The moment occurred when I was almost five. We had moved north at the beginning of the 1940's up Mattapan's common avenue, Blue Hill, to the adjoining but poorer streets of Dorchester. My mother did not keep a tight watch on my whereabouts once I was out the front or back door of the house, distracted possibly by my baby sister. I had just returned from a daring excursion a street across and a street down on my own to the nearby Franklin Field, where the long grass of late spring had grown so tall that, lying back in it, I was invisible. There, the blue sky of May and early June rolled over me. I thought about the world and wondered how old the universe was and what eternity meant as it went on and on. The latter speculation was so vivid and frightening that my head began to spin under the sky, dizzy. I pulled myself up and rushed home, with a headache, and afraid. My grandfather's death earlier during the year may have stunned me into such reflection. When I came through the front door of the house, I found my mother stretched out, lying half asleep in my room, sprawled across the big double bed that had left my parents bedroom to become mine, across from my sister's smaller one.

"What happens when you die?" I blurted out.

"I'm looking forward to it," my mother sighed. She looked at me with that strange, sideways irony I perceive in the picture where she holds on to her father's arm, an expression she rarely showed to the camera after her mother's death. "It will be a rest from you kids." She looked at me with a deadpan expression she rarely showed to the camera after her mother's death.

In the albums of photographs she meticulously assembled when my father first appears, she writes next to his picture, "old funny face." The photograph of my father shows a slim, handsome, young man in a bathing suit with his arm around her waist. The entry, however, that I would discover she wrote in his diary, the letters she wrote him

 in the first years of their marriage, from her post as a disaster worker in the Great Ohio Flood, tell a different story.

I am getting ahead of myself for I don't want to just tell the tale of how they met, those first years of their love. I want to talk as well about the letters she sent as a woman of fifty-four, fifty-five, to a son of twenty-seven, twenty-eight, in which I recognized the voice of a young girl of nineteen or twenty, ardent, romantic. Up to that point I had gotten instructions for buying sheets, pillow cases, kitchen implements, and a dry recital of family events, with orders to attend some of them. I suspect "the time is" always "out of joint."

For so began again the romance between a son and a mother, a romance only now fully apparent in looking back, that had flickered for a few moments for me, from infancy to ten years old; the mother, who would suddenly become a girl, slipping ahead of me.

Chapter Six

The mystery of the photograph above, which sat on my mother's dressing table throughout my childhood, together with portraits of her brother Bob and her sister Miriam, did not solve itself until I was finished with the first draft of this book. I knew who it was, my mother's mother, Annie. One could guess immediately that it was taken very late in my grandmother's life. What I didn't realize until I was reviewing the materials I had gathered from my mother's albums was that it was cropped from the very first photograph Mother had pasted into her first album, on the back of its front cover. It was the beginning of memory for her, and the last photographic image she had of her mother, a ghostly one. The original is at the end of the next chapter; Annie, with her youngest Mildred by her side is surrounded by grandchildren, Betty's daughter, Muriel, and Celia's boy, Mitchell, holding his sister, Shirley. My mother cropped all the grandchildren and her sister, Mildred, out of the photograph. It was her mother Ruth held close to her. My mother looked at Annie smiling out at her every day when she went to the bureau in her bedroom on which sat a sewing box, a chest of costume jewelry and a collection of powders and perfumes under her mirror.

Cut away from her grandchildren, what strikes me is Annie's enigmatic smile, slightly mocking, masking the pain eating in her that would, in a few years, end her life. My mother practiced that smile, slightly mocking, amused, scrutinizing, but also in its inquisition, loving. If I go back and look again at my mother on the arm of her father in the one photograph I have of them together, I can see some of that look as well and reinterpret it to show more sweetness.

But my mother keeps eluding me. I look again at the tight, tense smile in photographs from 1918. She is acting a role. She is part of a family whose cheerful poses in those pictures belie the strains. Her older brother, High, has been left for dead on the battlefield in France. Her adored brother, Bob, will run off with the receipts from the store to Arkansas (or Mississippi) for a year, returning when he falls sick and his mother retrieves him. Mother never mentions any of this. The Lesslers existed for me in childhood and adolescence in a romance of upward striving Americans with multiple happy endings. Only her brother Bob's death in 1944 falls like a shadow through this romantic production of my mother and her sisters; the circumstances surrounding his death shadowy ... suicide, an accident? The aunts and uncles mutter in the background in an angry chorus about his wife, and even our house walls echoed with

it. The few pieces of furniture Uncle Bob gave us when he broke up his household in Providence, his share of a business with his oldest brother, Simon, acquired a hue of sadness for my mother.

It is not until I go through her albums that I recognize my mother has left some pieces to the puzzle of her disappearing act. All through our life together, until her last six months, she has played a part for me, deliberately. Rarely did I see her backstage without her makeup. As I go through her albums, I realize that the first image shows her in costume and that her pleasure in the theatrical will be a constant.

I lose the actress who poses as my older sister in 1950. I am almost eleven and that is the last moment of romantic attachment to her in childhood. I can still recall the handsome young woman in shorts, socks, sneakers, leading my sister and me over a broken cyclone fence and barbed wire in the lot across from our new summer cottage in Hull, Massachusetts.

As I think about my mother, ransack my own memories, it's the death of Annie Lessler in 1925 that I think determined who Ruth Sylvia Lessler was and so I go back to her first album.

I turn her scrapbook to its first pages. There are no pictures of her in the year of my grandmother's death. Thinking about the photographs in the first chapters, one labeled "When We Were Young," and the earlier ones taken in Bridgeport in 1918 or 1919, I recall a remark of Aunt Miriam: "In grammar school days, I was sent and Ruth was sent to school for a year away from Betty's house. Something happened at Betty's house. Your mother went up to the bathroom and cried. Betty went up and said, "Why are you crying? You'll wake the baby."

"Ruthie answered, 'You don't care why I'm crying. You only care that the baby should wake up.'

"She felt very neglected."

Again, I go over those photographs from that first album, seeing that sense of "neglect" reflected in her face. What was it like for her, losing her mother, and the real head of the family just as she was entering high school, becoming a young woman? It could have been a catastrophe, but the older members of the family rallied to take care of the younger, and their mother had been careful to provide for them. Annie had left a "light small stone" from one of her rings to Ruth ("a large stone" went to Dorothy, and various stones were left to other women in the family). Ruth with her other sisters and brothers would receive a share in the family business. The Bridgeport papers refer to it in Annie's obituary as the Chain Silk Shirt shops. The stores in Bridgeport and Maine generated a significant amount of money through the next seven or eight years. My mother had a balance of $4,776 dollars on January 1, 1932; a year in which my mother would withdraw $1,145 dollars from that account, probably for tuition at Simmons College and living expenses.

According to the will dictated to her oldest daughter Celia, Annie specified that the house on Savoy Street in Bridgeport was to be "kept up with the income from the silk stores until all the girls are married," but this didn't prove practical. Miriam recalled, "We separated very early. We maintained the house for a while after my mother died. Then we gave it up. She [Ruth] went to live with Esther. I went to live with Betty. Mildred went to live with Celia. It happened right after Dotty [Dorothy] got married."

After her mother's death, Dorothy won the war to marry Willy Cohen, whom Annie had disapproved of.

The departure from Savoy Street did not happen overnight. The older sisters tried to sort out how to take care of the younger ones and what to do with their father. Joseph Lessler played no role in the stores that Annie had set up in Bridgeport and Portland, Maine, where her sons and son-in-law, Lewis, Celia's husband, worked.

Just how bitter some of his children were at Joseph Lessler at the moment of their mother's death can be felt in a letter that his son Bob sent addressed to his *Dear Brothers and Sisters,"* from Portland, where he reported that he and his older brother, Hyman (High), were sitting shiva, went to *"schul everyday 6 A.M., lay t'fillin and then [go for] Mincha and Maariv [the afternoon and evening service when the Kaddish is recited as well.] "Let us try to keep our spirits together and be in harmony, as our mother always wished and thus we will be a blessing and a blessing to her while she watches over us in heaven."* In his last paragraph, he adds, *"At this time, I do not believe it is advisable for anybody to notify J.L.; as I am not sure whether Mother would really care to have him say Kaddish over her."*

Ruth's father had been away in Palestine when Annie died; he had already been removed from any effective part in making decisions for his children, or the business his wife ran in real estate and retail. The year after her mother's death, although living under the supervision of her three oldest sisters, Ruth had to quickly become independent.

Was she enrolled in Bridgeport High School at the time of her mother's death, October 1925? My sister tells me that she once saw a school record in a desk drawer of our family house, which showed that our grandmother Annie had enrolled Ruth a year early in New York City, falsifying her birth by one year, claiming my mother was born in 1911 rather than 1912. Mother said she had skipped two grades. What is clear, however, is that she not only held her own with children a year older than she was, but skipped easily yet another year ahead. Ruth seemed to have spent only three years before graduating Bridgeport High School. By the spring or fall of 1926, she was enrolled. A clipping from a local paper pasted into her album, dated 1926, identifies her as one of the cast of a play put on at the high school.

The Footlight Club of Bridgeport High School will make its first appearance this *afternoon in a children's program including, The Birthday of the Infanta.*

My mother is in the second row, last person, identified as R. Lessler ("Ru"—the first and second letters of Ruth scribbled over her head) dressed in what looks like a toreador's costume as a boy. Despite the blurry pixilation, I see her characteristic expression, lips slightly pursed, between amusement and skepticism.

I want to linger over that image, one of the very first markers Mother chose to record, the first image I have of her from her own collection. She preserves herself in the role of an actress. In the photographs from 1927, the first ones after this newspaper clipping pasted into her album after her mother's death, the most striking also shows her in the role of actress.

She was obviously hurrying into a more mature role. Invitations to a prom, valentines from boys, crowd several pages of her album together with a number of photographs as she poses, to my surprise, as a "vamp." She scrawls under this "Rio Rita Doll."

I will find her again and again, "posing." Playwriting will be the high point of her senior year. I always assumed that I got my own theatrical bent from my father's side of the family, which brought me to a brief professional career on the stage as an actor, then a director, and even several forays as a playwright. He was the storyteller. My grandfather had a beautiful voice and his first cousin was a famous cantor, the youngest in history at five years old, performing in concert halls across Europe. The London branch of the Mirskys were all involved in the theater. Now, I realize how poorly I understood my own dreams. It was with my mother that I went again and again to the theater in downtown Boston to watch musicals or more serious drama and whatever was weekly at the cinema. My mother lived in a world of movie and musical comedy fantasies.

Who was Rio Rita?

It was one of the most popular stage musicals of 1927, produced by Florenz Ziegfield. It premiered on Broadway at the beginning of February, set attendance records that held until *Oklahoma* in 1943, and ran until April of 1928, almost outpacing *Showboat*. It was a musical based less on its narrative than on its capacity to loosely associate singing, dancing, with a romantic story. The shot above of Marian Benda, who played several minor roles, Conchita and Palomita, will give you some of idea of what the musical was all about. In my mother's album she has inscribed, "Rio Rita Doll" under the snapshot of herself.

The plot begins with posters advertising a reward for a dangerous bandit called the Kinkajou in the Mexican border town of San Lucar. A mysterious gringo has come to the town who turns out to be a captain in the Texas Rangers, Jim, who falls in love with Rita Ferguson, an Irish-American-Mexican girl who sings in the local hotel after being displaced from her family ranch along with her brother Roberto. The villain of the piece is the governor of the San Lucar District, Ravinoff, who is also in love with Rita. Ravinoff tells Rita that Jim is a Texas Ranger who has come to arrest the Kinkajou, who is is suspected to be her brother, Roberto. Rita turns against Jim, but later saves his life.

In the second act Ravinoff puts on a spectacular party at his gambling barge on the Mexican side of the Rio Grande to impress Rita but Jim slips onto the barge in disguise and cuts the boat loose from its moorings. Floating to the American side, Jim unmasks Ravinoff as the real Kinkajou, arrests the villain and *Rio Rita* ends with a wedding.

In 1929, a movie of the musical *Rio Rita* would be released by RKO, but in 1927, word of the stage musical had reached Bridgeport. Ruth

Lessler may have taken a trip to Broadway and seen it. What is sure from the snapshot and notation in the album is that my mother saw herself in one of the flamboyant roles.

The snapshots that follow in 1927 are taken in front of the family house being maintained on Savoy Street. How did my mother respond to the return of her father? What was it like on Savoy Street, where she poses with her sisters Miriam and Mildred? Only later would the three youngest girls be shuttled to their married older sisters. In the photograph, where her sister Mildred is still holding on to her doll (and not the sexy Rio Rita doll), my mother looms over Mildred, very much the older sister. The 1927 photographs show a laughing, confident Ruth, a girl in transition to a woman. Others, especially those snapshots with her sisters, Miriam and Mildred, reveal that Ruth is

only fourteen years old, the bloom of childhood still on her cheek. It is my mother who pretends to play the banjo that I suspect belonged to her older brother, Jules.

Three years later, my mother appears alongside her sister Miriam in a kick line at a pony ballet where my father will spot her. Is she still dreaming of dancers in *Rio Rita*?

She is fourteen in the winter of 1927, only fifteen through the summer and fall.

For most of her senior year she is only fifteen. She has been sixteen for barely two months when on June 26, 1928, she graduates Central High in Bridgeport. Her one act play, "The Gate," which takes place outside the ghetto of Prague, wins a prize and will be performed during March of the following year. In a photograph taken with the other prizewinning playwright, I know well the suspicious glimmer in her expression. She is one of four finalists for the Barnum Prize, her essay "Hurrying—Wither" was awarded one of the "coveted scholarship-leadership pins." She was on the honor roll graduating cum laude.

The most striking photograph is the one she has taken for her graduation, the bottom image on the next page. Immersing myself in the movies that helped form my mother's idea of whom she wanted to resemble, it is clear that she had carefully studied the glamorous image of Clara Bow. Her icy, but fragile pose might well have earned her a screen test in Hollywood.

Ruth Sylvia Lessler had just turned sixteen but the photograph taken in that year for her graduation shows that she can project the eerie beauty of a professional model, the glow of a Hollywood actress. It is that image that suddenly struck me some four or five years after her death, presenting me with a girl I would have fallen in love with, so that I did, and ached lying in my parents' marriage bed, despite the presence in the house of a girlfriend I was in love with and would marry.

Mother's photograph from 1929/1930, which follows the rather cold, dangerous screen siren, seems more natural, the kind of girl I might have had a chance to date.

What did she do after she graduated? If I read her handwriting correctly in March of 1930, she was staying at her second oldest sister Betty's house, when my father passing through Bridgeport, read the local Jewish community paper, saw her picture there in "the pony ballet" of a charity show and called. She would still have been only eighteen when Wilfred Mirsky, a twenty-four-year-old graduate of Harvard, restocking flower shops along the Connecticut coastal road from the New York market, tried to get fresh on a first date (a blind one) and she slapped him.

How young she was, and in a sense, vulnerable, though she pretended otherwise.

The spring and fall of 1930 in her album are filled with booklets for dances. There is a whole page in the album where dance programs from 1930 are pasted in, and the shriveled remains of a corsage from one of them; the Junior Dance, the Thanksgiving Dance, the Henry Barnard League, Christmas Dinner, the K.O.J. Washington's Birthday Dance. A newspaper article printed in September of 1931 in the Bridgeport paper with a photograph beside the column, reports that she attended night school at a junior college while in Red Cross employ and after that in the summer of 1931, took three courses at Columbia. In a second album that details her life in the early years of her marriage, which she must have finished just after I was born, she pasted a newspaper article that detailed some of her employment. "From 1929 to 1931 she served as Receptionist with American Red Cross in Bridgeport, Connecticut."

My sister says that Mother told her she worked as a secretary and that my mother's older sisters did not encourage either her or Miriam to go on to college. While Annie Lessler had left all her children shares in the stores she had begun, the older sisters urged the younger ones to save this inheritance for expenses when they got married. My mother, however, gravitated to more serious work than being a secretary or receptionist. A clipping dated September of 1931 from the Bridgeport newspaper confirms her increasing interest in social work. It reports that for the past six months, summer and spring, Ruth Lessler has been cheerfully working for the American Red Cross in Bridgeport, helping veterans of World War One.

In a scribble at the bottom of the newspaper clipping below in my mother's hand is written (not visible here); "Vanity thy name is woman." According to my cousin, Shirley Winnick, it was a supervisor at the Red Cross who took my mother under her wing and encouraged her to go on for a college degree. Aunt Miriam was even more specific: "We both went to business school after graduation ... The Red Cross saw to it that she [Ruth] went on to college. She got a job first with a contractor—wasn't happy with it, went to the Red Cross. A woman supervisor there was so impressed with her that she saw to it that she was admitted. She had a few credits from a junior college she went to at night. Generally you needed a B.A." During her work with the Red Cross my mother decided to use the money that she had been left by her mother, and with the help of at least one, possibly several of her brothers, enrolled at Simmons College in Boston. That was the sober face she showed to the world. The dreams of Rio Rita, however, were revolving as well. I will find her a year later on the bumper of her car, a cigarette dangling from her mouth, posing coyly according to her own handwriting as either Gloria Swanson or Joan Crawford, or as the notorious, if romantic, loose woman of the cinema, Sadie Thompson.

RED CROSS HERE HELPED 802 VETS TO GET $310,000 ON BONUS

Sunday Sept. 13 Post

Miss Lessler Relates Stories Told by Ex-Service Men Since Law Passed.

A total of $310,000 is a sum to be considered. This, it was announced yesterday, was the amount borrowed on war certificates during the first six months of the new law by Bridgeport war veterans with the aid of the Red Cross here. This total was paid to 802 ex-service men of Bridgeport.

It is an interesting fact that the money received by veterans through the aid of the Red Cross in most cases was spent for necessities. Very little, in the belief of the executive secretary, was squandered. This opinion is gained through the knowledge the organization has of each of the individuals who sought to make a loan. In other words the $310,000 was turned right back into circulation in business in Bridgeport.

Miss Ruth Lessler, who was in charge of this work at Red Cross headquarters, colorfully told the Sunday Post of the "Bonus Rush" and what it meant to Bridgeport veterans. To be sure, she stated, hundreds of men also borrowed through the United States Veterans' Bureau office here, through veterans organizations, and banks so that these 802 men do not represent the total number, merely the Red Cross share of the task.

In '49 the general cry was "Gold! There's gold in them there fields," and a rush to California," Miss Lessler said.

"In 1917 the cry was "Johnny get your gun and make the world safe for democracy"—and a rush to arms.

"In 1931 there was the cry "borrow veterans on your certificate if need be' and so 802 veterans rushed to Red Cross headquarters.

"Those were feverish days," she continued, "excited men trooping in and out of the Red Cross office asking always, 'is it true—are we going to get one half of our bonus'—for that meant to them a way out of debts, expenses, until a job turned up or work was full time We in the Red Cross office could only answer 'We don't know yet—it all depends upon Congress' to each eager inquiry.

"The bill passed both houses—the President felt it wise to veto it—it went back for more consideration.

"During this week of suspense with the newspapers still giving front page space a tall, sparse veteran of Lincoln type appeared at Red Cross Headquarters. At the 'What can I do for you' with which he was cheerfully greeted—for a smile helps much in these days—he hesitatingly stammered 'You know I've been reading the papers and it seems like there is going to be an awful rush when this bill is passed. The wife and I decided I ought to come here and file application—you call 'em Veterans Notes,—so the minit that bill is passed you folks can send it ahead then we will have the money right handy so as to pay for the hospital care she'll soon need, and our grocer too—he needs the money right badly—and there are shoes and coal. Men like me can't afford being out of work so long. Clara is that proud that she won't send the kids to Sunday School 'thout them having half way decent clothing.'

"The man had hitch hiked and walked all the way from Huntington where he lived in a broken, wooden, shingled bungalow off the main road. He had walked for the better part of the way along the cold frozen road.

"Very willingly the worker filled out the note, but smilingly warned him, not to count his chickens before they were hatched," since no one could say whether the bill would be passed 'but if it does the very first minute we will mail your note.'

"With a grateful 'thank you Miss' he shuffled through the door feeling that an end to his many troubles would be reached for months to come if he could carry on until business picked up. Like so many veterans—he did not want financial help—he would borrow on his one remaining asset—Uncle Sam's bonus.

"There were murmurings on every side like the threatening rumble of machine guns in the distance. Everywhere you went the soldiers discussed the pros and cons of the bill, on street corners, in their shops and offices—anywhere anyone would talk and listen. Financiers argued about the effect upon business—many told what they would do with it. In poorly furnished flats, in tiny houses, in big ones troubled husbands and wives after the children had been tucked into bed figured out how much could be borrowed and how long it could be made to last. Some feared having so much money after months of sacrifice would go to their heads, while white haired mothers anxiously telephoned for advice, and here and there a wife for the children's sake wanted to know what to do.

"Then came the headlines announcing that the deed was done—the bill had become a law! Those who could not read got the news over the radio, while others from their buddies who became town criers.

"'Groups of men within ten feet of the building were chatting with each other as I approached the office that next morning—excitement ran high. As I reached the head of the stairs I rubbed my eyes unbelievingly—a horde of men, some sheepish, others impatient awaited the office opening.

Ready For Work

"'Red Cross National Headquarters at Washington had sent to the 3,500 chapters instructions prepared in advance should the bill be passed—so we were ready. We three of the office staff gathered piles of applications beside us—carbons ready—seats arranged next to the desk—and the Red Cross was ready for action.

"'The men were shown in and formed in three lines so they could move along quickly. The lines reminded them of those old mess lines of '17 and '18 and of the canteens where, too, the Red Cross served them. Our executive secretary acted as traffic officer, greeting the newcomers, answering questions, and trying to cheer for once more she too felt back in the canteen days of '17 and '18 when soldiers sought Red Cross not singly but in ever oncoming masses.

"There were many, many new faces, serious hard working men, mostly with families or dependents for very few of the other kind came to Red Cross, although there are too, among the veterans— veterans a good cross country for a certa— typewriters clicked— pause or a le— man was—

Aided Ex-Service Men

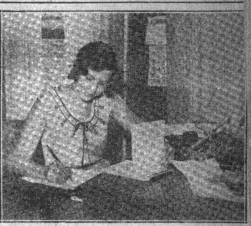

Miss Ruth Lessler shown at work in the Red Cross office where she aided 802 war veterans to collect $310,000 of their bonus money. She tells of the work for the past six months.

Vanity thy name is woman

Chapter Seven

In conversation (and in Mother's letters to me after I left home) until just a few years before her death, she rarely spoke without irony in regard to my father. "How did you meet Daddy?" my sister and I clamored in the pantry, inveigled by my mother into helping dry dishes. It was one of her few stories. My father had graduated from Harvard cum laude in Economics. He had gone down to New York City hoping for a career in finance with a letter from a professor to the president of a New York bank. It was 1929. When Dad arrived, he found the bank was closed and was told its president had just jumped out of an office window. My father, with no other prospects, took stock of his work alongside his father in the Boston Flower Exchange (popularly referred to as "The Flower Market."). Before the Crash of 1929 my grandfather had been a successful salesman on behalf of the growers to retail flower shops. Dad decided to start a business with a truck that would resupply florists up and down the Connecticut coast in the middle of the week from the New York Flower Exchange. Retail florists took the long trip into Manhattan once a week. Those who lived more than an hour out of the city and ran out of stock didn't resupply until the next week. The business was successful enough that my father kept at it for a year while he prepared to apply to Harvard Law. At twenty-four, an eligible bachelor, looking for young women to date, Wilfred read the local Jewish newspapers, hoping to find the picture of a pretty girl. In Bridgeport's Jewish newspaper my father saw a photograph from a play put on to raise funds for a charity—it featured a long chorus, or kick line, of young women—among them my mother, Ruth, and her sister, Miriam. Their long legs and faces were on display; their names under the picture. My father started calling all the Lesslers in Bridgeport and finally found Ruth, the eighteen-year-old girl who struck him as the most attractive. She was staying that month at her sister Betty's, the second oldest of her siblings.

Feature of Black and White Revue

"THE PONY BALLET"

According to Aunt Dorothy (Wilfred was six years older than Ruth), my mother was surprised by the call and was ready to hang up—a call asking for a blind date from a total stranger?

Dorothy, who happened to be beside the phone listening, urged her sister to take a chance. "He sounds interesting, Harvard?" her older sister, who had a zany streak, teased her. My mother agreed to go out.

"What happened?" my sister and I asked, whenever we got Mother to tell her version.

"He tried to get fresh and I slapped him."

Ruth was almost eighteen when my father, passing through Bridgeport saw that picture in the local newspaper, picked her out and started calling houses in the telephone book. I look hard again at the kick line and doubt it was her legs that attracted my father (the photo does not do them justice). Was it that intensity around the eyes, evident even through the crude dots of the newspaper clipping? I recognize that directness and suspicion, looking at me as a little boy, fascinated and appalled at what she saw.

My mother's decision to take a degree in social work at Simmons College in Boston brought her back into the social sphere of the young man who had rashly pushed his luck during that blind date in 1930. Was she very different at nineteen, a year and a half later, when she and my father met again in Boston? My father, Wilfred, had given up the hope of a career in banking and abandoned a business he had built up for a year, restocking retail florists north of Manhattan's wholesale market along the Connecticut shore and had left New York. He came back to Boston in the fall of 1930 and lived at home while teaching Hebrew school to pay his way through Harvard Law School. However difficult that first year was for my father, the next, when he began to court my mother, was more so.

In September 1931, Ruth Sylvia Lessler came to Boston to start at Simmons College. I see pasted into her album under the heading "Boston—Ah! School days again," a picture of Temple Israel, the Reform synagogue in Boston, from a program printed for its High Holiday services, Rosh Hashanah [New Year] and Yom Kippur [Day of Atonement]. She wrote on it, "Attended all days. Fasted Yom Kippur." There is no mention of my father during the early fall. She goes to the Museum of Fine Arts, the beach at Swampscott, where she poses "on the rocks." There are pictures of young men, one sitting on top of a car, others with their arms around her.

How did Ruth and Wilfred meet again? She was staying at the Franklin Square House, a dormitory for women in Boston. An anonymous person fixed them up, and, according to my mother's oft-repeated tale, it was a blind date. She told me she was surprised to face the fresh guy who had called her in Bridgeport out of the blue. My father laughed when I repeated her story to him in one of our conversations, after her death. "She wanted to meet me again. It was no accident."

How they met is less important than what happened. Here my mother's albums reveal to me much more than they did when I carelessly went through them as a boy, or even when I returned to them after her death and fell in love with the young woman there. My father too, left a journal, which reveals much in what it does not say, as well as what it says by accident. Unlike my mother's albums, it was kept hidden from my prying eyes or my sister's. Only after my father's death did I discover it in his bookshelves.

In Mother's albums the first indication that she has met my father are two phone messages. Numbered 445, on fragile yellow paper; messages jotted down by a receptionist at the Franklin Square House on the pad whose leaves stuck in the residents' mailboxes. In the album they are pasted in, folded over; one marked "personal," the other "private," in my mother's hand. They are both from the same date, 1-23-32. "Personal," on the right has the time as 7:15, but "private" on the left, has the 7:15 crossed out, and 7:45 P.M. written in. The message is the same "Wilfred called."

She must have suspected from those first calls that she would fall in love with Wilfred, though the album entries tease her own attraction. And perhaps they met at the very end of 1931, because there is poem of conventional sentiments (written by a Mabel S. Worcester) printed on a card pasted into Mother's album, which probably accompanied either chocolates or flowers. "If I could choose the rarest gifts at Christmas time to send," it begins. My father's handwriting has mocked the sentiment by writing in large letters under Ms. Worcester's name, "'Mother' Fatface," and in even larger ones "Sugar!!" In my mother's cursive script, under the card in the album is, "From Wilfred," and "Harvard Sight Seeing Day!" My father must have given it to her on a tour of the Harvard campus and Ruth, referring to him by his first name, seems to be taken with him, ignoring his irony.

There are excursions to the theater all through the winter, Katherine Cornell in *The Barretts of Wimpole Street*, Sophocles' *Electra*, and Bernard Shaw's *Too True to be Good* but no indication as to who took her, or whether she went on her own. Next to one photograph of my father, however, from the spring of 1932 she scribbled, "Funny-face himself." (That caught my attention as a boy, and even if the "ace" at the edge of the yellowed page has crumbled into oblivion, I remember wondering at the sarcasm as a boy.) Next to another she has scribbled, "My nemesis," but a third has the inscription, "Kissable?"

She may have been dating others, but the pages are filled with events to which Wilfred has taken her and cards from him. On Valentine's Day he sends both a telegram and a card. On May 28th, there is a flower from a corsage pressed into the album and beside it, "From Wilfred, May 28th. Wish I hadn't lost that orchid so I could have saved it too." There are other men mentioned, once or twice, and an am-

biguous note under a card that reads, "Harvard Class Day, 1932, Stadium Exercises, June 21st." My mother has scribbled under it, "If I hadn't been so conscientious maybe he would have taken me."

On June 28th, my father took her to the Boston Pops at Symphony Hall, signed his program and teasingly graded the musical selections, also adding from *The Merchant of Venice* the famous lines, "The man who hath no music in himself is fit for treasonous stratagems ..."

On the cover of another Pops concert program, his sister, my aunt Hilda has written, "To Ruth in sincere expression of undisguised affection, Sincerely, Hilda Mirsky." Mother's albums from the summer of 1932 are playful. There is no hint of a crisis. She worked briefly at the beginning of the summer. She refers to a trip to Manhattan on an envelope for a sugar packet with the insignia of *Ratner's* (a Jewish dairy restaurant). Beside it is written "Imagine eating blintzes at 1:30 A.M." and "Jack and Stanley, summer pals." On the other side of that page among pictures of her brothers and sisters called "1932 summer frivolities," a card from the Boston Dispensary reads "field work, July 1932" referring to the photograph above.

I began this book with my mother flinging herself into the air with joy in the summer of 1932. There was another photograph on that page that tickled me from the age of six or seven, when I first opened her albums as a little boy, but to which I came back again and again, in the years of my adolescence and directly after Mother's death. One can see the same large ship in the background that had foundered in a storm on Nantasket

Beach's sands, identified as "The Nancy." I have already plucked the one that has "Kissable?" inscribed. On the album page, right below the shot featured above, "Smile for the Birdy," is a romantic shot of Dad in his striped jacket. Next to it is written in block letters, "A page about

nemesis," and on the other side is a rectangle with Ruth's equally sarcastic comment "funny face."

What follows is a page in her album dedicated to my father and his family; pictures of Wilfred and his sisters; comments like "Hilda—Ever calm and serene"—a misreading of my tumultuous aunt. "Rocky, the youngest," refers to my father's half-sister, Rochelle, the child Israel had with his second wife, Gertrude, after Devorah's death and his remarriage. "Always Sunny," my mother puns on Aunt Sonia's nickname, "Sunny." My father's stepsister, Charlotte, has "sweet fifteen" written on the photograph itself. The most telling photograph is at the very top of the page. My mother and father are kissing on top of a bench, and she writes next to it "I [AM] CAUGHT IN THE ACT...TSK TSK...BLUE HILLS..."

There is no image of Gertrude, Dad's stepmother, not in the albums or the loose photographs that were stowed away in drawers. My father and his two sisters from Israel Mirsky's first marriage never made peace with Gertrude, who they claimed locked the refrigerator when they were children and fomented trouble between them and Israel. My grandfather Israel appears very late in the album pages, at the time of my mother's marriage. Her notation "Pops" beside the photographs at that time is significant and the omission of my grandfather, Israel, at this point in the album, equally so.

There was a crisis in my father's life. It would lead to a break with his father and I imagine my mother was aware of the pressures that had been operating on her "nemesis" Wilfred, even as he courted her. Her testimony comes from my father's journal, which I discovered after his death. His pages make no mention during the winter of 1931, the spring of 1932, or even the summer, of my mother, or indeed of any young woman, though his pages before that, in 1929 and 1930 are full of references to his dating, and even an ambiguous page about a married woman, estranged from her husband, that he danced with. The first notation of his to refer to my mother occurs in September of 1932.

On July 4th of 1932, however, my mother discovered the journal that my father had been keeping in a scattered and haphazard fashion since his graduation from Harvard in 1929. He had filled up fourteen pages until July of 1932, writing in a script that averages 140 words per page. There are only ten entries since the fall of 1929 when he began it. My mother, however, on the last page of his journal has written him a note. She must have come upon the diary and decided to write something in it, on the very last page of the whole, mostly empty book, under the heading in large brown type, "Miscellaneous." Has something happened (or not happened) between them?

> *July 4, 1932*
>
> *Wil-I have no right to write here but I wanted you to come upon this page some day and remember fondly—I hope—a girl's name who always had and will be wishing the best for you—who has appreciated more than you realized at the moment the sincerity of your feelings. Who knows whether our paths will meet after I leave Boston with all such pleasant and painful memories. But if fate should desire it so—at least know that you have always a friend.*
>
> *Ever yours,*
> *Ruth Sylvia Lessler*
> *Tis better to have loved and lost*
> *Than never to have loved at all.*

I see from the article above of August 1932 that my mother had volunteered to work, nine to five, at her former place of employment in Bridgeport for the Red Cross, "with compensation only of learning more and more." In addition to the page that talks about her eating blintzes at 1:30 A.M. at Ratners, she details a date with a "Rupert" at The Pine Brook Club, a program from the Harlem Jazz club Smalls' Paradise in Manhattan where Jack's photograph is displayed and "What a Time!" and "What a Dancer" writ large in her hand on opposite sides of a good-looking young man whom she identifies as "Jack." "Hatcha! Colored Nite Club," scrawled across the top, "High What a Chorus Yaller" on the bottom. (I journeyed to Smalls during my college years to dance unaware that Mother had preceded me.) There are photographs of her nieces, brothers and sisters from the summer, so she was traveling, as well as working. What provoked her to write such a farewell on the page of Wilfred's diary, which might well have been considered an intrusion by my father into his private papers?

A page in my father's journal on August 7, 1932, discloses a family secret carefully kept from my sister and me. My father's half-sister Rocky, or Rochelle, used to joke about my father's aunt Tsirrel, the powerful matriarch of our extended family in Montreal, that she was such a storyteller that she invented a tale about Mayor Curley of Boston having to talk Harvard into taking my father back at the law school after they had kicked him out. Mayor Curley's negotiations on behalf of my father may have been an invention of my great aunt Tsirrel, but it was only when I read my father's journal that I realized he had indeed been expelled. It was not part of the myth he encouraged about his uninterrupted academic prowess, which cowed me when I came home with Bs instead of As from public school. The entry reveals the pressure he had been under in this second year of law school at home. While he courted my mother, his father's flower business (a business that required my father to get up before dawn to help out in) was falling deeper and deeper into bankruptcy and his stepmother, Gertrude, went on complaining about him and his sisters, undermining his confidence.

> *August 7, 1932*
> *This is the darkest day of my life. Were it not for the fact that the family is gone and that the radio is giving forth some of Tchaikovsky's music I'd go crazy. I just don't know what I feel. My throat is stuffed; My heart is heavy, my head is aching. The real reason is probably that my reputation runs ahead of my ability. But to feel that I'm one of those that has to leave the law school because a man like Simpson who is teaching his first year and doesn't know how to judge men and read papers. What gets me is that Equity, the course I felt I did best in is the one I have to bust. I still cannot believe it. Its [sic] for Evidence I rightly deserved to bust for my mind just wouldn't function that day. You can't get up at five and work like a horse till 8:30 and run to Cambridge on a hot day and take an exam of a four hour type is just impossible and longer [sic]. Still, that's the way I used to take them in college. I should have learned from the previous year when I passed out at the property exam. But to refuse my father anything he asks would make me feel worse than examination busting.*

My mother was in Bridgeport when my father got the news. Did she have an inkling of what pressures my father was under? In her first album, on the last page where a valentine telegram from my father to her was pasted and a card (she was in New London on Valentine's Day

so this was probably spring 1934) there was a poem called "Pretense,"
typed up.

> *Tomorrow when I go to shop*
> *I'll buy a painted mask*
> *The brightest one on any shelf;*
> *And then when people ask*
> *Where you have gone, I'll be so gay*
> *No one will ever guess*
> *That now and then I catch my breath*
> *In sudden loneliness*
> *And heads will nod, and lips will say*
> *Once you were out of sight,*
> *Forgetting was an easy thing...... [sic]*
> *And I'll pretend they're right.*

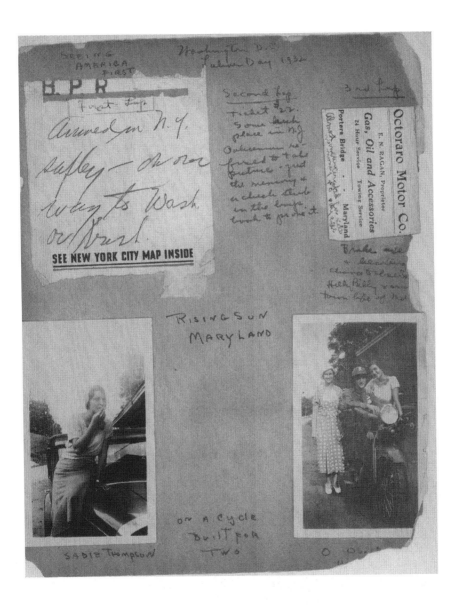

Was Ruth Lessler speaking about herself? She typed. My father never learned how to. Or was Ruth referring to what he was going through at home? Or had Wilfred sent it to her, having someone else type it up? Was it Ruth's reaction to his valentine and telegram, sensing what lay under his lighthearted banter? By Valentine's Day in 1934, my mother was in New London, Connecticut, and had embarked on her career as a professional social worker. Three hours or so of travel by train or automobile separated her from my father. She was probably waiting for him to make a decision about marrying her. In a sense, she had rescued him from his own loneliness. A year and a half earlier, on September 14, 1932—his 26th birthday—when my mother is back in Boston and his fate at the law school is still in the balance, he writes in his journal for the first time since August 7th.

1932 My 26th Birthday — Sept 14

A splendid day. The most enjoyable day I've had for years. The spirit of the day—Ruth Sylvia Lessler of Bridgeport Conn but a good Bostonian by adoption.

Here's what I accomplished with 25¢ in my pocket all day.

1. Had a nice breakfast served by Sonia [Dad's younger sister]

2. Enjoyed a tennis match.

3. Entertained at dinner at Franklin Square House by Ruth.

4. Surprised by Ruth in a colorful maroon robe which was worn special for the day and which lasted only that day.

5. Surprised by Ruth with "Dante and Beatrice" and "Beatrice" and a deep seated kiss that made me feel so touched that she thought I acted embarrassed but a Mirsky is never embarrassed especially on his birthday.

A photograph my mother entitled "Lovebirds" shows them snuggling at Axelrod Manor in September.

Somewhere between September 25th and September 28th, my father argued his case for readmission to the Harvard Law School. He notes in his journal.

> *I'm going back to school.*
> *It was my first case before the Board of the Law School. I know that my letter was a stirring one. There's nothing like developing the truth. You can write truth so much better and in so much more convincing a way. Nothing but the truth for me …*

And the following entry from the 28th of September gives some indication of the turmoil in his father's house, where his stepmother, Gertrude, who had tactlessly enraged the three children of Israel Mirsky's first marriage almost from the first week of her moving in and taking over the household, was making it very difficult for my father to get back on track as a law student. My father, Hilda, and Sonia had suffered through starvation in Pinsk, had witnessed the uncle who watched over them shot in a massacre of Jewish leaders by the Polish army.

Their mother had slowly died before their eyes on the boat that took them to America, just as my father, a boy only fourteen, saw his father for the first time in ten years. His sisters had no memory of Israel Mirsky. My father was devoted to his father, but the strain of getting along with Gertrude was showing. Getting up at five in the morning to help out his father in the wholesale flower market, where Israel was going into bankruptcy, then coming home to a tactless stepmother proved too much.

"A good lawyer is one who can concentrate under any conditions; the cry of children, the stenographer's finger taps or the barrage of the street cars." Thus Joe Beal began his lectures in conflicts today. What I need is time to concentrate in. I don't see how I'll be able to work it all in. That is, my teaching [Hebrew school], studying et al. What's more I don't seem to feel "am bestam" that stomach and gas escapes bothers me very much. It is all due to nervousness caused by the trickery of Mrs. M. may the devil take her. That woman is a curse to humanity and plain wickedness with malice aforethought. I'm actually afraid to live in this house. But necessity is a great force. On with the show.

The crisis in the house of Israel Mirsky would continue until my father and Sonia moved out. Hilda went to California to live, joining her fiancé, Joseph Levy. She left after punching Gertrude in the face after a dispute over the silver cups that the children had brought with their mother, Devorah, from Pinsk. Gertrude tried to appropriate them. Joe Kopelman, a cousin of my grandfather and the man responsible for bringing Israel Mirsky up to New England to sell flowers, came to the bus that took Hilda west and gave her a hundred dollars. Aunt Hilda told me that she realized how desperate her brother Wilfred was and gave most of it to him, leaving with barely enough for food on her trip across the country. My grandfather was so hurt by his two remaining children moving out of the house that he refused to speak to them for a year, until one of his close friends in the synagogue, Abraham Knight, gave him a stern scolding.

If my mother had lacked a real father in adolescence, my father had lacked a mother. They both lost a mother at about the same time, at thirteen and a half, if my father's date of birth is 1906. (Dad was unsure whether he was born in 1905 or 1906. His journal's reference to becoming twenty-six in September of 1932 suggests the latter.) I can't help but believe that it was my mother's steadying hand in 1933 and 1934, which gave him the "*betochen*" or confidence to soldier on through his last year at Harvard Law School, successfully pass the Massachusetts Bar, and begin to practice law. Israel Mirsky by now had gone bankrupt. My aunt Rochelle, my father's half sister, painted a vivid picture of her father's house; Israel Mirsky coming home empty handed, unemployed, unable even to afford the money for an anesthetic during a painful operation. On March 6, 1933, my father would write in his journal:

> *With the banks closed and with the bar closed, I wonder what we are going to do. We must fall back upon the state.*
> *We haven't missed a meal yet in this land!!!*

The last remark was not a cliché to Dad. He had come very close to starvation in Pinsk, when, between 1916 and 1919, only his grandmother's vegetable garden and his own wits had kept him, his mother, and his sisters alive. It had to be a reminder of just how bad life could get. A third of the population of that town deep in the swamps of Belarus died of hunger each year between 1916 and 1919. Just how important Ruth Sylvia Lessler's support was to Wilfred will soon become obvious, but despite Ruth's attention to Wilfred in the fall of 1932, she is hardly leaning on him. "Seeing America First," she writes cheekily in her album. On Labor Day she visits Washington D.C. She poses by a car, smoking a cigarette and writes under it, "Sadie Thompson." It's a curious inscription, referring to a film based on a scandalous story of W. Somerset Maugham's about Sadie Thompson, a woman of "loose morals and sordid reputation who travels to the South Seas seeking a new way of life." Sadie was played by Gloria Swanson in the movie of 1928. In 1932 another version appeared with the title of the story "Rain." Sadie was played by Joan Crawford. I've watched them both and it's hard to decide which actress my mother is impersonating. (They both appear with cigarettes dangling from their lips.) When I was a little boy I remember my mother acting in a play put on by a local synagogue, but that flair for role playing, and particularly for the romantic fallen woman was something she repressed in the role of mother.

SADIE Thompson

I should have guessed that her pleasure in going to the movies or taking me along to see plays was not just a desire to be entertained, but as is true of my own nature, a wish to escape into other worlds. She notes on the same page regarding a speeding ticket on a car trip south, "Second Lap. Ticket $22. Some hick place in N.J. [the] Policeman refused to take [a] picture—just the memory of a check stub in the boys [sic] book to prove." Under "Third Lap" and a card for an Auto Repair shop, she writes, "Brake work and bearing ... chance to observe Hilly Billy and small town life." Writ large is "Rising Sun in

Maryland." I can't identify the man she poses next to in several pictures for that trip, but there is another couple along, it seems, and he is snug against her back as she sits laughing, gripping the handlebars on top of a motorcycle in the rider's position. (She was in terror of me on my own motorcycle. Why did I never look back in these albums in my adolescence and ask her who he was?) Still, in the photographs taken during October of 1932 she is cuddling with my father in the Blue Hills, going to concerts, plays with him and his sister Sonia. There is no ambiguity about their being a couple in love.

While the fall of 1932 is crowded with photographs in her album, most of the winter of 1933 and early spring is a mystery to me. One moment, however, I recovered from my father soon after my mother's death. It occurred at the very beginning of that year, 1933, in which Ruth and Wilfred would become so attached that their marriage seems to have become inevitable. My mother's albums do not speak of the day; her silence is eloquent. On the first of January 1933, her father, Joseph Lessler, passed away in Bridgeport. It is the dead of winter and standing in a freezing graveyard could not be pleasant. Bridgeport, however, is only three and a half hours away by train from Boston. Her older sisters were there and certainly other family members would gather. My father recalled his surprise as a young man to hear that my mother expressed doubt as to whether she was going to go down for her father's funeral. The family did not bury him next to Channah, Annie Kurland Lessler, his wife.

Annie, their mother, had not died suddenly. Was she sick when he left in the late spring for Palestine? "She sent him off to get him out of her hair," was the import of some of the whispers. Still, he stayed a long time. He had received his passport on May 22, 1925, passed through the British Passport Control Office in New York on June 1, 1925, and didn't leave Palestine until October 7, in that same year, the day before Annie died, passing through Marseilles, October 13 and Cherbourg, October 16. He obviously did not arrive in time for her funeral. The contrast between the dapper young Isaac Joseph Lessler who married Annie in 1895 and the tired patriarch who appears beside his son of fourteen, Hyman, in 1914 is dramatic. Even more so is the difference of a few months in that summer of 1925. The passport

photograph, probably taken in May, shows a portly but still confident Joseph. In Palestine, the man who stands in front of a painted background a few months later, looks confused, his suit rumpled, and the third photograph I have of Joseph in the same jacket shows the same bewilderment.

His older sons never forgot how he pulled them out of school to help in the family shop. My aunt Betty's second oldest, Muriel, confirmed what her sister Margie told me, "My mother married young to get out of the house. He was a big man [Joseph Lessler]. I remember [after Annie's death] he lived with some people some five or six streets down from us [in Bridgeport] where we lived on Harlem Avenue.

"I remember when he came to see us, my mother would feed him but never with us. He would eat at the kitchen table where the maid ate. My mother fed him with leftovers. He was not the kind of grandfather you wanted to hug and kiss. He'd give you a penny to kiss him and then take the penny back.

"I think Uncle Dave was one of the few who understood that there was something mentally or physically wrong with him. I remember him coming to the house after he [Joseph] had a seizure and saying, "He's just had a heart attack," and we were frightened sick. Uncle Dave tended to his needs. I don't know where the money came from."

Even my aunt Dorothy, the only one who really defended her father to me, recalled, "Pop took Bob [out of school]. Bob ran away to Mississippi. He developed malaria. My mother sent him money to come home. Mommy said before she passed away, 'If it hadn't been for all the children and the business, we could have had a happy life.'"

It was my aunt Miriam, however, whose judgment I have on tape, which explains my mother's ambivalence. In Miriam's version, her older brother, Bob, took some money that was supposed to be deposited in the bank and ran away to Arkansas, where he found a job and stayed for a year, until he decided to return home. Miriam described to me her father's habit of nudging her mother to the point where this needling and wheedling approached the pathological. "He nudged my mother, he didn't nudge me," she says in a sharp voice. By the time my mother, Ruth, was growing up, Annie had displaced her husband as the authority in the house. I remarked to Miriam that the street records seem to indicate that Annie had taken over Joseph Lessler's business in cloth that he had begun, probably with his parents' help, on Orchard Street. "Well, she felt she had to," Aunt Miriam replies. "She was probably more competent to run it. And that could have probably also created problems ... He was very jealous of her ability ... and he resented that he did not have that same ability to do what she was doing. And one of the problems, as I recall it, is that he could not stay with it very long. In other words, he could start something, but then, he wasn't ... he did buy up a business one time and he thought he was doing a great thing, you know, he was going to strike it rich or something. And it was a disaster. And my mother had to finish it up because he walked away from it." Earlier in the interview, when Miriam told this anecdote, she talked about growing up in a home where her older brothers and sisters were already absent. "We were very close to our mother; we were more mother-oriented, than father-oriented. Both Dotty [Dorothy] and Davey were very helpful to us, in helping us with homework. They were surrogate parents. Especially Davey!"

I asked, "Was he the surrogate parent to everybody?"

"Just to the youngest," my aunt Miriam replies, "I only got to know Betty and Celia when I was older, when we visited them."

Earlier I mentioned the whispers among my cousins about my grandfather Joseph Lessler being committed to hospitals for mental problems or alcohol addiction in the years of my mother's adolescence. Clearly, when my mother's father returned from Palestine, weeks after his wife's death, he was not treated as the head of the family. Annie's money had been left to her children. It was to her older sisters and brothers that my mother looked for direction, and particularly to the one college graduate, Davey.

Who was my mother?

She talked so little about herself. Her secrets were locked inside so tight, the taboo of asking so strong for me, that it never occurred to me to ask about her father. It was only a month after her death that it dawned on me. The space on the wall where his photograph should have hung was blank. I turned to my father in the front seat of his car to ask, "Did she ever talk about her father?"

He thought for a moment and then, as if puzzled himself by where my question had taken him, drew a long breath, "No."

We drove on in the car for another few minutes when he turned from the wheel. "I'll tell you something strange though. When her father died, we were dating. I asked her when she was leaving for the funeral.

" 'I'm not sure I'm going,' she said."

My grandfather (it seems strange to call him that, since no one talked about him in

our house when I grew up) died in Bridgeport, Connecticut. In the 1930s, the train there took only three and a half hours from Boston, where my mother was at school, earning her degree at Simmons College as a social worker. In the copious family albums there is only this one picture of my mother and her father. It is not from her albums. None of my mother's albums contain a photograph of her father.

Her father, Joseph Lessler, has blown up in size from the early portraits, the marriage photograph, where he appears as a skinny, dashing young beau who married my *zaftig* grandmother, Annie—not fat, but with a robust, sweet beauty. (I would sometimes hear my older cousins talk about Grandma Annie, but never about him except to remark that they were not buried together, though in the same Bridgeport cemetery.) In that single photograph where my mother appears alongside her father, he is a comic figure, posed on a child's scooter, one foot on its diminutive running board, as if to take off. I puzzle over how to read her face.

My mother has put her arm through her father's. She has a half amused, but slightly deprecatory smile, as if she is putting up with the joke. In her pursed lips, I recognize an expression I memorized from hers, and put to my own use. It establishes distance, a play of ironic condescension, so as not to get hurt, and was one of her most familiar, if genial, masks. I guess that she is already out of high school, working at the Red Cross, not yet enrolled at Simmons College. (On the other hand, she has already assumed this persona by the age of sixteen as she graduates Bridgeport High.) She is self-assured, and perhaps more amused than I want to think.

My mother never said a word to me about her father. No image of him hung anywhere in the house, I can only guess at the deep-seated anger her ambivalence about attending his funeral concealed.

By the spring, both my mother and father were getting ready to graduate and go out into the world to earn a living in the middle of the Great Depression. The strain of competition at law school must have been particularly harsh on Wilfred Mirsky. He wrote in his journal:

Sunday May 14, 1933.
A week before exams. I looked at the catalogues and saw my name in the unclassified list and it was an odd feeling to have—I must jump a different hurdle than most of the third year men. Somehow I have faith in myself, but a little doubt creeps into my soul now and then as to making the grades. Those next few weeks will affect my life greatly, I feel but I'm cheerful with the beautiful May sun on Mother's Day. In these moments I feel I'd like to tie my soul to something someone but I can't. I haven't anyone and it is perhaps a good thing to stand alone—I offer a prayer to my dead mother.

There are happy photographs in the year before his exams, but even in June of 1933, when my father did well enough to graduate from Harvard Law School, and my mother sailed through Simmons College—why did my father feel so alone?

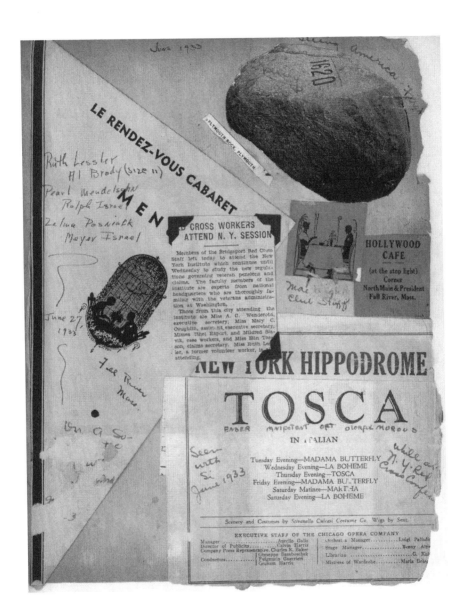

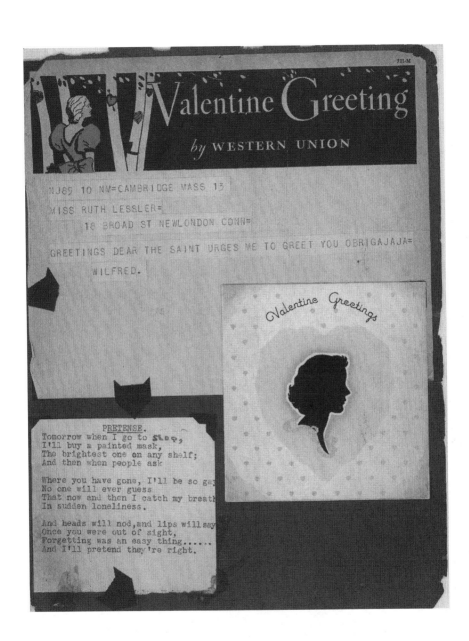

Was it just the tug of sadness from Mother's Day? Or was he truly confused about his feelings toward my mother. He was almost 27, but she was barely 21. Ruth Sylvia Lessler writes in her album, "All Things must come to an End. And so Goodbye Boston. Last Memories. June 1933." She goes down in that month to a Red Cross conference in New York City with a number of staff members from the Bridgeport office to study "the new regulations governing Veterans' pensions and claims." Under the heading "A New Beginning. Professional Days. Mansfield Training School, Connecticut. July and August 1933," she prepares for her new career but she is obviously enjoying herself as there are pictures of her in a bathing suit and scribbles in the margin, beside photographs, "Hot Dog Roast, Marshmallows too—country and water. Staff picnic." There is also a photograph of my father's arm around my mother, dated July 1933. And another dated, Labor Day, 1933, and inscribed next to it, "A glorious weekend at Lake Massa … in New Hampshire," mentioning my father, his sister Sonia, other mutual friends of theirs as well as petals pasted in with, "Flowers from that midnight dance."

• • •

When my mother took her first job after graduating Simmons College as a social worker in October of 1933, it was in Providence, near enough to reach Boston easily, only an hour's train ride away, an hour and a half by car. In her album she writes, proudly, "October 1933 Jewish Orphanage of Rhode Island, Providence, My new home as Girls Supervisor." And my mother has an automobile of her own that she nicknames, "Nira," posing behind the driver's wheel.

She labels another photograph "Nira on the job." She has pictures of

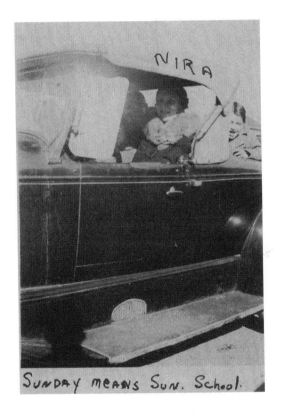

her charges, both girls and boys. She writes "Our Gang," and below another, "More of our Gang." There is a picture of my father in a coat, and tickets from the Harvard-Brown football game on Saturday, November 18, 1933. A better job will soon appear on the horizon, further south

OUR GANG

in New London. And only four months later, the orphanage gives her a farewell party, on January 26, 1934, at 7:30 P.M. A card is pasted into the album.

> To Miss Lessler,
> Just a little gift from all of us. "We hope you will have lots of luck and
> sucess [sic] in your new job."

And again, a card:

> Think of us often and use this
> writing case when you come back
> to us again to record our good marks.
> The Kids.

In a few months another album, Volume II, will take up the story of her life until my conception. I am not sure exactly when Mother began her first one, which she entitled on a page she painted with purple and brown, "Scrapbook, R.S.L." The last page of her girlhood album ends with a valentine telegram from my father, Wilfred, as well as a card from him, so she had already taken up residence in New London and started a new job by the middle of February. The poem about forgetting is pasted there as well, perhaps a bittersweet sense that despite the valentines, "R.S.L." might be forgotten by Wilfred. Her stay at the Rhode Island orphanage was brief but the outpouring of affection from her charges shows that she was certainly a success. In fact, it is the only employment I recall her mentioning frequently. It is the first page of this first album of Ruth's, though, that makes me suddenly nostalgic, returning me to the girl of thirteen, who has just lost her mother. The poem above the photograph of her mother with four of her grandchildren, probably a year or two before Annie's death … was it pasted in first or last?

All about me—Ruth Lessler
Just a scrap or two
That would not mean much to
you
But really brings back to me
Such pleasant days in memory

The "pleasant days" in the album except for that photograph where Annie Lessler appears with Ruth's youngest sister, clinging to Annie's side, and her first grandchildren surrounding her, all lie after the death of Mother's mother. Still, it is with a photograph from that previous era that the album begins. Nothing else from the period before my grandmother's death was pasted in and my mother, Ruth, hardly spoke to me about that early childhood, try though I might, to draw her out about those memories.

Chapter Eight

No girlhood nostalgia begins my mother's second album—neither poetry, nor images of her dead mother, nor any nephews or nieces. The book's first photograph is of the orphanage in Rhode Island and echoes the sadness of what she probably felt, eight years before, when her mother, Annie, died. Mother must have begun her second album in New London. Most of the photographs and memorabilia from her position at the Jewish orphanage in 1933 lie back in her first album. She left Rhode Island in the winter of 1934 for a new job, but the second album begins with a look back at the orphans she left behind. This scrapbook has a larger page-size than the first. In the flyleaf there are no pictures or poems, only an austere inscription by her at the top, "Vol. II, 1934."

That first picture is so large that the earlier album could not have easily accommodated it— a formal photograph of the entire orphanage and its staff, with the signatures of almost all the children. Seated in the second row, among the six staff members, she is not only sober; she almost looks like an orphan, young and old at the same time, as if she felt she must fall in with the faculty. Her departure was certainly regretted and the children missed her. Ruth returned to observe the Passover at the Jewish orphanage and the poem the children wrote welcoming her back, the birthday card they sent in April, speaks to their affection.

The backside of the page with the large photograph of the children and orphanage staff pasted onto it, the next in sequence, holds a newspaper article about her new place of work in New London. Throughout the first album there are references to Red Cross conferences that my mother attended. Evidently an opening for a social worker in the new center for the unemployed that was operated by the Works Progress Association had been advertised and my mother must have jumped at it. She had done this sort of work with veterans of World War One in Bridgeport. On April 9, 1934, the New London paper *The Day* lists Ruth S. Lessler as the social worker for the Federal Transient Center set up at Broad and Cottage Street in the former offices occupied by Palmer Brothers Co.

New London was several stops further than Providence on the train from Boston, and a much longer drive. It must have taxed my father, who was just beginning to build a law practice, as he continued what would be a long courtship. On April 4th, her birthday, he sent a telegram, which she pasted into her album.

HAPPY BIRTHDAY DEAR. SORRY. COULDN'T ARRANGE. STOP. WILL WRITE. WILFRED.

And there is a card that must have been attached to a present. It reads, "To keep you in humor in the evenings while I read the law. Wilfred. April 1934." On the card in another hand, possibly my mother's is written, "God's gentleman." "Bar to admit 218 April 25" a newspaper clipping announces, which must refer to my father. On this page at the top, she marked the formal beginning of her New London career, writing in block letters, "Home is Where Career is 1 New London Federal Transient Bureau." Under it "Happy Nights" penned in thick

letters, below that in thinner ones, "Working Days." Another page has
an elaborate corsage ribbon and flowers, pasted in and written on it,
"*Shavuoth*, Boston, June 7th, 1934, gardenias and dancing, Maimon-
ides affair." Another flower, possibly a rose, is pasted in next to the date
June 9th with "Farewell to—" but the word is indecipherable, and sadly
a missing photograph next to which my mother has written, "That
famous Chez Mirsky domicile, father and son." The most striking photograph is that of my father slim and handsome in a three-piece suit,
posed in front of my mother's car, Nira, and under it my mother has
inscribed, "Nira's favorite driver."

In July, my mother was off to
Chicago for another conference.
Her brother Simon took her to
see a performance of Tosca at the
opera. The next months, for some
reason, go unrecorded; no theater
stubs, no newspaper articles, no
telegrams. At the end of March
1935, my mother evidently decides
that she needs a vacation regardless
of whether Wilfred can go along.
She pastes the receipt from Ka-
plan's Travel Bureau on March 29th
and the brochures of the Ward
Line. "6 Days, all Expenses, 55
dollars, Cruise to Havana, Ward
Line. Havana at the Peak of the
Season. T.E.L. Oriente."

Wilfred's sister Sonia as chaperone (or vice-versa?) perhaps needing
a vacation as well, signs up for the trip alongside my mother and just
before Ruth's birthday they sail off to Havana.

My mother kept a careful and detailed log of her trip, which was
pinned into the album. I quickly rifled through it as a boy. Finding
no obvious secrets, it made no impression. Mother left from Boston
by automobile on April 2nd. There is no mention of my father but she
drove up from New London to say goodbye and fetch his younger

sister, Sonia. The two women travel together to the dock in New York, where my mother leaves her car. It takes them three hours and forty five minutes to get to New London, which gives me some sense of how much time it took Ruth Lessler during 1934 and 1935 to drive back and forth to see her beau, Wilfred. My mother and Sonia spent the night in New London, calling Boston and Bridgeport. My mother records that her sister Miriam "thought I was 'crazy' to go to Havana this time." In 1930, the two had gone to Bermuda together. I can feel Ruth's pleasure in shocking her older, apparently more conservative, sister.

The pages of Mother's journal are fastened with a rusting pin. It has a ball of topaz ceramic at the end, the kind that might have served to pin the folds of a dress in place or a man's shirt when it came from an expensive store. They hold together fifteen pages written on the ship company's stationary, the Ward Line (some are sheets folded in half to make four pages. She saved menus, brochures, entry-cards in Spanish for Cuba, and took lots of photographs.

From New London, my mother and Sonia reached New York in 3 and 3/4 hours (that would be good time, even today). Another hour's train ride and a cab brought them to the ticket office where they discovered that "there were only 22 passengers—but our stateroom accommodations were changed for the better—so tho[ugh] we missed the hubbub which usually greets one at the pier, we went immediately to our stateroom and decided it was for the best. Room 326 ... outside, rose bed spreads...but no washing accommodations, spacious, superb ..." Two friends, Moe and Al, knock on their door, having come on board to see them off and then on at 4 P.M. on April 3rd the boat sails. "Al and Moe waved on the pier faithfully until out of sight. There were only a handful of people on board and on the pier but one grey-haired Irish was cutting up and made the leaving quite a humorous chain of witty repartees."

Aunt Sonia had survived a harrowing crossing of the Atlantic as a child of nine in the midst of the worst storms in twenty years, waves swamping the tiny French steamer that brought her mother, brother, and sister to America. Sonia had sea legs, but not my mother, who as the boat pulls out to sea is immediately dizzy; but going in to take tea in the dining room with Sonia is not too faint to notice that they were attracting attention.

My mother's jaunty slang surprises me. I hear the voice of the actress, the woman who perches on the hood of an automobile with a cigarette dangling from her lips, imagining she is Gloria Swanson or Joan Crawford. "There was eyed by a short blonde fellow at next table. We turned up our noses and went our way. Soon to be followed by the same gent. Well what the hell—all's fair on shipboard. Finally we all introduced ourselves and the ice was broken."

My mother takes up her journal two days later, but goes back to the evening of the 3rd where "a wave of nausea" overtakes her on the deck as she and Sonia talk to the strangers they

have met. She notes that they sat talking "of this and that" as she fought off the seasickness, "still dressed in our respective grey and blue suits." My mother and Sonia go back to their room, rest and wash up. They go to dinner and find that the elderly ship's physician is at their table. "We were shown to table 49—the only other occupant Dr. Noonan, ship physician—an elderly grey-haired 'amateur philosopher' self-styled—with a Van Dyke Beard. And a very interesting dinner companion was he. We now know the following—he is a vegetarian—a lover of flowers, abhorrer of liquors and a native of Oakland, California. When we exhaust table topics, we can always listen to and discuss stories of the Morro Castle—where he was formerly [assigned] until he was transferred only a short time before the disaster.

"The doctor prescribed a capsule and pill for my illness and it did help a great deal. Blondie—Vic Seward, a cotton salesman, attached himself to Sunny and his friend, Bill Planz, another salesman of some sort, to myself. After dinner we danced a bit in the ballroom—what a ballroom! Small trees geometrically placed about the glass enclosed 'veranda' with tables set for four and in the middle a large floor for dancing. Alas we found that apparently we were the only young four on boat and the others preferring chess ... with such small passenger list (only 22) the music was furnished by orthophonic radio rather than orchestra." My mother heads for bed at 10:30, seasick. "Sonia dutifully following, although she was not affected at all by the roughness of the sea."

So my mother wakes up on April 4th, and finds herself, "rolling, rolling—light-headed and giddy—not all energetic was my lot. I forced myself to smile and dress and sit at table with Sonia. The meals I shall not describe but enclose menus instead. Only peculiarity—the Doctor Noonan's idiosyncrasy of breakfast tastes. 1.—tomato juice 2. orange juice 3. grapefruit juice. 4. sauerkraut juice. And so on thru all the juices on the list. A little hot water and orange juice was all I could stand—but Sonia ate heartily.

"After breakfast a brief spasm of vomiting," and so she rolls between her deck chair where she meets an older Scotch couple, the Browns, with "delightful accents" and her bedroom. "It wasn't until noon that I realized that it was my birthday." By 3:45, she is recovering, taking a long nap, and when she and Sonia are invited by the Browns for drinks in the smoking room before dinner they put on their velvet gowns and happily go for a social hour. "At their advice we both had a brandy—I felt much better for it and went down to dinner a new person though I cautiously ate lightly."

"After dinner having eaten more than I expected, at the waiters kind concern we went upstairs to the drawing salons. Mrs. Brown was playing piano. Mr. Brown accompanied her with a nice tenor. We joined the group & before long Vic & Bill did too. Two dowagers applauded vigorously from the corner & soon the stray men (the important looking ones at The Captain's Table) peeked in the windows. A Mr. Campbell, age 53, designer of the Oriente & what a truly lavish ornate well looking ship it is—also joined us & he had a beautiful tenor voice—he sings over the little radio hour too. The others in the group were 3 men—one a married dark-haired mustachioed polite, about 40, one of the freight agents of the Ward Line & the third, a candy manufacturer (I think?) At the completion of 1-1/2 hour group singing we had a round of drinks at Mr. Brown's, & then Mr. Campbell's expense, Sonia and I had a Bacardi and an orangeade. After that we returned to the ballroom and there danced from ten to one. With three women and eight men you can imagine how popular each one was. Later sandwiches, dainty, and hors d'oeuvres to take away the liquor effects were served.

"A short walk around the deck with three escorts between Sonia and myself. We were in the Gulf Stream—and the breezes were so warm—and refreshing—the sky was dotted with stars—but no moon.

"And so to bed at 1 A.M., Sonia and I both tired and happy for the first time since sailing—because I felt myself again." To which, she writes a "P.S. Later learned the third escort was a Mr. Bittles, a wealthy N.Y. with a private yacht; going down to complete a business deal in Cuba."

On April 5th Ruth is up early. "Arose at 7. The day is beautifully clear and warm whereas yesterday AM was rough—cold and foggy. We showered, donned summer clothes and colored hair ribbons and breakfasted gleefully. We spent an hour at the gym on the bicycles—horses—& lifts. It was fun—the Capt. comes thru & what a grand looking old gent is he—all dressed up in white today as were the other staff members. Then rounds of shuffleboard—deck tennis & ring goes, the whole group of last night joining. Then under sea spray—O—grand but here again we were fooled, expected a swimming pool, some [thing] as a planned recreational activity. And the quiet—reserved 'stuck up' purser…a man of 32, invited us to cocktails before lunch. So we dressed up in cotton frocks and had a sweet martini on the veranda with the several gentlemen of last night's party. The conversation was all about horses—and why we were asked except to grace the table with femininity I don't know.

"A light lunch—because of a dizzy feeling and out on deck again to find the flying fish. And we actually did see some—also porpoises on the side of the ship.

"At night having dined in our green and brown gowns respectively, we walked the decks with the Browns, Bittles. Beautiful night. The colorful lights of Miami Beach quite apparent and a sympathetic warm breeze…" I find myself typing up much of her journal, striking out summations, substituting exactly what she wrote. I realize I want to write not just a memoir meant to unravel my mother's secrets but a ghost book; to enter the world she lived in, recover her footsteps to her cabin, on the dance floor; her observations about the good-looking guide, the "blondie" who eyes her, and wonder about her reticence in saying more about Vic. Even her spelling mistakes and shorthand seem precious.

"April 6th, 1935

"An early arisal [*sic*]—a quick shower and a shower on the Oriente is grand, an attentive steward in the background anxious to please. And in to breakfast... Dr. Noonan was late, so we ate with the Browns. Then on deck to view the skyline of Havana. And what a beautiful view—the Morrow Castle Fort, standing in majestic [outline] against the lilac sea. The city of tan and green stretched out before us beautifully laid out—a few smoke stacks of chimney in the distance and the round dome of the Capital Bldg [*sic*] resembling our own national one. The brown singing diving boys—gracefully finding the pennies the few passengers threw down and screeching their singsong Spanish out, entreating to throw coins & they would dive. The coins were placed in their mouths once they retrieved it from the waters.

"After an unfortunate [scrutiny] by the Cuban health inspector we donned our best summer togas and started down to be met by a reporter of *El Paiz* and had our pictures snapped.

"Then the large steel pier and there met by the tourist guide. Only the police inspector's party seemed to be interested in the excursion, the others having work to do. In two cars we were bundled, long open Packards. Sunny and I were placed in one with dear old Mr. Baldwin and a lovely blonde young tanned driver—Mr. Kelly by name—we later learned—in Cuba yrs [*sic*] and married to a Catalan—meaning on the borderline of France but of Spanish nationality.

"In we got and no sooner did the car leave the pier when we were surrounded by tens of beggars—girls and boys from 5 to ten with pathetic ragged appearance 'please lady, money, money, money, the penny': When they got their penny off they'd rush to an orange vendor who with a delicate machine peeled the orange skin and gave them the large sweet fruit."

My mother drives on to see gardens, "enjoyed a tasty beer at 5 cents a glass, and had our pictures taken by a persistent semitic Cuban. Then to a sugar plantation—the farm—and a cock fight."

Who did she write this journal for—herself, my father, or friends? That single notation jumps off the page to me, "had our pictures taken by a persistent semitic Cuban." Was Ruth not a *semitic American*? My father and Sonia's first language was Yiddish as was Mother's parents. Both families had come from Eastern Europe. Sonia was right beside Ruth in the gardens. Is Ruth Lessler swept up in a role she wants to play on shipboard and in her tour of Havana—just an American girl, free of any ethnic identity? Her jaunty first remarks in eying the men takes me back to that photograph of Sadie Thompson. It was obviously charming to be Scotch, if not of old Anglo-Saxon stock. The day before this excursion to the gardens in Havana, on the evening of April 5th, she had remarked, after noting "the sympathetic warm breeze … Later, a round of orangeades and punchades with the La Belles and Mr. Baldwin and the Browns on B aft deck talking of this and that, mainly Scotties. A general get-together in the smoking room, quite cliquey—:"

Mother and Sonia were evidently the most attractive women on board and they were included in the clique, though it meant listening patiently to their elders. She observes of her inclusion that it meant "leaving Sonia + I to the mercy of Mr. Baldwin & Mr. and Mrs. Brown. Enjoyable discussion of Señoritas—life in the tropics & then a professional talk on prisons + reformatories with Mr. Baldwin who is the Inspector in charge of 20 schools in N.Y. dealing largely with problem boys. The tales he described of N.Y. hoodlums were quite interesting …" Mr. Baldwin offers to give Ruth and Sonia his "kindly let alone card" if they find themselves "in trouble in New York City." She kisses the night goodbye with the sentences, "Then another Lasting round of drinks and so to bed, tired but happy, tomorrow we would be in Havana—Hurrah!"

What did she hope to find, apart from better weather than New England could offer in early April—romance, a sense of herself as an all-American girl? What did she recognize in that photographer who shadowed her so that she puts him at a distance with a racial cliché *"persistent semitic"*? The most interesting passages are the early ones on shipboard when she first meets passengers and passes judgment on them. With the exception of the child beggars who assault the tourists leaving the boat, begging for pennies to dive after, and some observations on the cemetery and the orphanage ("an immense building housing 1500. Private clinics are plentiful but few real hospitals. The only relief given is food & clothes & shelter y [*sic*] relief station method"), her journal is a dry account of meals and drinks. She does note the atmosphere of Havana in the streets. "Blue-coated policemen in groups of twos + threes were all over the city, part of martial law also tan uniformed soldiers. Most of the policemen were young + immature looking. Traffic seemed to be with no direction at all, tho [*sic*] there were traffic lights at a few corners. Cars invariably bumped each other around corners— but instead of breaking out into a volley of curses—the two drivers usually bare their teeth + smile + go on." After detailing a lavish supper before departing Havana and reboarding the ship for the voyage home and the lights of the city as the boat sails north Mother stops recording except for a brief note. On April 7th, when she mentions getting up at 7 A.M., taking a shower, "a quiet day."

Evidently the three-day return to New York held no charms though she kept the menu of the farewell supper. On the next page of the album there is a cocktail napkin folded over and stapled. Under a picture of a merry-go-round, the name of the bar in large letters curving in a semicircle, on either side of a drawing of a tiny cocktail glass is printed, "Plaza Merry Go Round." "Ruth" is written on one side of this glass and "Wilfred" on the other. Stick figures sit on the merry-go-round, and in tiny handwriting, my mother has drawn arrows and identified them as "Ruth" and "Wilfred." She has written underneath the merry-go-round, "Age 23 1935" and under that "Copley Plaza Boston. The inscription over the napkin reads, "Make up Celebration."

My mother is back in Boston. My father and she are celebrating her birthday (since the actual date occurred while on the boat) at one of my father's favorite hotels in the city.

Was the trip a subtle warning to my father? She could go off on her own if he didn't make up his mind to marry her? What does "make up celebration" imply? By traveling with Sonia, however, my mother had basically included herself in Wilfred's family, as he had included her in his.

I am struck by my mother's will to be independent, not just to enjoy herself. She would go off again, by herself, despite her attachment to my father. How much did she resent the limits that taking care of me, my sister, placed on her independence? My father's political career will cost her a share of her cheerful sense of fun, no matter how much satisfaction it brings her.

"You were an accident," that remark she made to me as a little boy—was it just the streak of cruel teasing in the Lesslers? Was it anger at how my birth had changed her life or simply a way of putting a cocky child, who assumed his mother should adore him, in his place?

I suspect it also echoed a rueful sense that all the fun and adventure that she had been enjoying through the 1930s, even after marriage, might have gone on for another four or five years.

Hearing her footsteps across the deck, fighting her nausea, determined to have a good time, I know I am near her.

The page in the album after this trip, follows up a year later, in the spring of 1936. The first line of its notation laughs, but it is followed by a cry from the heart that strikes me as I see into her thoughts through the pose of the professionally smiling, buoyant social worker.

"And now we skip one Year to June 14, 1936
Heart's Desire Won—"

The inscription in the album pages is between two telegrams congratulating Ruth and Wilfred S. Mirsky on their marriage, one from my father's cousins in Montreal, another from the Mattapan Zionist Federation, and a handwritten note from the Lessler family congratulating them.

The photographs of the wedding are scattered throughout boxes in the house. My grandfather, Israel, was beaming. His sister, Tsirrel, came down from Montreal for the wedding, and his closest cousins, the Kopelman sisters, joined the celebrations; my grandfather prominently in the midst of them, Gertrude is noticeably absent from the photographs retained. My mother pastes her father-in-law's photograph into her album with the notation, "Pops." According to Dad's sister, Rochelle, Israel Mirsky had caught Ruth and Wilfred kissing passionately on the back porch of his house and pulled his son aside to insist that he marry the young woman. If so, Ruth was obviously grateful.

Though my mother skips a year in her album, from that trip to Havana to her wedding, there is a final notation in my father's journal some months before the wedding that speaks to the fact that they are being knit closer and closer.

Sunday Dec 8 1935 Just had a good meal made by Sonia: Soup— chicken—meat loaf—pickled tomatoes, sweet potatoes—sweet mickes at Ruth Lessler's suggestion tea, plum cake et al. A good dinner in presence of happy countenances turns the food into manna & that is why I feel good but when I feel good I feel lazy & lackadaisical. For instance I have a pair of Cohen wills to [do] but don't feel like doing them. Lucky I have a driver in Ruthie Lessler. She'll see to it they are done ...

Whenever the decision to marry was made, it must have also been taken as my father's law practice began to develop. And my mother was evidently further along in her career as a professional social worker. The newspaper article pasted into the back pages of her album record, "From 1935 to 1937 she served as Field Supervisor of Emergency Relief and Works Progress Administration in charge of government family case work in twenty-three towns including Lowell, Massachusetts." The dates may be approximate since she was working in New London in 1934 and 1935 and that from December of 1936 through the late spring of 1937 she was in Ohio. Did she come to Boston before the wedding to find an apartment for them? In the formal portrait of my mother and father she radiates the poise and glamour of a Hollywood actress. There seems to be just a touch of sarcasm in my father's eyes but not in Mother's, as they pose side by side. She had to be caught up in the excitement as my grandfather's close friend, the chief rabbi of Boston, Joseph Soloveitchik, performed the ceremony. (Soloveitchik was one of the founders of Modern Orthodoxy, and known popularly as "the Rav,") Since Dad's sister Hilda was coming all the way from California to attend, my grandfather had decreed that his youngest daughter Sonia should marry her fiancée Harry Schatz, at the same time. I suspect that the Lesslers were outnumbered by Mirskys and my grandfather's large social circle at the ceremony. As the shamus of Beth El, popularly known as the synagogue of Boston's Orthodox scholars, Grandpa would have proudly invited many of the congregants. What did my mother think of her immersion in this world? My father called himself an agnostic when I asked, but he was proud of his Jewish learning, and admired his father's formidable Talmudic education, a bit regretful that he had not risen to the same level of study. In choosing my mother, my father had stayed within the circle of the Jewish world but also stepped into a modern American one. And my mother? In one sense she had chosen a family whose intellectual life was closer to her grandparents on her mother's side, the Kurlands. Their men still put on phylacteries in the morning and went regularly to synagogue. Her breezy "Pops" next to Israel Mirsky's photograph signaled that she had adopted him, as he had her, but … It was as much on her terms as his—she would keep a kosher house, but she had a career, dreams, and would make her own decisions.

Chapter Nine

When did Ruth Lessler return to Boston? Did she take an apartment before or after her honeymoon across the country with my father? "Connecticut comes to Mass.," a photograph of my mother beside her car proclaims. The FERA (Federal Emergency Relief Administration) plate above her Connecticut State plate identifies her as a worker for the federal government. It suggests that she is posing before the honeymoon since it is not snapped with Blue Hill Avenue in the background, the address of their first apartment, but on one of the Avenue's side streets.

Mother's second album has pages and pages devoted to that American ritual, the honeymoon. During their trip across the country with my father, I see her as a young woman, a wife. I search her face for changes. These are the last years in which my mother will be alone with my father. Staring at the two of them, Mother obviously in love, I step into the album's privacy. "Connecticut comes to Mass," was taken somewhere in the Jewish streets of Dorchester or Mattapan. I will be born nearby three years later on Blue Hill Avenue, the district's thoroughfare at the corner of Hazelton Street. I suspect that they took this apartment right before or after their honeymoon. Under a photograph of it at about this time is written, "At Chez

Mirskys." There is an article from a New London newspaper about Miss Ruth Lessler, being named "chairman of the case work committee" of the New London Council of Social Agencies at a meeting in the city hall. The "Miss" seems to date the article to before the wedding. Their honeymoon was a leisurely car trip back and forth to California. Ruth and Wilfred drove west and east. They stopped along the way to say hello to the extended Lessler family. The photographs of the trip begin after the pasted-in telegrams of congratulations, under the handwritten notation, "But still Happy Moon." There are two pictures of my father, one on Revere Beach in Massachusetts, the other with the inscription under it, "En route to N.Y. by Bridgeport Ferry." Then in the middle of the page, "Hospitality of the Nishballs," my mother seated and my father standing at Ruth's sister Esther's house. Esther was eleven years older than mother, married to Harold Nishball. Ruth's surrogate mother after Annie's death—sharp-tongued, strong-willed, with uncompromising rectitude, I found Aunt Esther forbidding even before the early death of her oldest son Jerry. Esther's integrity and quiet generosity, however, had formed the character of Ruth.

Esther and her husband lived modestly, but she had inherited her mother's authority in the family. I can never recall Esther teasing, and while her remarks were often uncomfortably direct, there was an underlying concern in them that took the sting away, even when her sense of propriety seemed old fashioned. As a child, an adolescent, a young adult I felt my mother's awe of her older sister. Despite Esther's critical remarks about the "dirty words" in my first books, Mother's obvious love for her sister held me in sway as well. There is a photograph of my mother and father on a picnic blanket, and one called "A bit of croquet," with her oldest sister, Celia Greenbaum, who also lived in Bridgeport, and another with her brother Davey, his wife Claire, their first child, Adrienne. Mother's older brother High was living in California with his wife Celia, and two children, Kenneth and Richard. My father's sister Hilda lived nearby and my parents decided to visit both families.

A photograph of my mother and father seated with her relatives, the Gamzons in Chicago, appears on a further page but there are no clues in the album to where they traveled until my parents reach Detroit, where they dip into or out of Canada at Windsor for "Canada Phooey," as is written in the inscription on a picture of my mother at the doorway of a cottage.

Next came the Badlands in the Black Hills of South Dakota, Mount Rushmore, Montana, Wyoming, Montana, Yellowstone National Park. I want to linger with Mother. She is not just happy, she is the mother I too rarely caught sight of—funny, mischievous; her delight in everything around her infectious. Above is one of my favorite snapshots. High in the Rockies I feel her bubbling over as she touches the snow bank.

They drove on, stopping to tease each other on the courthouse steps in Reno, Nevada, until my mother and father reached Dad's sister Hilda in Berkeley, and my mother's older brother High's house in Long Beach, California. Hilda is photographed visiting High and Celia's house, so my father must have gathered her into the Lessler family world. The brochure from "Knott's Berry Place," which is pasted in, testifies to another trip south of Los Angeles. On their return, my parents also passed through Iowa and the wheat fields. The inscription on this page is "Gotta go Home Sometime." A rippling line is drawn in the album and then the notation "Homeward Bound. Extra Passenger. Celia."

Celia Lessler chose to ride east with them, leaving her young children, Kenneth and Richard, behind. She stands in the wheat fields, and with my mother's arms around her in the tall Iowa grasses. (Was there already trouble in the marriage between Celia and High?) "Resting at B[ridge]p[or]t. Conn at the Lessers," reads a blurry photograph with a picture of my mother, her back turned, and her brother-in-law, David Lesser, her sister Betty's husband in the frame. "Settled again

in Mattapan" the page reads, and there are two photographs, one of my grandfather Israel and another with Israel, Sonia, and her husband, Harry Schatz. "Our own veranda" it reads and it is the apartment where three years hence I will be born.

This is where I will find my mother's affectionate scribble under her father-in-law Israel's photograph "Pops." Aunt Sonia told me how her father (whom she adored) slapped her once as a young woman for saying, "You lucky dog," to him, in all innocence, after he had won something.

"You call your father a dog?" Israel asked, incredulous. Sonia's half sister, Rochelle, born in the 1920s in America, complained that he insisted on a formal title, rather than the American "Dad," which irked her, along with his distant manner and his fondness for European and Yiddish expressions. (By way of paradox, Israel insisted that the children of his first marriage, Wilfred, Sonia, and Hilda, when they arrived from Europe, address him only in English, wanting them to achieve fluency as quickly as possible in the language of their new home.) My grandfather evidently felt a special fondness for his new daughter-in-law, and she found something of the warm, affectionate and intellectual father that she had missed in her own.

My grandfather often appeared in our house directly from his duties as the presiding figure in the Beth El Synagogue in his elegant frock coat, and striped pants. My grandfather was, according to his friend the Rav (Rabbi Joseph Soloveitchik, professor of Talmud at Yeshiva University), one of the few who understood every word of Soloveitchik's complex Talmudic discourses. After his humiliating bankruptcy, my grandfather had found a post as the figure in charge of the Beth El synagogue on Fowler Street in Dorchester, which possessed a handsome Moorish hall and whose leadership was both wealthy and educated. My father adored his father, Israel, despite his bitter resentment of the stepmother Israel had taken as his second wife. My mother evidently felt close to my grandfather too and her lighthearted title for him in her album confirms it.

Was my mother commuting to her job in New London when she returned from her honeymoon to Boston's Mattapan? Did she have new responsibilities with the Federal Emergency Relief Works and Progress Administration in Massachusetts? She ruthlessly cleaned away old files (unlike my father) so it is hard to know. What would prompt her to go out to Ironton, Ohio, just a few months after returning from the West Coast? Was she ordered there? It was still the Depression and my father's law practice would never be particularly successful. (She would complain, tongue-in-cheek, that he had done a million dollars' worth of free law work.) Still, it's a mark of my mother's independence and Dad's admiration of her spirit that she left for a six-month stint of work in a dangerous flood zone, miles away and only six months after their honeymoon. Although she is happy in all the photographs of her in the Ohio flood zone, she still retains the aura of a professional social worker. In the snapshot labeled "Pocahontas" she seems like a girl of sixteen not a veteran government administrator of twenty-five.

The photograph that follows it in the album was shot in front of the apartment building on Blue Hill Avenue, my mother's hands in a warm winter muff indicates that it was taken just before she departed for a six-month adventure in the "heart of the heart of the country."

In December 1936, six months after being married, Ruth Mirsky left Boston for half a year as a federal disaster worker. She went to Ironton, Ohio, which had been struck by one of the great national disasters in the United States during the twentieth century, the Great Flood of 1937. She was there to help with the recovery until June of 1937.

The photograph below that she entitled "By the Banks of the Ohio" shows her on her own again and, at least at the beginning, liking it. Before I reconstruct what was obviously a thrilling moment in her life, I have to address her silence to me on the matter later on in her life. She pasted in many snapshots of the Great Flood. Mother's date of departure from Boston suggests that she was in Ironton or close by before the waters struck, devastating the towns along the river. What a story she must have had to tell, and if I had urged her when I was in high school or college, she might have told a tale of perils and disaster. She had plunged into it at the very beginning of her marriage, not that many years away from admiring the adventurer Sadie Thompson in films. Who was the Ruth who had more than a sneaking curiosity about these tough women wandering the world, fleeing a life of criminality and prostitution, but ready for romance? Sadie Thompson, whose role she obviously enjoyed slipping into, sits on the hood of my mother's car, a cigarette dangling from her mouth. What a fool I was to miss her in this moment, and never to ask her, for my sake, to return briefly for a moment to the her memories of the Ohio Flood and tell me , what she saw, what she dreamed about when she was there. She left me only her footprints in the albums.

My mother had gone off as a professional to help in an American disaster, whose story of nightmares has largely been buried in the course of the years. The length of time she spent in Ohio meant she was already in Ironton in early 1937 when the river overflowed, caught up in the days of confusion and fear. Ironton on the Ohio River was one of the places devastated as waters rushed through its downtown, destroying it as an industrial center. I remember talk of her serving as a social worker in cities near Boston in the wake of calamities, but never about this long separation from my father or the scale of the Ohio flood's destruction. Since she never told me the story, the reader will have to bear with me as I try to reconstruct it.

The Ohio River is one of the three great arteries, together with the Missouri and the Mississippi, of the United States. "Navigable for its entire length, the Ohio flows 1579 km (981 mi) from the confluence of the Allegheny and Monongahela rivers in Pittsburgh to its mouth in the Mississippi River at Cairo, Illinois. The Ohio provides a vital commercial link for industrial and agricultural interests in the Midwest, and barges on the river carry products such as coal, steel, crops, chemicals, and petroleum." [MS Encarta] So much for the dry ground, economics and geography; the Ohio was subject to terrible floods in the early twentieth century before steps were taken under the Roosevelt Administration to control its waters. In the twentieth century it crested twenty-one times over the sixty-foot mark at Cincinnati, which was downstream from Ironton, and sometimes in quick succession. In 1913, two major floods were only months apart, leaving hundreds dead and thousands homeless. On February 1 and February 12, 1918, great chunks of ice floated down the river and crushed the hulls of steamboats, effectively ending their commerce on the Ohio. Again on March 21, 1933, the water reached 63.6 feet and on March 28, 1936, it was only slightly lower at 60.6 feet.

The worst flood yet to be recorded, however, was the Flood of 1937. In an online article about the flood, Owen Findson and Cameron McWhirter quoted the following report from *The Cincinnati Enquirer*:

> *Two days before the crest was reached, the city experienced its worst day, the day called "Black Sunday." At least 10 gas tanks exploded, and there were oil fires on the Ohio and in the flooded Mill Creek Valley.*
>
> *"Valley is Inferno as Gasoline Burns," said an Enquirer headline. "Disaster is Worst in City's History."*
>
> *The city's power plant was shut off and emergency power tapped in from Dayton, Ohio. Residents were urged to use only one light bulb and one radio. No water came from the taps. People filled buckets at ponds, springs and artesian wells. The Milling Machine Co. was converted to a water bottling plant with volunteers working on the production line.*

Cincinnati was a city under siege, sliced in thirds by water for 19 days. Travel between neighborhoods was only by boat. The entire population was divided into two groups, those who were victims of the flood and those who volunteered to help them.

At the '37 flood's crest, nearly one of every eight people in the Tri-state was left homeless. Almost one-fifth of the city was covered by water. In Northern Kentucky, about one-third of the river communities of Kenton and Campbell counties were flooded. In Indiana, Lawrenceburg, Aurora and other river towns were inundated.

Damage was about $20 million.

Ironton was hit particularly hard. Ginger Gillenwater, in an article published in 2007 entitled, *"Ironton, Ohio—The Rise and Fall of 'Little Chicago,'"* lamented the lasting damage imposed on the formerly thriving county seat of Lawrence County, which was a promising urban center called "Little Chicago" before the Flood of 1937. [Text published online, Sep 06, 2007.]

It is a sad sight when traveling the downtown of a city that now has a mere 11,000 residents versus the 30,000 it had just seventy years ago ... The town peaked for many years from its conception and still continued to flourish even after the last of the furnaces were shut down right after the start of the 20th century. Due to the porous nature of pig iron, better iron creating methods were developed, which put the pig iron industry out of business. The city still had the shops and other industries that were popping up everywhere, but the city met a terrible disaster in 1937 when it rained for many days causing the Ohio River to swell beyond its banks. Before they knew it, many residents were on the top floors of their homes waiting for boats to come rescue them. Many of the business collapsed on themselves, caught fire, or were severely damaged by floodwaters. Lives were lost and because of the future threat of such a flood, many moved away ...

There was millions of dollars in damage from the flood of 1937 and a couple of years later the city decided to build floodwalls to prevent such a disaster from happening again. Those same flood walls and floodgates are still in use today despite the fact the city has been in need of new floodgates for quite some time.

Just a few miles downstream from Ironton, Ohio, on the other side of the river is Greenup, Kentucky, also a county seat. The WPA Guide, written when memories were fresh, records its fate in 1937:

> *Greenup is no longer an important river port, and only a few farmers use the old ferry between this point and Haverhill ... Greenup was almost obliterated by the disastrous flood of 1937 when the entire population was suddenly marooned and desperate efforts had to be made to prevent destruction.*

The pictures my mother posed for and possibly snapped in a camera speak louder than words. On January 28, 1937, the city's local paper *The Ironton Register* looked back in shock at the last two days.

> *Rain, incessant, fearful, appalling rain of a weeks duration enveloping the Ohio River watershed, assembled all the destructive forces that are embodied in the word "flood" and sent them hurtling down the Ohio Valley, laying waste a fertile stretch after rain that extended from Pittsburgh to Cairo and thence down the Mississippi. The flood eclipsing the record of the 1913 deluge by five feet caused a monetary damage that is at present inestimable and claimed many lives.*
>
> *The city of Ironton was covered by the onrushing tide and only about ten per cent of the entire area was left untouched by the ochre solution and not a single person in the entire valley was left untouched by the effects of the extending catastrophe. The toll of these angry waters has not been fully levied even though the crest has been reached and recession has been noted.*
>
> *In the wake of the chaotic disturbance will come the horsemen of the Apocalypse who are astride the scourges of Pestilence, Famine and Disease.*

There is not a single soul in the entire reach of the Ohio Valley who could have predicted the terrific, ever rising rush of the maddened tide. Certainly none among us would of ventured to presage a stage that would exceed the 1913 forage of the mighty river, that then laid waste its fertile valleys, causing millions upon millions of dollars of damage and levying a heavy toll of lives.

The river observers had held fast to the belief that a snow deposit in the Pennsylvania and West Virginia mountain chain was necessary for a flood of major proportions in the lower Ohio. This belief and this conclusion was blasted by the forces of nature in this Year of our Lord. A drenching, driving rain that continued hour after hour, day and day and stretching on into a solid week furnished the Ohio and its tributaries with a mountainous stream of water. It rushed into every lowland section, engulfing each like a tidal wave, forcing the inhabitants into the higher and more habitable regions, laying waste their homes and ravaging their possessions.

The photographs below are from my mother's albums but there exist many more outside them.

In Ironton alone 12,000 people were left homeless, the surrounding towns added another 31,000, taxing the emergency services in the area, but it is estimated that a total of 350,000 people had lost their living quarters in the Ohio Valley. One hundred homes had washed away in Ironton, and nearby Coal Grove and Hanging Rock and 90 percent of Ironton was covered with water. Many buildings downtown had collapsed, while others floated from their foundations. Returning businessmen and residents alike found a sea of mud, sections of street subsiding, the debris from smashed porches scattered everywhere.

There are bleaker, more dramatic photographs of the flood damage in Mother's album. Some emphasize the sense of her command of the situation with her fellow disaster workers. They look out confident, almost triumphant, against a background of the water's destruction.

What were her feelings during the worst of the flood? She left no clue.

I found two letters of hers to my father in a box at our beach cottage just a few years ago. They were written in April and May, when the river had receded and the work of reconstruction was in full swing. They are both on the stationary of the Hotel Marting. ("Fireproof" it offered "European Rates from $1.50 to $4.00 and 130 Rooms, 105 with private baths.") At the top of the first letter, she promises in capitals: "P.S. OVER THE WEEKEND I AM GOING TO MAKE UP FOR THESE SHORT NOTES BY A REAL LONG LETTER."

April 30, 1937

Darling,

Your letter sure tickled me.-about the novel name of the novel you sent and the episode about the night-gown. Have you "madeup" with Sonia about the car?

It is sixty forty five PM, and still light outside. I had my supper- a fruit salad plate-all fresh fruits, coffee and spice cake for 40¢. I just bout a half dozen more oranges for my breakfast-the grapefruits are going out of season now.

I have completed all the data on my grocery business case and going to write it up tonight—or else the figures that are dancing around on several sheets of paper will be lost forever.

Please don't forget to straighten out the bank account at the Home Savings-or there may be trouble in with-drawing the money when we want it. O boy! $353. Isn't that grand. In a few more days, probably by Monday, I will get another $65. That will bring us into the $400 mark-I may have to use the very last one to take me home, if our plans for June 30th don't coincide with the Red Cross. But just how soon we will close up is still not certain. So- here's hoping.

The trains still whistle horribly at night- -I could SCREAM. But that wouldn't do any good because they would still whistle.

The weather is so perfect out here Wil- -though it isn't at all peppy. I have some fresh redbuds in my room-gathered the other day- tomorrow is Saturday-Gosh, just a week since you were here- it seems to be much longer- doesn't it? Wilfred, what do yu [sic] suppose it is that keeps us so much in love- for I surely do more and more—how about you?

Ruthie

When I found the letters they set me thinking about how concealed my mother's emotions were. I had never suspected such tenderness between my father and mother.

My father, obviously, had visited my mother in Ironton just a week before in the middle of April. She is still in the glow of it, as the last lines of the letter beg an answer.

The second letter was written seven days later.

Friday night

Darling:

Today the green skirt came. Thanks a lot. Keep your eyes open for the white shoes-but hold them there. I will want them when I come.

Starting May 15th, the girls will be sent home. They will go in groups-from then until the 31st so- be patient.

You know the expressage on the tires from New York would be considerable-wouldn't it have been wise to get them locally to get service guarantee?

Did I tell you Will, that I saw a movie camera here, projecter and all, for $25.00. It is a Univex make. What do you think about it?

Charlotte, Mae, Grace, and Sophie went to Louisville for the weekend to see the Derby with Mr. Gardner, the building advisor, and the accountant. I wasn't asked but I don't feel badly, first because they will be riding three in front and three in back and 2nd because I don't feel the urge to gamble on the races— third because I don't know whether you would have approved.

Sweetheart- I'll call you at 7, our time EST that means 8 your time, Sunday-you'll be at Sonia's won't you.

Yours,

Ruthie

JUMPING WILLIKERS WILLIE, i feel humble at your outburst of love expressed by your letters."

The surprise comes for me when I turn the single sheet from the Hotel Marting over and see

typed in capital letters in the middle of the page.

I ADORE YOU

She has turned into a teenager. Had she ever been that in Bridgeport at thirteen and fourteen, when having skipped two grades, a guest in her older sisters' houses, she had to compete in a class of older girls?

I suspect from the hint in her letter of April 30th that Ruth is ready to pay her way home if their plans for June 30th do not jibe with those of the Red Cross for dispatching her back to Massachusetts. The separation was beginning to grate on my father. My mother it seems, weighing her subsequent behavior, did not really want a full-fledged career once she had married my father, or was at best, ambivalent.

As I child I heard something about this flood but she told no stories. Until I began to go carefully through her albums, where she did, in fact, leave a narrative of her life before I was three and a half or four years old, and I could observe her. From her laughing face, the way she seems to twirl in her coat before the camera, "on the banks of the Ohio," despite the human misery, she must have felt elated to be able to put her training to use in the midst of one of America's great emergencies. Still, the adventure went on too long for a young bride. She would tell me in her late forties, when she assumed a full-time position that she would have preferred to stay at home, to preside over a house full of grandchildren. In her smile on the balcony, crouching among the plants, I see a flicker of the pleasure she showed in her last few years, scattering flower seeds and bulbs in the back lots of our beach cottage.

In September, two months after my mother returned from Ohio, she took a job in Boston. The newspaper article is pasted into the back cover of Volume II, her second and last scrapbook. The article read as follows:

Mrs. Ruth L. Mirsky Chosen as Case Worker by Family Welfare

"Jewish Family Welfare Society has engaged as case worker Ruth Lessler Mirsky ... The case worker received her education in social work at Columbia University, Harvard University, and Simmons College School of Social Work.

"From 1929 to 1931 she served as Receptionist with the American Red Cross in Bridgeport, Conn. In 1933 and 1934 she was Girl Supervisor at the Jewish Orphanage of Rhode Island ... From 1935 to 1937 she acted as Field Supervisor of Emergency Relief and Works Progress Administration in charge of government family case work in twenty-three towns including Lowell, Massachusetts." The article continued in boldface, "In engaging Mrs. Mirsky as case worker, Jewish Family Welfare Society has endeavored and we believe succeeded in complying with the recommendations of the recent Providence survey and of the Providence Community Fund. She is fully qualified by education and field experience to bring to her work the most modern methods essential to do a good job. The Executive Committee has paid particular attention to obtaining a worker of such personality as will bring to families in need of care a thorough kindly spirit and a warm interest in their welfare."

At the bottom of this page was a photograph of a Maryland facility and a picture of a Federal Co-op Housing Project, inscribed "Washington D.C., Conference, Social Work."

It is Mother's handwriting at the top of the page that catches my attention. As a chorus to the flattering newspaper remarks, she added over the headline "Chosen Case Worker" the comment, "Until the Mirsky addition entered, Sept. 1937 to May 1939." I hear a tinge of regret. My mother's independent life was over.

With this the albums end, but not the photographs. Whatever her real feelings when she found herself pregnant, now I enter the picture as the "accident."

Chapter Ten

Above are nine of the twelve brothers and sisters with their mates at a reunion near Bridgeport, Connecticut in the mid 1950s. From left to right: the oldest brother, Simon, his wife Ruth beside him, then David Lessler, and his wife Claire, Louis Greenbaum and Celia, Miriam (partially concealed by the camera), Mildred Ruderman, Esther Nishball, Willy Cohen, Harold Nishball, Betty Lesser, Dorothy Cohen, my father Wilfred, my mother Ruth, and Saul Ruderman. Jules and his wife are not there. Hyman (High) was in California and Bob had died.

In 1956, David died; ten years later, her brothers and sisters began to disappear. Simon, Jules, Betty, and my mother felt the loss of each one. Her siblings' deaths did not loosen her tongue but I felt her emotions nonetheless. At one point she asked me to go down with her to one of her siblings' funerals. I think it was Jules's in 1966. Mother, who often seemed like a haughty, reserved Yankee matriarch, not the voluble Jewish mother of Philip Roth's cartoons, has begun to look at me too like a young girl. I sensed that something had changed between us, the prelude to that moment when she raises her blouse and shows the telltale sign of her secret illness, hidden from us all. Four months later, what would turn out to be in the last months of her life, she shocks me. As I kiss her at the door of the hospital ward where she has followed me to say goodbye, she bites my lip. This is the moment, I think, when she realizes she is dying. My time with my mother in this world is about to end, though in one of those moments when life turns into what would seem to be fiction, I face at first not the exhausted matron who can not rise from her hospital bed, but a young woman I knew when I was four or five. Later, as her flesh first swells, then falls away from her skeleton, dream turns into nightmare.

As she raised her blouse at our beach cottage at the beginning of September, to show me a hard, swollen belly (five months before the kiss at the end of the hospital corridor late in the winter snows of February) I was shaken even as I scolded—the price of this intimacy was staggering.

My mother kept her own counsel like a close-mouthed banker, rarely showing any emotion but irritation, and could quickly put anyone in their place whom she came in contact with, from Beacon Hill blue bloods to my sister's formidable mother-in-law. Not simply to defer to me, but to invite me to examine her was unthinkable. Yet, she chose on that day to show me, not my father or sister, the secret that must have been gnawing at her all through our last summer.

Anxious to get to know her two grandchildren better, my mother had asked my sister to come east, in the summer of 1967, offering to take care of the two girls and give my sister some welcome relief from watching over them, and time with her husband. The ferocity of my mother's embrace of my nieces was a sharp contrast to her deliberately blasé attitude toward me, and possibly my sister Deanna, when we were growing up. Mother was especially solicitous now toward Deanna. I was happy that she was at the center of attention, relieving me of Mother's sarcasm. My mother was being very cool to me. The year before my parents had visited me for an extended vacation in California and my girlfriend, who was not Jewish, arrived during their stay. Mother was visibly angry that I was not giving her my full attention. Despite that, I felt the tug of a powerful, if irascible, affection that summer, which drew me toward the beach cottage and my parents, and in particular, Mother. So I was there, alone, for that last weekend, summoned to say goodbye to my sister and her girls.

I had returned east at the beginning of the summer of 1967 after teaching for a year at Stanford University. Albert J. Guerard, one of the two professors I had studied with at Harvard, arranged for me join an experiment with freshmen students there called "The Voice Project." It had been a year crammed with excitement. I was given a chance to try out all sorts of ideas in the classroom and on the stage. Forming a freshmen drama group with a young professor whom I had known at Harvard and with whom I had staged readings of Shakespeare's plays in Cambridge, I directed one of the medieval mystery plays, *The Magnus Herod*, during Christmas. It put into practice skills I had developed staging the plays at Saint Mark's Church on the Bouerie through the fall of 1964 and the spring of 1965. (Several of the actors I directed had or went on to have distinguished careers; Judd Hirsch, Frank Langella, Warren Finnerty). My students at Stanford were brilliant and the university offered me a position as assistant professor. My first novel, *Thou Worm Jacob*, had just come out and my parents wanted me to stay at Stanford in Palo Alto, rather than return to City College, which had offered me the same salary.

Dad's law practice had tumbled into disrepair after he left the legislature and my mother's term as a commissioner on the Industrial Accident Board of Massachusetts was over. The district, Ward Fourteen along Blue Hill Avenue, which had elected my father as a state representative from 1949 to 1958 (with the exception of one term in 1953-54), was changing rapidly. The middle-class Jewish inhabitants were moving to the suburbs at an accelerating rate. African Americans from the South rented the empty apartments, bought houses and some of the streets were now hostile to the old men and women who had stayed. Crimes like murder and armed robbery, practically unheard of when I was growing up in the neighborhood, were now being reported. It would be easy for my parents to give up their rented apartment in Boston, hold on to the beach cottage in nearby Hull, and instead of travelling south to Florida for the winter, go west to California. My sister now lived in Portland, Dad's sister Hilda, in Pasadena. My mother had several nephews and nieces in California as well. Visiting me in Palo Alto while I was at Stanford, my father and mother had found inexpensive rooms and they dreamed of returning to live nearby.

My decision to take the teaching position at City College in Manhattan upset them. My students at City College were just as acute at that moment in history as those at Stanford, though without the time and focus that comes from living on a residential campus. I found one of my letters, arguing about my return to City College to my parents. My tone was callow, insistent, condescending. Looking back at my words, those envelopes sent from California as well as New York City, all of which my mother kept carefully catalogued, I am ashamed.

Equally aggravating to my mother was the fact that I had come back to live again with the girl I had been with for three years. Mother let me feel the depth of her displeasure at what she considered to be "living in sin."

Still, there were those long letters I sent Mother. Six years before, in 1961, I followed a professor who would become a lifelong mentor, Albert J. Guerard Jr., when he left Harvard to teach at Stanford, and I became a graduate student there. I had spent the sum in my bank account gathering interest since my bar mitzvah, together with a piece of my Woodrow Wilson Fellowship, on a childhood dream—a motorcycle. It left me with just enough for rent, but not for food, clothes, or an occasional luxury. Mother wrote me a check when I appealed to her— but she was furious that I would buy such a dangerous machine. (As I sifted through her albums writing this book, trying to imagine her life just after she graduated high school, I was amused to find a photograph of her on the back of a motorcycle behind a handsome man obviously some years older.) She sent me monthly supplements to my income, but only, "On condition that I get at least, a five-page, single-spaced letter from you once a week." It was good discipline for a writer. (I was also corresponding at length with a girlfriend at Radcliffe, where my attempt to maintain a long-distance love affair was less successful.) Returning to Stanford in 1966, however, and no longer needing any financial assistance from my mother, I found myself again writing at length to her, in part because the tenor of her letters had begun to change. I was used to laundry lists: the thread count in cotton sheets, the best ratio of metals in stainless steel, and cheerful reports about the neighbors, together with bland accounts of her trips with my father to see relatives. Now I found her letters personal, intimate, evoking without pretension the atmosphere of the house, her life, and inviting me to write back in the same vein.

She kept all of my letters to her, carefully arranged, but where are hers to me? It is not my autobiography that I care about but hers. Many of the letters that she sent in those last few years have disappeared, I did find one addressed to me, dated March 20, 1965, that would have been two years before her death. She announces a literary project, that, like the photographs, I have revisited in her albums, speaks more about her than I realized. She was being ruthless with my old toys, lead soldiers, cannons, teddy bears, my prized lemonwood bow (I traveled across half of Massachusetts at eleven years old to purchase it, although I could hardly draw its string back at first); all the memories of childhood fixed in things were being emptied out of our house's closets and the summer cottage attic, either thrown out or given away. (Just as she had immediately given the extravagant wedding gown she was married in, to a bride who could not afford one.) The notion of me succeeding in a profession was never discussed. I don't recall praise, even when I began to crawl out from under the weight of my parents' early disappointment in me and win prizes at the one thing my fantasy life had prepared me for, acting. My father didn't praise me either, but occasionally my career in the theater, my admission to Harvard, and my fledgling attempts to write, drew a smile of appreciation. When I inched into adolescence, tore at my face, hid in my room, trembled with fits of depression, Mother decided that she had to play a different role with me. Whatever melancholy obsessed her, she no longer showed it to me. She insisted on optimism, that I adopt a positive attitude and she scouted out free dance classes at the Arthur Murray studios to try to develop my social adeptness. She found free vacations to take me out of Dorchester, Mattapan, Roxbury, like Boy's State, a political farce run by the American Legion. But the cosmetic smile barely hid her perpetual pessimism about her son.

Here is my father and mother, circa 1965, at the pier by our beach cottage in Hull, Massachusetts.

March 20, 1965

Dear Son:—

It is a Sat afternoon—the day is damp and a wet snow is falling. Dad had to be in the W. Roxbury Court this morning defending a Russian whose Ukrainian wife left his bed & board & wants $60 a week when the man only earns $67. Dad is not expected back until 2 so I am amusing myself by chronologically assorting your letters from California to your service days through Woodstock & N.Y. The story of your life and your changing attitudes towards the world & women—When you are ready to write an autobiography—or become that famous author that some other writer wants to know of your life & background, these letters will serve to help the world know you. Some of your sentiments, you would hardly recognize yourself!

[Talk of a special election, candidates] Dad wants to take another crack at it again. The old story of advertising his name around—the law practice this year has been very poor in contrast to former years. We really are not worried because law income is on an annual basis & one never knows when a big

case can come his way. However for the first time we have to
draw from savings to pay our income tax. Not that we are com-
plaining—for these are savings from which to withdraw & life
has been kind to us. This past year Dad has not pushed to get
business—& has taken life more leisurely—which is only right
at his age & with his responsibilities for his children's care over.

[Enclosed with the letter was the death notice of one of my father's political rivals, Julius Ansel, with a tart comment about his financial dealings, which the article of course omitted, ending with] ... *he would have been thrilled with all the flamboyant publicity that accompanied his death!!*

My only instruction is [to] get your income tax done—the deadline is April 15th & the same as your plays so you'll have to spare the time now!!!

Your ever loving,

Mother

Given Mother's mask of disapproval through adolescence and college, it was a surprise to find from the carefully preserved packets of letters I sent her that she thought someone might make use of them. It contradicted the myth that I still half believe—that I was a disappointment. What did she think of me, finally? What did she mean by "your changing attitudes toward the world and women"? She saw something about me I did not, but I was too anxious, in awe of her, to ask.

This was 1965. Two years later in the summer of 1967, my mother, caught up in the role of a grandmother, was increasingly unsympathetic to my confusion about a woman with whom I was searching for an apartment, large enough for both of us, after I had finished my year of teaching at Stanford University. We were ready to try the experiment of living as a couple.

We had met when she was barely sixteen, started dating when she was eighteen. She had come to Manhattan, leaving college abruptly after two years just before I left for my year of teaching in California. She visited me there for a month. My mother, who had come out with my father to see me, was not happy about my being on intimate terms with someone to whom I was not married. It didn't help that the girl was without a professional career. Something else was astir as well in my mother, though I was insensitive to that. I felt her stern eye follow me, angry when she visited me in Palo Alto in the winter of 1966-67, even angrier when I went up to Boston after I returned, to report that we were planning to find an apartment and move in together.

"Make up your mind!"

I didn't say anything. I was afraid of Mother's habit of relentlessly pressing a point. She could send my father screaming with rage, running down the back steps of our house, afraid of his own violence as she nagged and nagged, helpless to control the way she got under his skin. At twenty-seven, twenty-eight, I was just as vulnerable and it made me just as crazy, so that I wanted to smash the telephone receiver into the wall when she started. In the past it would have taken me hours to recover my calm after one of her calls to me in New York City, but I was not prepared for her next remark.

"I want to know whether I should love her or not."

I couldn't answer. In the last year, even more than my girlfriend, Mother had confused me. I felt her draw me close, need my attention, in a way that was intimate, and even in her letters she speaks to me as if we were the same age, but at the same time I felt her maternal disapproval. Preoccupied with her grandchildren, during the summer of 1967 she looked at me with a cold eye. The beach cottage was at the disposal of my sister, brother-in-law, and their two children, one of them still a toddler. Most of the beds were occupied. I made myself scarce but came up to say goodbye to my sister, her children, my brother-in-law (who also happened to be a classmate of mine from Harvard), before they flew back to Oregon.

I stood on the front lawn of the cottage in the sunny blaze of late August heat, to greet my father and mother, as they returned in their automobile from driving everyone to the airport. Mother stepped out of the car and came up to me. Instead of avoiding my eyes, or walking past me with a perfunctory greeting, she stopped, just a foot away from where the car was parked against the edge of our tiny front lawn. In her eyes there was a look I had never seen before, quizzical, but tender, not frightened, as if she were on the edge of a confession.

"You were a medic in the Air Force."

When I left graduate school at Stanford, the draft for the Vietnam War was universal, so without a deferment for education, I was subject to military service. I was not particularly patriotic at that point but my father, whose sole tie to his political past was a post as the appeal agent for the local draft board, had insisted that I not try any of the dodges that many young men of my generation practiced to evade the draft. "You are not going to make a fool of me in front of those Irishmen," he snapped, when I proposed it. Having watched his uncle shot by a marauding Polish army in Eastern Europe as a boy, he believed in serving in the American Armed Forces, and wanted me to be able to handle a gun. I opted for what I thought was the least objectionable duty, a slot as a psychiatric ward assistant in the Air Force Medical Corps. And for the next five years, I would spend a fair amount of time in both mental and medical wards.

"Yes." I looked hard at her. She knew all about my time in the military, the hospital duty. My heart jumped, "Why, what is the matter?"

My mother was the one my father, my sister and I went to when anything was wrong with our health. She was the expert, the caregiver.

My mother's smile, half apologetic, was piercing, frightening, naked.

"What do you think of this?" she asked, drawing up her blouse.

I had only had one glance at my mother half-naked, and it was by accident, as a teenager, dressing, in her brassiere and girdle. The door of her bedroom was open as I passed to the bathroom, which was on the same corridor. The look that she threw me went through me in a hot blush of shame. Her nakedness was forbidden. She was careful never to appear disrobed before me and I had no right to look in, even if she had forgotten to close the door.

I stared now at a huge distended belly. She had hidden it under loose blouses and dresses for several months.

My look must have told her what I thought. Without asking I put my hand out and touched a swollen stomach as hard as a drum.

"How long has this been going on?" My surprise lifted my astonished voice into a loud cry.

"What is wrong?" she asked.

"Are you kidding? This is the belly of an alcoholic with advanced liver disease." I had indeed seen stomachs like this in Newark's Martland Medical Center, where I went for weekend duty as an air force reservist once a month. The psychiatric wards were where they sent the habitual drunks who were dying and beyond hope.

"You are going to the hospital, now!"

I was shouting. "Dad, what is going on here?"

My father came running out of the house. "What is it?"

"What is it? What do you mean? You haven't seen Mom's stomach?"

He looked at me, dazed. He had assumed that she was monitoring herself. "Let's go!" I cried. "She is really sick."

It was Sunday. It may have been the Labor Day weekend. My mother looked lost, but she agreed with my father that they wouldn't be able to find a doctor they could trust. Only the emergency wards would be open. They would make an appointment right away. It took an hour of my mounting fear and exasperation as I screamed, "Get into the car, now, now!" before they could calm me down. I was scheduled to go back to classes at the beginning of the week, but I warned them, if she didn't go to hospital right after the weekend I would throw up my classes at City College, and come back. That alarmed the two of them more than my mother's condition. They knew what a loose cannon I was. In giving up a position at Stanford and coming to teach in New York City, I had only a tenuous hold on a job that didn't promise tenure. Anything that jeopardized my employment threatened their own fragile sense of security. I knew they had to agree to make sure I showed up for my classes.

Mother had taken my harangue about driving immediately to the hospital meekly, and though she stubbornly deferred it for a day, preferring first to see a private physician, she scheduled a doctor's appointment the next morning. Her operation followed swiftly. She did not let me know, if indeed she knew, the extent of what was wrong with her. The doctors and my father had begun a game of deceptive reassurance. No need to come up for the operation, she insisted. "It would be minor surgery."

Better to come up just after, she said, and my father concurred.

I was reassured for a brief eight hours after seeing her in her hospital room the day after the operation. The weight she had accumulated over the last ten years or so had melted away.

• • •

Only six years before, she still retained a lot of her youthful beauty even under the stress of serving as a commissioner of industrial acci-

dents for the Commonwealth of Massachusetts. At my father's request, Mother took a position the governor had promised Dad for leaving the House of Representatives, where he was a thorn in the administration's side. For those four years she served as a commissioner, she was the principal breadwinner for our family. I have a photograph of her at Miami Beach in a bathing suit dated 1961, where her figure and face reflect the older girl I remember from childhood. The last snapshots I have of her, taken shortly before that first operation, reveal more than I want to admit. This is how she looked in her middle fifties, 1965 or 1966, but at the time I thought the careworn lines in her face, the added weight, were just the inevitable signs of aging.

When I cried in frustration to my father months later, "Didn't you notice?" he looked at me baffled. My mother was the expert on medical care in the family. "She was a commissioner of industrial accidents! She dealt with all sorts of doctors for four and half years," he answered. Now, after the operation, she is briefly a girl again, the delicate young woman I will find in her albums at seventeen, eighteen, nineteen. She smiles at me when I come into the hospital room from the train station and we spend a half hour or so in pleasant conversation, my father hovering at the back of the room, warning me not to tire her. He and I come home from the hospital together, having heard from her lips with a kind of resigned sweetness, her understanding of the diagnosis, "It's chronic; chronic inflammation. I will have to learn to live with it."

My father, standing beside me at her bed in the hospital, said nothing. His face showed nothing. We drove back to the family apartment, one floor of a two-story brick house that my parents had rented for the last fourteen years or so in Mattapan on a quiet, shaded street; the same street on the corner of busy Blue Hill Avenue where they lived at the time of my birth twenty-eight years ago.

In the hospital, my mother had glowed against the white pillows and sheets, looking as if she was eighteen, nineteen again, not much older than when my father had first met her.

I go to bed early, reassured. It is two or three in the morning, September 1967, when he thunders out of his bedroom, in his white cotton T-shirt and boxer shorts, the varicose veins bulging out of his elastic socks, crying out so that I jump out of my bed and meet him in the hallway outside the room that has been mine since high school, "She's dying! She's dying!" The nightmare has flung him out of his bed, and frantic, terrified, composure like the bathrobe slipping from his shoulders flung open. I've never seen him like this. Mommy, now Dad, naked in front of me, a sight I can never quite cover up.

Later, many years later, I will understand what he is seeing—not just his wife, but his mother who died before his eyes as a boy of thirteen crossing the Atlantic in seas that threatened to swamp the boat, sailing toward a father his two younger sisters have never seen, whom Dad only vaguely remembers from the age of five. My grandfather, Israel, a handsome young husband, slipped out of his father-in-law's house, pretending to be going by railroad to investigate a job in a brother-in-law's bank and fled to the United States. My father is now facing a new trial and an old one that he has never talked about, and is cracking apart. Even when I pry out the details: a journey across famine stricken Poland, Czechoslovakia, Austria, toward the Atlantic ports; then his mother writhing for ten days in a ship's bed across from him and his sisters, her dying as they sail into New York harbor, Dad hardly acknowledges it. Only when he is felled by his second heart attack years later in 1980, passing his hospital room, do I hear him cry out, "Mother, Mother."

I am left alone, in a sense, with my mother; my father cannot bear sick beds, the hospital.

• • •

Did Freud really understand anything?

The Oedipus story is not necessarily a paradigm of the love between a mother and a son. It is the exact opposite of the real tale of many mothers and sons, the touch of the mother, particularly the young mother, her hands on the boy child, the weeping, toddler, hugging what may remain a memory of Paradise. What could a crying child exposed on a hillside know of her perfume, absorbed through the pores of his body?

Oedipus meets his mother as a mature woman, a widow with all the weight of her boy's death on her shoulders. My mother was still a girl when she held me close, almost a sister.

I will see that older sister, that girl, again, sixteen years later in the first of those last eight months in 1967 and 1968 when I hurry to Boston, over and over on weekends, from my job teaching at The City College of New York, to spend as much time as I can with her. I lose my sense of what is real, harried both by the toll of the train and bus trips and the knowledge of her approaching death, and I walk through grueling hours in the hospital into a state of semi-insanity. My mother too, her body rocked by the agony of malignant cells, begins to pass in and out of lucidity. The first time this absolute authority on good and evil, on my choices—from girlfriends down to the minutia of taxes, loses her clarity—the experience sends me reeling into medical shock. Coming up from Manhattan, and seeing her this time in late February of 1968, unable to recognize me, making no sense, as I enter her room at the Hospital for Chronic Diseases, I get dizzy, feel the blood pooling, and have to rush to the men's room to pour cold water from the faucets over my wrists. Happily, the fluid rebalances in her body by the end of that week, and the woman I know lies in the bed again. The same rational, curious eye meets me, as she regards her son from the skeletal wreck of her body, but the fear of it happening again remains.

"Do I have...?" the question comes at last from her, which we (because my father cannot bring himself to tell her) have dreaded, in the last month of her illness. Though I suspect she has known it from her return to a hospital bed in December of 1967. No one has the courage to let her know that "chronic" in her case, means fatal, and very soon. Meanwhile my father is in the grip of memories he has long suppressed.

My sister visits from Oregon during December with her children, but has to go back there and will not return until the very final weeks.

"What do you think?" I answer, letting Mother know in my equivocation that she was indeed the victim of a word we had been avoiding, but as always, making her the arbiter of truth.

"If I have another six months, it will be enough." She is waiting for her grandchildren to come east again. They will be by her bed in a few weeks, my father and I urging my sister to come early before it's too late.

Why do I have the illusion in September and October, in the hospital and at home when she briefly returns to our house in Mattapan, that I am talking to the older sister I last saw in 1950 looking at her as a child? In the first months of that last year of her life, she is moving between our home and the hospital. My parents live through most of the year in a comfortable, but modest apartment, renting the bottom floor of a two-family house on a tree-shaded street. Through late September, October, even early November, Mother walks in a futile attempt to build up her strength since our front door lies about three quarters of an hour away from the Hospital for Chronic Diseases where she receives treatment. Soon she will be hospitalized there and not come home except for a few hours. Did I walk alongside her, or follow in her footsteps to see her in a brisk walk, half of it along the edge of Olmstead's Franklin Park with its lordly stands of trees, and wide green pasture? In that brief, surreal interregnum—September, October, early November—I walk beside the girl I remember when I was a ten, eleven year old, sprinting over the cyclone fence to go exploring in the abandoned army fort that lay just over the hill opposite our summer cottage.

So the curtains part between my mother as a young girl and me, in my father's shoes, courting her. My father's cousin Lily, who saw him at thirteen, having just come over on the boat to America, losing his mother as he landed, and then later as a high-school and college boy visiting Lily's house, told me that he had "hungry eyes." Those eyes are softer in the snapshot I have of him, a passport photo taken just before he leaves Pinsk, his town in the swamps of Belarus, but I see the wolf gleam from the corner in the pictures that are taken in the succeeding years. His name in Hebrew, *Zaav*, means "wolf" and it is as a wolf that he will meet my mother.

My father fades away in the last months from my mother's bedside, frightened by what he sees. He hates hospital rooms. We are both cowards and when I vent my frustration at the constant traveling, he explodes with his own frustration. Nothing, though, will be as awful as the moment early in the autumn, just after her first, futile operation, when the calm mask falls away from his face. Yet, as she greets me for the first time after her operation, she has never looked so beautiful. A line from a fellow novelist, Seymour Simckes, who grew up a few streets away from me in Mattapan, echoes in my head. "All great tragedies are about the family."

• • •

Was I cruel? My cry keeps echoing as our roles suddenly changed. "How long has this been going on?

We were brutal in the name of being honest with one another, as if what came to mind at any given moment had to be spoken—in the moments that followed, when it might easily have been contradicted, rarely to be unsaid, a characteristic of the Lesslers.

The scrim had parted to show me a distended belly above the belt of her slacks. She was so careful to conceal her nakedness, so suspicious of my rapacious eye, having caught me several times in a bedroom half-clothed with a girlfriend, and let me know that she had absolutely no trust in my character in this regard. She knew far too many of my secrets than I care to reveal here, but I knew nothing of hers. Years after her death my sister, three and a half years younger than me, revealed to my surprise that Mother had lost what would have been our youngest sibling in a miscarriage when I was eight years old and away at summer camp. And now, like a guilty child, Mother had revealed a stomach swollen well beyond her gradual surrender to the dimensions of fifty-five years of age, and had spoken to me as if I was suddenly the adult.

In the pages where my mother pastes the congratulatory telegrams for her marriage she includes two photographs of my grandfather Israel. Her scribble, "Pops," is telling. Mother admired Israel Mirsky, not only because of what my father did but because despite Israel's domestic problems, he was the traditional Jewish father that she had always lacked. This brings up a subject that I have skirted. My mother was poorly educated when it came to Hebrew, Jewish texts, and general Jewish scholarship. For many years after my grandfather's death, our house was strictly kosher, but outside of the home we ate whatever we wanted. Eating at restaurants or visiting friends, "When in Rome, do as the Romans do," was my mother's watchword. Slowly, during my adolescence, except for a brief period when my sister became intensely religious, silverware and dishes, previously kept separate for meat and milk, began to mingle on kitchen shelves and cutlery slots. None of Mother's eleven brothers or sisters had any real background in Jewish learning and their houses and their children's attitudes reflected it. The kitchens were often kosher and they celebrated the High Holidays like Yom Kippur, Rosh Hashanah. Passover seders were traditional in some homes, while in others they became an excuse for comic food fights with little attention to the prescribed ritual. Mitchell Greenbaum, Celia's oldest boy, whose father had been the "socialist among the Lesslers," influenced perhaps by his wife, embraced a true Orthodox world. Uncle Simon's house in Providence, to which we went for

Passover, did observe a traditional seder, including the long series of prayers after the meal.

I understood from the hostility Mother showed when I brought a non-Jewish girl home as a serious candidate for affection, the strength of my mother's attachment to Judaism. She was rude, often to the point of cruelty. My father, who had a thorough Jewish education and could lead High Holiday services and explain a Talmudic passage, whose speech was peppered even on the floor of the Massachusetts legislature with anecdotes of the rabbis, was hospitable and never raised the question with me of marrying in or outside of a world to which he was loyal. It was to my mother, however, that I talked (or cried) about the girls I dated. Their rarely being Jewish was a sore subject, though hard for her to speak about. My girlfriends, of Scottish and English background, while Mother was alive, might have been willing to convert if I had asked. My father, despite his agnosticism, had brought Mother back to roots that then became stronger and more important to her own identity. I suspect this was even more so due to her attachment to my grandfather, in whom Jewish Orthodoxy was alive, witty, full of joy, as he sat at the elbow of charismatic scholars and rabbis in America, and brought traditions from Pinsk that helped reshape it into what was to become Modern Orthodoxy. My father could articulate some of my grandfather's genius to me. My mother never revealed any knowledge of her father or mother's Judaism, but nevertheless she conveyed her attachment to it.

I cannot say to what extent her spirit, while she was still alive, guided me back to my grandfather's world. In every sense, her death did. We were in deep grief, my sister and I, in the days after her death. Mother died on a Friday night, and according to Orthodox custom not to inter on the Sabbath, she was buried immediately on Sunday. Her funeral was huge, since my father was still a public figure in Boston. An overflow crowd filled the auditorium of Temple Beth Hillel, which was also the main hall of the Dorchester-Mattapan Hebrew School, where my grandfather Israel's name was inscribed inside the doorway on a white marble tablet as one of its founders. The funeral chapel brought the little wooden benches that it was customary for mourners to sit on during the week of formal grieving, the *Shiva*, and after the seven days was over when people came to the house to pray with us, my father took me by the arm and led me to a local synagogue on Woodrow Avenue just off the main thoroughfare of Blue Hill Avenue where there was a daily *minyan*. He purchased a small set of phylacteries from the *shammus* there, showed me how to put them on, and announced, "You will say *kaddish* [the mourner's prayer] for eleven months. It's an honor for your mother."

My father's favorite Jew was Spinoza. While Dad could lead services with a practiced skill that underscored his employment during law school as a Hebrew teacher, later as a cantor, and did say *kaddish* twice a year on the anniversary of the deaths of his mother and father, he didn't care for synagogues. His presence in them was largely dictated by his desire to make contact during his political career in the district with its Jewish voters. Except for Rabbi Joseph Soloveitchik, my grandfather's friend and the most compelling figure in Modern Orthodoxy, Dad had little respect for rabbis. His attitude toward his own brother-in-law, Aunt Rochelle's husband, Maishe Cohen, one of the leading Conservative rabbis in Montreal, was affectionate but critical. Still, Dad made it clear that there was no choice on my part. Whatever he thought of the effect of saying *kaddish,* morning, noon, and night for the next eleven months, showing up at a synagogue wherever I was, New York, California, or Boston, it was my duty.

I fell into the rhythm of it, dazed and frightened by Mother's death. For the first time it was not Judaism as an idea, or as a culture, but as a practice that I was involved with on a daily basis. I have written about it elsewhere, the strange effect of rowing through the service with a group of men toward the common chorus of the *kaddish.* Some were older, some younger, but most of them were in the synagogue because, like me, they had lost a parent. It brought relief from my load of grief. And for the first time, picking up a book that my friend Rabbi Ben Zion Gold had given me, eight years before, Gershom Scholem's *Major Trends in Jewish Mysticism,* the search for the other world had meaning. Before my mother's death it had seemed strange and impenetrable. In the tremor of anxiety that I could not shake, I also asked my father to take me to hear Rabbi Soloveitchik speak. I did not know at that point how close my grandfather had been to a man known as "the Rav" or "the Teacher." My mother returned me through her death to my grandfather Israel's world.

And what about the girl I had lived with on and off for six years? We broke up. Did I want someone who had more of my mother's qualities? It wasn't just a question of being Jewish, but rather that stern quality of oversight, of integrity. As my father and I wrestled in the wake of her death, I realized how much discipline she had brought to his behavior, and how much I missed her often grim, but truthful eye, even if I had resisted her judgment.

• • •

And there was another aspect of my mother, which I have been reluctant to talk about. "Use it," she had ordered me in the final days of her agony as I stared at her face, her emaciated frame, wasted away to the bone sockets. "It's material." Her voice was steely, despite her broken body in the hospital bed.

The dreams that followed her death were so disturbing that I got up from them in the half-light of her dying, and had to fight my way back into the morning, leaving a damp, awful world behind. She was angry in these appearances. She was alive but in a half-life, disgusted with me, my father, the whole family, refusing to acknowledge us when she walked the corridors of the house. In some of these dreams I had the sense that she had moved out of our home, was living a separate life, wanted nothing to do with me, my father, even my sister.

In childhood, adolescence, and my life up until the age of twenty-nine, I had felt again and again the weight of her disapproval, but never the cold, hostile rejection of the figure moving through these fantasies before dawn. Why was she so angry? My father had fallen in love with his young secretary right after Mother's death. My sister and I were worried about him and it seemed, at least to me, important that he find someone who could take care of him, wake him back up to a new life after his career had turned into what he regarded as a dead end. I wanted him to be happy, to have another chance and if he wanted it, another family. We knew, my sister and I, that he loved us, though I doubted that he would ever find a woman who was the equal of my mother. In his heyday in the legislature my father had the wits and agility of a young man, but his political career had already been over for ten years. Now as he tried to keep up with a twenty-three-year-old whose world was very different from his own, it proved to be too much. He rose no later than 5:00 A.M., conditioned by his work as a boy beside my grandfather in the Boston Flower Market or Exchange, and was used to going to bed by 8:00 or 9:00 P.M. at the latest. In my teenage years, he had wangled a license for me a few months earlier than technically allowed so that I could drive him home from midnight sessions of the Massachusetts House of Representatives, because he had a habit of falling asleep at the wheel. When he tried to stay up dancing until midnight or one in the morning with his new girlfriend, it took its inevitable toll, on top of his smoking and carrying too much weight on legs roped with varicose veins. It brought on angina, and so, despite their mutual affection, the romance did not last.

Throughout it all I felt that Mother was crying out at all of us, however, and I rose frightened from these dreams in which she was there, sick more often than healthy, not wanting to be with us anymore. I rose and typed up everything I could remember of these spectral appearances before dawn, happy to have even her anger, to have anything of her presence in my life.

In the fall of 2008 I searched for the typed sheets and handwritten pages on which I set them down as they came; which were at their most intense in the third year after her death. The folder I thought they were in was eluding me in spite of an ardent search through my papers, as if not wanting to bring forth those nights into public view, but let them remain in the privacy of the shadows through which she had appeared. Then, in yet one more exasperated shuffling of files in a dusty corner of my shelves, a manila envelope into which I peered, preparing to dump it into a wastebasket full of other meaningless paper, surprised me with the pages, typed on the thin cotton bond that I had favored in the days of portable typewriters.

I could recall the dreams even before I found the pages. It was perhaps because the most powerful one had come on the night of her death, and was etched beyond the scratching of words so that I had no reason to write down the memory to recover what I could never forget.

• • •

I have taken up this story, a march to my mother's last breath; a journey I have started and stopped so many times, but happily the dreams take me beyond her death. Months before it, she had been strong enough to walk through the fall season from my parents' rented apartment in Mattapan over a hill of pleasant, well-shaded streets to the Hospital for Chronic Care. Even at a quick pace, past the edge of a bucolic Franklin Park, it was almost an hour's trek. Now, in February of 1968, the disease began to race. I have already spoken about that awful moment, when, taking the train up to see her, I found she had lost lucidity—a result of an abnormal water balance in her body. Up to then she was the authority, consulted on taxes, bank accounts, apartment rentals, my strategy for receiving tenure at City College. Now she did not recognize me. What did I see in the woman thrashing in her bed? I had rushed from her room to the lavatory, turning the faucets open, running cold water over my wrists, blood pooling in shock, to keep my own sanity intact.

I was losing her months before I had prepared myself, before I had exchanged the intimacy of being asked, and answering the question, "Do I have cancer?"

The words touch my lips like a curse. In the corridor, when I queried the doctors about her chances, a thin young man, with a pallid complexion and a German accent, expressionless, answered brusquely, "She has none." There it was. Pronounced from his bloodless lips, the "lack of affect" expression struck me as brutal and inescapable.

The efforts of her doctors at the hospital—or her own strong will—brought her shaken body back to a tenuous equilibrium. Her eyes cleared. She spoke to me with her old authority intact.

She came home several times after that episode of losing lucidity. I was almost sure that she was there for our Passover in April, though my memory may be playing tricks on me. I know that I took my motorcycle out from our garage when the weather was still very cold in March, so I could drive back and forth from the house without borrowing the car from my father. I had bumped into another car in the parking lot a week earlier. Normally she would have ordered me to go down and leave a note on the windshield, admitting my culpability, but small details of moral rigor were now a matter of indifference to her. She shrugged, forgiving me, adjudicating. This time, she would rule in my favor. Life was unfair and a small dent was inconsequential.

The doctors could not tell my father or me how long she would live after that spell of confusion. "She has a strong heart," they said. "Your mother could live another six months, even a year." They had done all they could, we were advised, and asked to make arrangements to move her to a nursing home.

My father was in dread of their medical insurance running out, and evidently small charges were beginning to accumulate that it did not cover. One could see, however, that except for her swollen belly, she was being eaten alive. The bones of her face emerged as the last bits of flesh sank away, the face, not of her mother in those plump-cheeked portraits of Annie toward which my mother had been verging in her early fifties, but the classical Sephardic features of her father as a young man. In the last stages of the illness, her nose and forehead prominent, seemed to reveal the stern face of an Egyptian pharaoh unwrapped from its cerements, only where the sockets of the mummy would be empty glancing with grim hawk's eyes.

My sister had come in the depths of the winter with her children, summoned, begged to come, by my father and me. Once again we pleaded with her to leave the West Coast early since she and her husband would be coming east from Portland, Oregon, at the very end of the spring. He was to take up a new position as a professor at the University of New Hampshire. It might be her last glimpse of my mother, and my mother's last chance to see her grandchildren. And we, my father and I, needed my sister as well. I had wept in my father's law office that the strain was driving me crazy.

I was coming in now at every spare moment from Manhattan. I am almost certain that my mother came home one last time for the Passover celebration in the middle of the month of Nissan, April 12th. It was a Friday evening. She would pass away on Friday evening three weeks later. These are dates confirmed on a calendar I kept at the time. My memory, however, plays tricks on me. I remember my mother being allowed to come home after we pleaded with the doctors to let her partake in the traditional meal, the Passover seder, at our table at home in Mattapan. Was this the moment that my father stumbled by mistake into her bed, forgetting that it was where one of Aunt Miriam's sons had been staying for the night? She was far too ill to leave the hospital for more than a few hours. It is a measure of my own imbalance that according to my sister I have transposed the Passover at which she and her children were not present since she arrived after the holiday, with an earlier family meal that took place in the winter when my mother was entering the most critical stage of her illness. It was at that meal, my sister assures me, that the following incident took place.

I see Mother's angry skeletal form seated in the midst of our family at the elaborate table we set in the dining room. We have brought out from the very top of the pantry shelves, where they have been carefully wrapped and rewrapped, the sacred icons of the house since I was an infant, her crystal wine glasses. The fragile goblets were a gift from her sister Esther for my mother's wedding. They only graced our table for special occasions, once, maybe twice, a year, far too precious for ordinary meals and even holiday ones.

One of my sister's two children, either the toddler or her older sister, reaches across the table and knocks a goblet over, spilling a sea of red wine across the white linen tablecloth and shattering the crystal. My mother shrugs. Her expression forbids any scolding. The child's good humor is more important than glass. Yes, we all silently agree, but the red stain is like Mother's blood, and the shattered goblet mocks the wedding ceremony, when one is broken underfoot by the groom for good luck. A chill runs through me and in memory I confound the two meals so that it is the ceremonial spilling of red wine into a plate that symbolizes the twelve plagues in Egypt at the Passover seder that has run wild. It blots the table in a Red Sea, a sea of my mother's blood. I see it happen again, my mother at Passover, her grandchildren, our last meal, our last supper, before I am engulfed in Mother's death.

April 21 [1972]
A dream of my mother. Her face is filled with the anguish and unbearable pain of her sickness. It is too awful to look at. I cover her eyes with strips of white adhesive tape. Then I cover the

grimace in her cheeks, the wringing of her lips. Still out of this partially masked face, the pain rings and I begin to wind the white tape from her temples slowly down around her face until she is entirely encased in white cloth.

This is how I saw her last. A white mummy. I looked at the blank figure of my mother and seemed to see her move, up and down.

"She moved," I cried to the nurse. "I saw her chest move up and down." But they, the nurses in the room, smiled knowingly and took me away.

The night before, I dreamed that she had begun the long sickness but was still alive. We were at a political meeting in Dorchester on Morton Street [one of the main thoroughfares of my father's district]. Someone called out, "Nominate Ruth Mirsky for the committee!"

My father sadly replied, "No, you can't anymore. She's not well."

Again, the brooding presence of my mother, home, sick, dying slowly, but still alive, a ghost in the midst of the living, one of those who have not been given their allotted time.

You cannot understand this dream without me telling you about the night my mother died, returning to the end, before going beyond it.

• • •

We had no idea when the end would come, only that my father, my sister—who came after Passover—and I, were in a state of suspension watching my mother's body deteriorate. The coffin screws tightened each day; but the prediction of doctors that she might go on for months, was increasingly doubtful. She was probably going to have to go to a nursing home. In order to lighten the gloom, my sister, who had hurried to us with her children ahead of her husband, whose semester teaching at Reed College still had weeks before it was over, prepared a Friday night meal. She had become a skilled cook since her marriage to the delight of my mother and father. I had come up from Manhattan and gone to the hospital first. It was frightening to see the disease progress. Only a few weeks before I had turned my mother's body in the bed, almost naked under the shift, to keep her from developing bedsores, in the absence of her favorite nurse. She was so light, not quite a feather, but almost. I had done this turning as a hospital attendant while serving in the U.S. Air Force Reserves, and it was gratifying to be able to call upon my experience, to hold her as a professional and carefully move her back and forth. I had brought her, surreptitiously, a cold can of pear nectar. She could not keep down the fruit juices they offered her in the hospital, too acidic for her stomach. She had complained that the ice chips that kept her mouth moist were tasteless. We both smiled at our successful variation on the hospital diet.

Now, she was at a further stage of deterioration, a dramatic one, almost all bones, trembling uncontrollably, surrounded by nurses. Seeing me, she shot me a distressed look of recognition, raising her arm, firmly for a moment, signaling. "Do not look at this! Go away. It is not for your eyes." It was not a rejection but a gesture in which she demanded with all her authority that I respect her privacy. She did not want me to see her in this state.

I left the hospital, calm, but deeply dejected. I went home, only a few miles away by automobile and asked my sister if I could invite a guest, since my girlfriend was back in Manhattan. An old friend Mary, from my years at Harvard College, had just returned from working as a volunteer in the poorest districts of Caracas in Venezuela and my focus on my mother's condition had made it difficult for me to find a few hours to drive into Cambridge and sit over a cup of coffee with her. I called Mary, and took my father's car to pick her up and drive her to our house. The route from Mattapan to Cambridge ran by the hospital and normally, I stopped to go in and check on my mother's condition, sit by the bed for awhile, but Mother's peremptory gesture earlier seemed to forbid me from returning so soon.

I have no memory of supper that evening, only that the aura of Mother's condition lay over the table. When it came time at about 7:00 P.M. to drive Mary home, I asked my sister if I could take the older of her two daughters, Emily, with me for company. I was afraid to be alone returning from Cambridge in the automobile, a thirty-minute ride. Emily was wide awake and it was between eight-thirty and nine when we passed the Shattuck Hospital, coming back to Mattapan, which lay only a few minutes away by car. I thought again of stopping to check on Mother but it seemed unwise to expose a little girl to the shadowy, dimly lit hospital corridors at night, particularly given my mother's condition earlier. In a story called "Memory Candle," I detailed that moment. "I remembered my mother's hand pushing the air, pushing me away. My niece beside me, I went on driving, went to what had been home to my mother and father for fifteen years, a rented floor in a brick Mattapan two-family house." I wanted to turn into the parking lot, but with an effort of will, I drove on past the Shattuck.

At home I turned my niece over to my sister, fell into bed, exhausted, and slept. The call from the Shattuck came about midnight.

Did I go alone to the hospital? How did I get there? This is a blank space in a morning of wavering reality. I fall back on the story I have just quoted, which, closer to the event, is probably more faithful than what I now recall.

"The call woke us two hours later. It was Friday night. Later that would mean something. I only recall starting up in the sheets as my father cried, "She's dead," at the telephone, ripping my white undershirt in two, as if making up a bandage right away against the terror, although it was because I had been told that you were supposed to tear your clothes. I wondered what else I should tear, my hair, my suit, the bedspread. I drove to the hospital but Mother's body was already wrapped, even the face. "It's moving," I told the nurse. I see it.

" 'No, no,' they said gently, pushing me out of the room, away from the body to which I had bent, trying to bite through the white adhesive tape which was wound around it from head to foot. 'You are imagining it.'

"I wasn't. I wanted it unwound. Only it was too late. No one will do that for you. So I let myself be taken home. I went to bed. That's when it happened.

"I felt her. She came for me. Lying in the bed, in the darkness still, two or three in the morning, I was not asleep, not awake. When I felt her, saw something of her, a force, a wind, come down and begin to pull me up after her, taking me with her, toward something I knew (and now, remembering, I do not know) was evil or dangerous and I pushed her away.

"Why did I do that? Was it you? What could I have wanted more, Mother, than to have gone with you? Yet, I too pushed you, pushed you away. For you were angry, so angry, I was afraid.

"I was alone. Afraid to lie back, go to sleep, knowing that in sleep, she would come again, and for some reason, I was in fear.

"In that moment I did not let myself take the hand that had only twelve hours ago pushed me away. I recognized my mother's face in the spirit furious over me, wanting to tear me away from the bed. But I recoiled from the force which had half drawn me up in the sheets after her."

As I recalled the moment again in the summer of 2008, "Hovering over the bed, reaching for me, asking me to come, her fingers just inches away—why did I pull back? For I did pull back afraid to join her in that flight beyond the world. You can tell me that it was a hallucination, but as the room whirled around me and she was there, tugging me up, it was no illusion, for I cried out, and she understood, I would not go then."

It was that meeting with my mother's ghost on the night of her death, which gave the dreams that followed some of their disturbing power. There were many nights in which I passed into a world where I wondered what was real. Four years after her death my mother still haunted me. I wrote down very few of those nocturnal visits because they upset me. Their tenor was reproach.

Here is the second dream that I wrote down in that summer of 1972, though it was one of many.

Dream, June 26th. A large house. It becomes clear as the dream progresses that it is the house at 92 Hazelton Street, my parents' old apartment. But are my father and mother alive? One of them, or both of them is dead, but the dream does not make that clear, only that something has altered radically in the house and in my welcome in it. I am sleeping in one of the rooms, here it seems more like 136 Hazelton Street [we lived

*at the bottom of Hazelton Street for several years in the early
1950s] where I slept in what was meant to be a dining room
but was made into my bedroom. When it is time to take a bath,
someone, a boyfriend of my sister, is in residence, not taking his
bath but about to, and I am only suffered in a very condescending way to go quickly in and out of the bathtub. Somehow at the
end of the dream I feel as if S [the girl I lived with for six years
and broke it off with in the second year after my mother's death]
was still my girlfriend and I protest that at least I was with
a steady girl while my sister and unaccountably, other people,
have brought back much more temporary partners to occupy,
usurp our house, making me a stranger in the house.*

In the summer of 1972, my father was alive. A young Norwegian
woman, who would become my wife, had come to visit. The breakup
with my former girlfriend was still disturbing me. She had known my
mother well. My sister, who had divorced her first husband, was seeing
the young man who would become her second husband. These are the
shadowy facts in the background of the dream. I speak about sensing
the presence of a man my sister is dating in the house, but what is perhaps strangest is that at the bottom of the page I have written a line.

"My name is Israel, Ruthie."

This is uncanny. I was not married. Just the year before, I had met
the twenty-one-year-old Norwegian whom I would marry. My son, Israel, would not be conceived for another eight years, and my daughter,
Ruthie, for nine and a half.

*July 25. In the past week, three dreams about my mother. As
I dream them, I resolve to write them down, but I always forget
during the day and slowly they face into obscurity.*

*The first dream. She is alive again but sick. This sickness
being rescued from death, but obliged to live a half-life, a life in
which one walks half-dead, like a corpse from whom a certain
hope is missing, talking, walking, but not animated by the sun,
is quite terrible, and so the dream, like the several that have
come before it, is tinged with melancholy. But I am glad to have*

my mother speaking to me in any way, walking beside me and I prolong the dream and wake up happy.

Is it a paradigm of what might have happened, if indeed she had been given the two years more of life she begged for? Or even the four or five months in a nursing home, or better still [had been] taken home as she begged [for] in the last few weeks of her life?

The second dream is one of the most difficult and provoking I have had. It is not like the repetitious first dream [where] she is alive, but sick, a dream of a simple return. For the first time we question the illusion of her coming to me in a dream. We are in the family house on Hazelton Street. It suddenly fills with her relatives and she is very happy. Much happier than I can remember her in any of these ghostly dreams where the prevailing tone is melancholy. Somehow we fall into talk in the office study, which is in the middle of the house (with no doors, really more of a foyer or passageway than a study, but my father has put his desk and bookcases in it, so that everyone is privy to everyone else's phone calls).

She is gay, almost dancing at the company of so many of her family, girlish. I ask her, "But Mother, isn't it all an illusion, the family being here?" (For, in fact, they have never been in our house like this, Boston being too far off for Lessler family meetings.) And she says, both of us understanding, that it is all an illusion, that she is dead and that both of us are only enjoying each other's company in a dream, yes, but if you believe in an illusion hard enough it will be so, and suddenly as if to prove her point we both see my cousin Judy dancing merrily in the passageway to the front door, winking at us. She is there. Judy [my cousin, Aunt Dotty's daughter] is in the house and we both laugh happily hearing the din of the rest of the family whom we believe [are] in the living room.

The third dream is a dream of duty. We are living not in our own house but in a drugstore down on the corner of Wellington Hill Street and Blue Hill Avenue. [Just a street over from Hazelton but Wellington is extremely steep since it climbs

*the hill. At the bottom is] High's drugstore. This drugstore, half
pharmacy, library, variety store, was the focus of my adolescence
as I sat there reading erotic paperbacks and sipping raspberry
sodas after junior high and high school. [The druggist,] High,
a curly-haired pharmacist had the kind of serious respectability
that is the mark of character in the Jewish middle class. Somehow, the one-story brick building that housed his pharmacy has
been transformed into a wooden three-decker, almost a Gothic
three-decker. We are living in the rooms on the third and second
floor. But the bottom, where the pharmacy used to be, is full
of old furniture and dusty, like a cellar or attic. To please my
mother I set to the task, without being asked, of cleaning these
rooms up, throwing out broken furniture, washing the floors,
walls, putting the junk of our family into the garbage cans outside, restoring the rooms to use and life. She comes down to look
and gives me one of her rare looks of approval. Somehow I have
opened the house up, given life.*

*In this dream, the stairs between the downstairs street-level
rooms and the rooms upstairs where we live are very vivid and
important. She stands on the stairs in the back of the house looking into the rooms I have cleaned, freshened, through the dream,
beaming approval.*

This next dream is undated. It must have been dreamed at some
time in the very early 1970s. My father was alive then. It is a dream
that touches with that uneasy, ominous sense of prophecy. When he
died in 1982, he collapsed first in the vault of the First National Bank
where he returned over and over again to check his bank deposit vault,
afraid that someone was gaining access to it and possibly stealing from
him. He was pronounced dead by an incompetent doctor at the bank,
but was revived by the paramedics, though with so much damage to
his brain in the interim, that he never came out of the coma and passed
away several days later in the hospital.

A dream that my mother is still alive.

It begins in a haze with my mother still about the house. My father is there. He goes out. An enormous hurricane comes up. I look out the window and see that a brick skyscraper, a red brick skyscraper rising on a slender column, then spreading out to a pyramid inverted of red brick, somewhat like the First National Bank building in downtown Boston is shaking, shaking, tipping, yes tipping; it's going to fall. I watch it incline until the last possible moment though I am far away I know that pieces of it will shatter everywhere and then I duck, fall face downward into a doorway hearing the roar of it going over. Or perhaps I have been watching from a tiny window in my house. I go downstairs. My mother is there. It [the house] is [left] alone, we are alone in the house but worried. Where is my father? Will he remember to duck down and take cover from the flying debris? We move about the house. Worried. After an hour or so, a knock at the door. My father!

He is clutching his shoulder. He appears to be badly wounded. Is there a blossom of blood on his shirt as we take his coat off, dreading the worst, a great splinter of iron?

No, it turns out when we have peeled his shirt and white cotton undershirt off, that he was badly frightened, exaggerating. It is only a bad bruise on his chest. It has to be cleaned with alcohol. I want to do it but my mother insists. She flies to the cabinet, comes back with a bottle and cotton.

As she bends over the wound I want to snatch the cotton out of her fingers I am so horrified. I see that her fingers are swollen with water, baggy, green and white with death. The fluid that is collecting in her body has made the fingers like the hand of a monster. I am crying, but she tenderly leans over my father with her swollen, distorted hand and slowly, awkwardly manages to brush the wound.

Oh my mother. I realize at that moment that she is only half alive. That she moves among us as a ghost. Again I wake up trembling to know that only in dreams can I encounter her and then, again and again, even there, as a dream within a dream.

The final dream in the file is handwritten sometime in the late 1970s.

> *A dream of my mother—July 25*
>
> *I am on the slope of a hill with some friends when I see across grass and the road a picnic stand my aunt Miriam and her family, the Pozens. I start walking toward them filled with laughter at the surprise they will have in finding me here. I make a wide circle and as I come close they stand up and are smiling, half unable to believe it is me. But they wave me on [to] the next hill where there is another family reunion. Here in the valley between two grassy slopes I discover Aunt Esther, Aunt Claire, [her daughter] Adrienne, the strange (to a boy) secret circle of ladies, which possesses the inner secrets of the domesticity of Bridgeport, the crinolines, silk, ribbons and dresses. My mother is there too but she is dressed in a black tuxedo, very white in her face, with a white dress shirt and yet with sneakers on her feet. She seems abstracted from the rest of the group and wanders sadly limping away from them.*
>
> *My Aunt Esther is speaking enthusiastically to the group and as I realize that she is not the old Aunt Esther I have always known with puffed out features, but the beautiful girl I have seen in the picture of her youth in New York and Bridgeport, I cry out, "Aunt Esther!"*
>
> *She stops with a smiling face and reproves me [mildly for interrupting.]*

What did the dream represent? It was a good dream I remember, but tinged with sadness, the understanding that my mother was never quite a member of that "inner" circle of the family, which Aunt Esther presided over, subject to the reproof that my sister and I felt from the aunts and uncles who dominated it. And yet, it was also a dream that promised some sort of rapprochement with her family even as she drifted away from it, lonely, misunderstood. Who was she—never quite that girl in crinolines, and ribbons, the image of her older sisters—despite her need for their affection?

The dreams would change back briefly after my father's death. My mother's perturbed spirit returned tinged in the bitter shadows of her first appearance. She seems to have taken body in the confusion and anger I felt in the wake of my father's death. I typed them into a notebook I kept while in Israel in 1982 when I went there with my wife and my son, who was ten months old.

April 25 [1982—the year of my father's death]

Last night, a nightmare of my mother, the familiar one that she has been alive all these years, a strange variant of the Hitler theme [that he never did die] which, having dreamed, I remember that I have dreamt before ... She is alive but has been living away from the house, angry, living in Florida. My father has concealed [this] but it [her disease] has been arrested and she lives on in a half-life. But now the agony of this dream is compounded by the knowledge that my father too has taken on this half-life.

Now in the light of his dream-like existence, she has come up from Florida to live with us again—but her life is like one of those terrible angry afternoons when she walked in a sick headache through our childhood, abstracted, untouchable, removed from us—so that we felt as if a ghost [and] not our mother inhabited the house.

I am cursed that I did not rise to write the dream in my notebook, I only remember now, hours later, that somehow the ... those miserable people next door were involved in our attempt to live again as a single family, father, mother and children at the beach house.

I find a second entry in the notebook I kept during those months of April, May, and early June 1982.

A dream of my mother. It is discovered that my mother is alive, all these years ... but living in Florida. She has been renting a small apartment. I say to my sister, "Let us give her an allotment from the estate so that she can buy a condominium, or have a better place." But my sister in some stubborn, adamant way does not want to admit that she is our mother and has any claim on the estate. And so somehow our mother begins to drift away? I can't remember the end of the dream and I think I am woken up from it. Do I intend to provide for her from my own share? All I feel is the strange lonely apartness of the Lesslers, as if that threat to cut herself off from us had been true and she is only partly attentive to us, her children. Of course the opposite was so, but the threat of the latter alternative hung over us.

I am being unfair to my sister who bore the brunt of my father's last months as he suffered a series of small undetected strokes and wandered between lucidity and darkness. The only conversation about condominiums we had was our attempt to jointly finance one for my father in his last years. In my notes after the last dream, attempting to understand it, I spoke about how angry I was at myself, how guilty. My father's death, I felt, might have been prevented, but it broke open the deep well of despair, my inability to hold on to either of my parents. Since my father's death was too close to grasp, did my dreams draw my mother's ghost?

For fifteen years she came, more often as an angry presence through our house, or living elsewhere, letting us know she was there, but that she no longer cared. It was a distance more brutal than any I had felt from her in life. And yet, there is that dream above, where she tends to my father's wounds, in a guise of compassion made more awful by her corporal dissolution. Slowly, though, the apparition gave up her bitterness and resumed a happier form.

• • •

During the eight months through which I had watched my mother die I did not feel the need to be religious. Or rather, I felt that it would not help to beg, to pray, to try to avert the oncoming catastrophe through an intervention of a power beyond this world. I had, however, at Stanford the year before begun to attend the Saturday services on an irregular basis. During several weeks ahead of the first classes,

I wandered with faculty privileges into the university's library stacks. I came across the Soncino edition of the Babylonian Talmud on the shelves. I began to thumb through pages, but overwhelmed by the material and without any preparation for finding a way through it, or a system of study that would allow me to filter it, let alone understand the arguments, I turned to the index in English.

In retrospect it would seem ominous. I picked the topic "Death," following the references through the set (seventeen seperately bound volumes, thousands and thousands of pages) though it took me weeks. The death of my grandfather, Israel Mirsky (who was the only ghost I had seen before the night of my mother's death), and the laments of the Talmud intertwined in my head. By this time the synagogue had been abandoned, where Israel had served as the guiding force so that Rabbi Soloveitchik would exclaim to me recalling my grandfather, "he *was* the synagogue!" The Jews had fled their old district in Boston, and so my father's career in representing those streets faltered; a sadness I could not identify went through my throat as I read the entries for death in the Soncino's translation. That September of 1966, a year and a half before Mother's death, something else happened that tickles the funny bone of superstition in my own religious belief. The Saturday service on the Stanford campus brought together Orthodox and Conservative Jews with the reform rabbi from its Hillel House (the umbrella organization that represents all sects of Judaism on college campuses) and some Israeli members of the faculty. I attended sporadically, but was identified as partly clueless when it came to the conventions of Orthodox prayer. My Judaism at that moment was basically "cultural," a remnant of the rote memory I practiced at Hebrew school that let me stumble through the Hebrew of the prayer book, moments with my father as he prepared me for bar mitzvah, the echoes of Eastern Europe that coursed through the Jewish streets of Dorchester, Mattapan, Roxbury, and some of the rabbinic texts in English that I had assimilated through my friendship with the rabbi at Harvard, Ben Zion Gold. My first novel, *Thou Worm Jacob*, a violent cartoon, reflected the social life of a decaying Jewish Boston, though the language wished for more. One Saturday I was called to the reading of the Law, *Torah*, for the biblical portion about curses. In Eastern Europe it was often given to the poorest and saddest member of the congregation for according to superstition, its curses attached to whoever was called up to receive it. (The chanter or *baal kriyah*, usually recites the passages assigned to members of the congregation, since the recitation requires that one knows it by heart—it has no vowels in the scroll and is sung not spoken.) In America, the rabbi usually takes the passage, as a way of obviating its ill effects. I didn't understand the protests from several of the more knowledgeable members of the congregation as I was called up by the stocky, arrogant graduate student who handed out the honors. It was a studied act of contempt. Later I understood, and I still feel the omen's shadowy stain.

My mother's death now swept me into a world I had never understood. As I mentioned, Rabbi Ben Zion Gold had given me Gershom Scholem's *Major Trends in Jewish Mysticism*. It is a revolutionary text that has influenced Jews and non-Jews, from the Yale critic Harold Bloom to Jorge Luis Borges, the towering literary figure of Latin America in the twentieth century. At twenty-one years old its first pages were meaningless to me, dry facts and a puzzling terminology that appeared inscrutable. In the wake of Mother's death it became a handbook; a place to search for her, to find some comfort from my own stiff horror by following the search of earlier generations within Judaism for what they feared to have lost forever. It was a chart to a forbidden place, the "other world."

Major Trends read from this perspective is the record of Jewish mystics climbing the ladder that Jacob on his rock pillow saw as the extension into the heavens beyond the physical heavens. I didn't hope to find my mother in the elaborate visions of antiquity or believe that the image of my mother, leaping in her bathing suit, would appear in the Neoplatonic romances of its classic work, the *Zohar*. Even its foremost scholar Gershom Scholem smiled at what he identified as plain spoof.

I understood, however, the emotions that created its stories, the need to go beyond this world not to escape it, but to follow the strongest attachments abruptly broken. Later I would recognize it as the preoccupation of Homer and Virgil, Dante Alighieri, and in the twentieth century, Robert Musil. Fiction no longer seemed a form in which to catch the follies of my neighborhood, the surrealism of the Boston streets I had grown up in, and my father and grandfather's world. Even the vagaries of American politics that I had witnessed as a child in a political household, as my father associated with governors of Massachusetts, presidential candidates, were less compelling. Fiction was not just a means; it was the only way I had to riddle the mystery, even if it could never be solved, of where my mother had gone.

Who was she?

I keep coming back to that, turning to her sisters, my older cousins, trying to undo my carelessness in not coming to my mother and pressing her to answer the question herself.

Would she have surrendered any of her secrets? Could I, as I would with my father in the wake of his heart attack, have unlocked memories of her childhood, adolescence, first steps?

The moment in December, when Mother understood that she was not going home from the hospital, and accompanying me to the door, suddenly reached to my face for what I thought would be her usual, light peck on the side of my cheek and instead, bit my lip hard, as if to hold on to me—what was it meant to say? That bite at the end of the hospital corridor might have been the key to some of her mysteries. Later I would not lose the opportunity to question my father in his last years. Almost fifty hours of his voice exists on tape as he recalled for me his childhood in Pinsk, my grandfather's absence, the brutality of its streets during World War One, the nightmare of the voyage to America, the bitter aftermath of a reunion with my grandfather and the stepmother he married. Like the bewildered knight of the German epic *Parsifal*, I was too well trained, too polite as I approached my mother in adolescence, in my early twenties, at her deathbed to ask of her spiritual life, "What ails thee?"

"*Iz pasht nisht*," my grandfather Israel would hush his children when they brought their personal troubles to him at his job, their quarrels with their stepmother, "It's not befitting." One does not talk about such things. My mother lived in another world, ignoring Freud, almost all of her thoughts concealed from me, only her disappointment and melancholy apparent.

Still, as I turn to the pages of her albums and sift through the boxes of my letters she collected and find several that she left for me, present time begins to exist as a dream without the sequence of a sun-centered planet, circle following circle, where child follows parent in one cycle of separation after another that only death's snapping interrupts. I remember my mother as a girl as well as a mother and in her albums, and the photographs taken just after the second album was finished, when I was on the edge of speech and then possessing it, the images of her draw me into the glow of her secret life. After I have thumbed them, and begun to write in my notebooks, trying to assemble the fragments and live it again beside her, Mother seems to hover closer.

Four years after her death, when I first looked again at albums that had lain closed in the attic of our beach cottage in Hull through my adolescence and afterwards, the shape of her flitted out into the damp air of the upstairs bedrooms at our summer home. I lay back in my parents' bed, almost faint with the painful sweetness of her images, sick with puppy love. For the first time, I was as in love with my mother as Freud had promised, though I had never desired my mother, never thought of her in the sexual sense. It seems as if the Hebrew taboo, her own deep sense of rectitude, the equal affection in which I regarded my father and his generosity, all held her in a frame of idealization without the murderous or erotic implications of the Greek myth, In pre-adolescence, as she existed for me, leaping the fence into the abandoned fort beyond our summer house, she is a sister, loved almost impossibly and always out of reach. I have such a powerful fantasy life that it is enough for me to see a woman briefly, to carry the wish to enter her with me, and the dream of doing it, for days. My mother remains in a world of ethereal space. I want her most intensely in a time of boyhood, eight, nine, ten, when sexuality was absent, or more probably, to fall into the jargon of psychiatry, "sublimated."

There is a line of the poet Neruda's, "From the foam chastity ..."

Again, in thinking of the afterlife and the puzzle of time, whom, if resurrection were possible, would we become: the child, the young man, the older one, and Mother, when would we live in moments of lost time? Day or night? Any and every moment is possible.

My father told me that he was an agnostic. My mother never told me what she believed, apart from that long sigh when I was four or five when I asked about what lay ahead in death. I imagine that her reply so discouraged me that I refrained from further inquiries. Her difficulty in accepting my non-Jewish girlfriends who seemed like serious prospects for marriage (she was unfailingly courteous even affectionate to the others) speaks to the hold that tradition, which rests on belief—examined or not—had on her. My father, the agnostic, after his second heart attack called out, "Mother, why is this happening to me," as I passed the open door of his hospital room. My mother kept her lips sealed as far as I know.

I wonder if she could have subscribed, as I do, to John Stuart Mill's austere but searching thought at the end of a paragraph on irrational belief and death: "The mere cessation of existence is no evil to any one: the idea is only formidable through the illusion of imagination which makes one conceive oneself as if one were alive and feeling oneself dead. What is odious in death is not death itself, but the act of dying and its lugubrious accompaniments: all of which must be equally undergone by the believer in immortality. Nor can I perceive that the skeptic loses by his skepticism any real and valuable consolation except one; the hope of reunion with those dear to him who have ended their earthly life before him. That loss, indeed, is neither to be denied nor extenuated." Mill's mockery of "lugubrious accompaniments" speaking of the funeral rituals, was not, however, my experience of mourning for my mother in the tradition of Orthodox Judaism. Nor do I agree that "the cessation of existence is not evil to any one." My mother finally wanted desperately to live and her premature end still shakes me.

• • •

The photograph below was probably taken in late 1937 or 1938. It is labeled, "3 sisters" on the strip above, and "On the Charles," below. Miriam is in the middle, my mother and Aunt Dorothy on either side. It is on a page on the other side of which has an article from the Yiddish *Forward* about my father's candidacy for state representative from Ward Fourteen. He lost the election, his first, and my mother has written in humorously, "Fakers, *Ganoviim*," under the article, echoing the Yiddish English of Dorchester, Mattapan, Roxbury, the Jewish district,

Ward Fourteen, where in 1948, my father would realize his dream and enter the Massachusetts legislature.

I asked Aunt Miriam about what their life was like, when she was visiting her daughter-in-law Janet, who was married to Miriam's son, Michael.

Janet: Did you share boyfriends too?

Miriam: No, she had more than I did.

Mark: Why do you think that was so?

Miriam: She had a nicer personality than I did.

Mark: Why? In what sense?

Miriam. Well, she was more outgoing. And she, your mother, had a love for life.

Mark: Dotty blames my father for ruining my mother's taste in clothes. Sort of shutting her up ...

Miriam: Well, you see, Dotty feels that material things are very important. Your mother, as far as she was concerned, it didn't matter. She would go out and look at a flower, and she'd say, isn't it beautiful.

Janet: And she was always that way, not just after she was married.

Miriam: No, and she had this ... She just loved life.

Morris: She had a green thumb.

Miriam: Yuh, and ... Dotty, to her, and to Willy Cohen, they thought *we* were *terrible*. We had an old television set that we had bought when Michael was born, after Michael was born, and we must have had it for about twelve or fifteen *years*, O my God, you know, they ...

Morris: Pilot, I don't know if you remember that company, Pilot ...

Miriam. The Cohens had this sense of grandeur, you know. And we never, your mother never had it. I don't have it. Even now they think ... They just did things in a big way ...

(I publish this remark with some reluctance and only because it speaks to the tensions within the family as brothers and sisters went their different ways. Aunt Dorothy was endlessly generous to other members of the family, taking nieces and nephews into her home for extended periods when the need arose. She greeted my girlfriends, then my wife, with an affection that immediately made them feel accepted.) My mother [Annie] would have the boys throw him [Will Cohen] out. She didn't want her to get involved with anybody at that age. She made her a sweet sixteen party and wouldn't let her invite Will ..."

One of the questions that I ask, over and over, looking at the tenderness of my mother towards my father in the years before I was born, is to what extent I embittered my mother's life. Why was she so depressed that day I came up from the high grass in Franklin Field? To what extent was her father's "state of mind," consisting of problems that, according to cousins, landed him in a mental hospital for a short stay, excluded him from control over the family business and made him a petitioner in old age in the kitchens of his older children, inherited?

The remark about Joseph Lessler's nagging, which Aunt Miriam recalled, echoes in my head. I remember my father, rushing out of the house in Mattapan, by the side stairs, not wanting to be seen by the neighbors on the front porch, screaming in rage. She could push his buttons with a cold, sarcastic set of critical questions. At first I always sided with her, but slowly I realized that she wanted this outburst from Dad; it was a way of releasing her own anger. She would do it to me as well in adolescence, either provoking me or withdrawing into a cold silence. I mentioned the back and forth with her, when I was about fourteen or so, after a bout of nagging to which I refused to respond, she admitted to me and to herself, asking rhetorically, "You know what I am doing?" She could not admit to me that her favorite brother Bob had committed suicide in California, in the midst of a failing marriage. Silent about her father, all her older brothers and sisters were held up as models. Even Jules, the brother who was closest to her in age and whom she obviously had disputes with growing up, was spoken of with affection, welcomed into our house when he came to Boston, his penchant for "kidding" or "teasing" her as a child brushed over and never referred to in his presence.

My father leaned hard on Mother every two years from 1948 on, as he won his political campaigns for election to the legislature. She was his real campaign manager, making thousands of calls, supervising the mailings, stepping in when his former students or friends found the volunteer work beyond their capacity in terms of time and labor. She also came in periodically to straighten out his desk in his law office. At some time in the 1940s, I remember he had his own secretary, or shared one with a lawyer who rented an office on State Street with him. Later, on Beacon Street, he may have used some secretarial services, but my mother was called upon over and over. We mailed fifteen to twenty thousand pieces of literature every time he ran for political office from the house and from the storefronts he rented in empty spaces along the main avenue, Blue Hill. When workers who had promised to help did not show up, my mother did.

Dad was proud of her and not all of what she did on his behalf was secretarial or managerial. She served as the president of my junior high school's Parent-Teacher Association. In Dad's first terms in the legislature, when he had the ear of the governor, Paul Dever, she served without pay as chairman of the Immigration and Naturalization Board of Massachusetts. None of her sisters achieved that public a role. I can feel my mother's charisma in the photograph below, where her oldest brother Simon and his wife Ruth beam as the governor shakes Mother's hand in my

father's presence, congratulating her. I smile bitterly now, thinking of how inept I felt as a boy at that time, how distant I was from that glamorous woman who so often shook her head, looking at her son.

My father did give her the scope to realize some of

her professional dreams. And she did not always accede to his demands. She sympathized with his political ideals, but balked when he proposed buying property for her to manage. She refused to be a landlady. I recall him showing her a motel for sale at a bargain price in Nantasket, but she quashed that idea quickly.

Did my father really expect that several of her brothers who had become wealthy would finance some of his dreams of acquiring real estate? I am afraid so, for I remember him kicking the corners of buildings in downtown Boston and remarking on how cheaply he could have bought them with their help.

He was obviously jealous of the financial success of her brother David Lessler, to whom Mother had felt particularly close as a young girl. My uncle David also retained the striking good looks of a movie actor into middle age and my mother's admiration continued until his sudden, unexpected death. Our house was thrown into turmoil during the days between the heart attack on the tennis courts and his death. One of the few items added to her albums after she closed them just before my birth, was a clipping from a Connecticut newspaper about David Lessler's death in 1956.

None of the other brothers and sisters who died before her would have death notices preserved in the album. Uncle David had a certain sardonic sense of humor toward me. I recall him teasing me about having a "tail" when I was too old to be teased in this fashion but "Davey" was a particular favorite of my mother, and she felt very close to him. She was outraged when I shared my father's rather cool view of "Davey" and let me feel her anger when I did not immediately respond to her grief. In 2011, out of an old file found in my father's law office, I discovered a painful letter from my uncle to my father, in which he tries to explain why the fee my father thought his brother-in-law owed him, could not be paid. And Uncle David goes on to remonstrate my father, who could never forgive a slight within his own family, for the note that my mother must have sent to his wife Claire, at Dad's direction.

May 20, 1952

Dear Wilfred,

At first I was not even going to write to you but then I thought I would try once more to open your eyes to the Boston situation in which we were involved. You, apparently, have no conception as to the actual facts or otherwise Claire would not have received that unpleasantly cold note from Ruth, stating that, "as of now, the children and I will be at the confirmation."

My uncle goes on to give the details of a case in which meeting my father in the Boston District Court by chance, he invited him to participate. Evidently it turned into a "fiasco," since the parties involved and my uncle lost thousands of dollars in the course of a bankruptcy proceeding. Although my father had done some work on behalf of my uncle's clients, they felt it had been useless. But in any event, according to Davey's letter, they had no money. The anger I hear in my uncle's voice as he concludes is obvious.

I personally tried to salvage something out of these losses by having suit instituted against the parties responsible for the fiasco. I advanced $50.00 of my own money and sent it to you as a retainer to bring suit. You not only refused to bring suit and kept my money but refused to even answer my letters. I still intend to hold the parties responsible for the "fiasco" liable for the damages they caused.

If you still feel that these facts warrant you being disturbed, then there is nothing further that I can state. That's your privilege. It would appear to me, however, that you, of all people, certainly have no right to be disturbed.

I trust that this may clear up the picture. If it does not, just let's forget about it because there is nothing further that I care to add.

I see my uncle's side of the case, and I see just how sharp his tongue could be from an earlier case that he and my father were involved in (Davey writes, in April 1945, "I am glad that you woke up out of your sleep even though it is to ask me for a check and the original note, which I enclose ...") but I grieve in particular for the distress the rupture in 1952 had caused his sister, my mother, and how little I understood of it.

How was I to do so, when she had told me nothing about her feelings for Davey? Nor would she discuss her brother Bob. I only learned about his possible suicide in my late teens from cousins. To have asked my mother would have brought a look of outrage. Why do you want to know? Worse, it would have brought that look of suspicion, in which she regarded me as an interloper intent on soiling her memories. Her attitude of cold realism and yet her fierce guard of the idea of family, her brothers and sisters, recalls for me the observation of the poet, Charles Olson:

It would be poor Romanticism if it weren't good realism;
it would be poor realism if it weren't measured (measured so
at the End of the World) of Romanticism.

She was a romantic though I did not recognize it when she was alive as I fought off her hope that I would embrace a safer course, a conventional job, an equally conventional marriage with a girl who embodied the values of the Jewish middle class: become a son who would win the approval of her older sisters and brothers. And, of course, that I would provide children she could dote on. After her death I would fulfill some of those expectations but too late in the world to gratify her and receive a glint of the reflected approval.

Mother was kept alive through those last months of her life in particular by a young Irish nurse who meticulously turned her patient's body in the sheets to keep it from the plague of bedsores, carefully watched the administration of medications ordered by the doctors, adjusted and readjusted the fluid intake, intravenous feeding, and brought to the room a brisk but loving bedside manner that buoyed my mother's spirits and kept her hopeful. This attractive, always cheerful young nurse echoed in some ways the mother I remembered from childhood and so transformed the grey corridors of the Shattuck, its rooms of dying patients, restoring the ambience of a normal, well-endowed hospital with first-rate personal care.

The TV sets in the rooms were the basic staple of the Shattuck's entertainment and recreation for its inmates, the major link apart from visitors, and the only link for the unlucky and friendless with the world outside. As I was visiting on a Friday, April 5, to be exact, the aftermath of Martin Luther King's murder the day before was flashing on the screens. Riots had broken out in the poor, African American streets of Boston. Some of the worst of the burning and looting took place in Roxbury, streets we knew well since some lay in my father's old political district, Ward Fourteen. Police and firemen were stoned trying to drive in and put out the flames.

Boston was still an Irish city, and it was stunning to hear that a part of it was basically in rebellion against that hegemony. "I'm going to go

down and teach those people a lesson," the Irish nurse cried, outraged at the scenes of angry mobs, the senseless burning, as African Americans seemed to turn with the worst fury on their own property and possessions.

My mother's gravelly voice sounded from the bed where she too was fixed on the TV screen. "When I get out of this bed, I'm going to go down there and help those people." That was the voice of the young married woman who went off to help in the Great Ohio Flood. I saw her often when I was a boy, the smile of the girl in Ironton, beside a bicycle.

Chapter Eleven

How do I end this?

My mother's story does not end for me with her passing into another world, whatever that may be, but is part of my own passage
there. As I review all the documents, albums, and materials again and
again, her story changes. Even in the two photographs that begin and
end this chapter, obviously taken in the same place and on the same

day, the story to read on my mother's face and mine, changes. In the photograph above at twenty-two months, I stare warily into the camera, while my mother seems detached. I have no memories of myself at this age.

I used to think that my first memory was at three and a half, just before the birth of my sister, when I smacked my head against a tool chest, lost consciousness and my grandfather, Israel, rushed from the synagogue to comfort me. The baby book she kept about my first steps, words, books, experiences, opens up earlier pages in my life, some that I do or do not recall. She meticulously sets down the date my tonsils were extracted and that memory is still vivid.

The baby book confirms an even earlier memory—though its date depends on my recall, rather than Mother's notation. It happened sometime between October 1941 and June 1942, but the scene of being dragged from under my crib, screaming, because I did not want to go off to the nursery school on Wales Street has been vivid for the last seventy-three odd years.

[Under Nursery School in the Baby Book]

Date entered: Oct 1941 Jack & Jill
Wales Street
Teacher: Mrs. Goldman [Goldner?]

From Oct to June he "hated" it & cried & had to be bribed with lollipops daily. This was a necessary discipline as mother returned to work for the Red Cross during this time. Nov 1942. We entered him at Hecht House & here he "loved" it and went joyfully.

I noted in my journal as I read this entry a few days ago. "Yes, I remember that first nursery school, though I was only two years and two months when I was first dropped off there. I was dragged from under the crib in the southeast corner of the bedroom, in tears. Whether it was my mother, father, or some other adults (I have a hazy sense of more than one person and no recall of a lollipop) remains obscure—only the sense of a dingy, boring place, an unsympathetic person in charge, my mother deserting me, hours of loneliness with nothing and no one to play with. The Hecht House where I was sent the following autumn was basically the Jewish Community Center for Dorchester and Mattapan, I spent a lot of time there in later years, but retain only the sense of its nursery as having wide, sunny rooms and friendly playmates. When I entered the Hecht House I was already three years and three months old, and ready to entertain myself without my mother or another adult close by. I don't think I ever recovered though from being dumped for most of the day for almost a year at two years old, when I couldn't speak or read, in a strange place, with my mother, father, grandfather, nowhere in sight. I imagine that my mother's salary was a necessity as my father's law practice grew very slowly, but my sister's birth when I was three and a half, meant that my mother was home until I went off to kindergarten and that was a blessing, which I only understand now in retrospect." As I go back to check what Mother wrote about me in my baby book, I notice her exact list of everyone who came to see her in the New England Hospital in Roxbury where I was born. Most of her older sisters, brothers,

their children, who were within driving distance of the hospital, came to visit her. The list is interspersed with my father's family and my father and mother's friends, but the Lesslers make up a large number—though Mother does not distinguish between visitors to the hospital or the house. Only Celia, whose ill health was a family legend, and Davey, did not make the drive—though Mother notes that Davey and his wife sent greetings the next day on the list she made of everyone who

wrote or telegraphed. Her second oldest brother, Hyman (High), was in California.

The number of those who did make the trip to see her strikes me; especially her second oldest sister, Betty, to whose house in Bridgeport Ruth was sent at seven and eight, long before Annie Lessler's death, when Annie was still living in Brooklyn. Miriam too lived at Betty's and went to school from that address. It wasn't, as you have read, an entirely happy time for my mother. Her older sister, Betty, had her first child in 1917 and when my mother arrived in 1919, at seven years old, there was another baby in the house, Muriel. In her own mother's house, Ruth was already sandwiched in between Miriam, who needed her mother's attention since she was often sick, and Mildred, who was the youngest of them all. In that photograph of Annie with her grandchildren, Mildred is sticking to her side as the baby. Mildred remained the baby until Annie's death in 1925. It was Betty, however, who dispatched her fifteen-year-old daughter, Doris, in 1939 to help my mother in the days before my birth. Mother refers to it in her notations of the day on which she went to the hospital. *Went to hospital 9:00 in morning. Woke Father at 5:30 A.M. Doris did the timing. Painless.* And later on in my baby book, Mother proudly reports that Betty has given her the family bassinet. *Baby slept in the family bassinet. The 11th baby to sleep in it belonging to Aunt Betty who used it first for Anne ...* (I wonder who these babies were between Betty's fourth child, Anne, and me.)

Mother's oldest brother Simon, his wife Ruth, their children Abby and Arlene (whom I knew by her nickname, Cissy) came; so did Betty and her husband Dave Lesser. Their daughter Doris was already at Mother's bedside, but they brought the next youngest, Ann. The list is dizzying: Mother's brother Bob, his wife, Sara, their children Alan and Gloria; Mother's older sister Esther with her husband, Harold (in whose house my mother lived, when Annie's house on Savoy Street was sold after her death), their son, Arthur; Mother's older sister Dorothy, her husband, Will Cohen, their children Joel and Anne Lee; Mother's older brother Jules, his wife, Lillian, their son, Paul, and daughter, Ruth; my mother's closest sister Miriam, unmarried at that time. Sadie

Dinegott, Aunt Esther's closest friend, who lived in the Boston area with her husband visited as well.

I suspect that the twenty-six or so from my mother's family made up a majority of the visitors at the hospital. Mother records 28 visitors to her bedside in the hospital, 78 visitors to the house, and 150 to 200 at the *bris* or ritual circumcision. At that event a week later, my grandfather's position as the *shamus* at the Fowler Street Synagogue meant that the Mirsky side probably overwhelmed the guest list. His sister and her brood came down from Montreal, together with my grandfather's friends in the congregation whose faces appear in the photographs I have of the ceremony.

Why do I reproduce the visitors' list? It suggests just how much her brothers and sisters, as a group, loved her. Twenty-three Lesslers, possibly twenty-five, showed up though none of them lived in Boston. Mother was never very close to her younger sister Mildred, who is missing, and though she loved Celia's children, the daughters in particular, Shirley and Elaine, I don't recall many visits to Celia's house. Celia does not send greetings the next day, though her daughter Elaine joins Arthur and Jerry, Esther's children, in doing so. Mother's brother Davey and his wife Claire send greetings but are not among the visitors. The quarrel I referred to in the chapter preceding, however, was in the future. Did Uncle Davey and my father always eye each other warily? Whereas there was tension between my father and the other lawyer in the family, Will Cohen, her sister Dorothy's husband, Aunt Dorothy and my mother were too close for my father's grumbling to be taken seriously. Aunt Claire, on the other hand, seemed to remain aloof. When I visited her shortly before her death, I found a charming, very funny woman, whose first language was Yiddish. Did my father know that? It might have brought our two families closer. One of the photographs Mother preserved was of her visit to Davey and Claire in 1932. And Davey, who sent my father a case in 1945, was obviously trying to help him out when he invited him to join the case that became a "fiasco." Davey had been my grandmother's right hand, when it came to real estate dealings. He had a brilliant career as a lawyer and some of his cases, his son Stanley, told me, established Connecticut state law. Davey had watched over his father, Joseph Lessler, caring for him right to the end. Davey and my mother were the only two of the brothers and sisters to go to college. My mother didn't just admire her brother Davey. When she talked about him, one felt both love and loyalty, a share of the "adoration," usually reserved for my father. Without the moustache, as I remember him, he looked like Cary Grant, and I suspect all his younger sisters had a crush on him.

When Davey's letter, quoted in the previous chapter, fell out of the folder of my father's casework with his brother-in-law, I was ashamed. I understood my father's point of view and knew how generous he usually was. When Mother's brother Jules came to Boston, he slept on our couch and Dad would call his contacts in the Boston retail world, trying to open doors for whatever products Jules was selling. When Jules got into an altercation with a traffic policeman in western Massachusetts and was thrown in jail, my father called judges, the head of the state police, the governor's office, to get Jules out. Our summer cottage was open to Miriam, her husband and children for extended stays, to Jules' family, any and all of them who came by. All my mother's nephews and nieces were treated by Dad as close family. Whatever the tensions between Davey and himself, I wish my father had repaired the breach, despite whatever condescension he felt from a brother-in-law, who was more successful than Dad was financially and with a reputation as a lawyer's lawyer.

I wish this reconciliation had happened, for it would have prevented me from hurting my mother. When the news came that Davey had suffered a heart attack and it was not clear at first whether he would survive or not, my mother's distress was visible. I made some idiotic and smart remark, inappropriate to the moment, and she flashed at me with an unexpected anger so hot and violent, I understood that I had crossed a line. For days the house was tense with the pain that she felt as she retreated into a silence that none of us could penetrate.

Looking back I wonder why I didn't ask her about Davey and what he had meant to her. Why was I so insensitive to her?

Mother was surrounded by her family throughout her life and when her sisters and brothers began to die one by one, she could not hide the wolf cub eating at her. It was perhaps the first time she turned to me to ask a favor—when one more brother passed away, she wanted someone to go down with her on the train to Bridgeport where he would be buried.

Despite her obvious affection for her brothers and sisters, my mother's attitude toward her family must have masked conflicting emotions. She felt like an orphan in childhood—the sisters were not her mother, but rivals for attention, and after Annie's death, the older ones had families of their own, and the brothers soon had wives. In marrying my father she entered a very different world than the glittering F. Scott Fitzgerald world of mansions and fancy cars traversed by the wealthier of her siblings, or the less romantic world of those who struggled on salesmen's salaries. (I wasn't alone in this—my cousin Margie wrote to me once about feeling the Lessler obsession with material things.) My father was a public figure, an intellectual, someone at home in the world of books, and, in a way, a throwback to the religious world of the Kurlands to whom Orthodox Judaism was a way of life. Dad was more of an Eastern European than an American, despite his Harvard degrees. He was a bit of a snob about the latter. I grew up influenced by his values and condescended too often to my mother, who never had a chance to gain his sophisticated level of education. Mother was born into a shift in the sociology of America's industrial revolution that changed the way siblings related to each other, as education, culture, wealth separated them despite their common desire to be close to each other.

The story of the Lesslers is also the American story of how families slowly grew apart. Some siblings succeeded and others struggled between the 1920's through the 1950's. (If one followed it through to the next generation, the tales of my cousins would have many bizarre turns of fate.) My father, however, was always dreaming of how his brother-in-laws would help make his fortune. We would walk around Boston in the early fifties, when real estate was beginning to revive, and he would kick the granite walls of sturdy office buildings of ten, fifteen floors. "I could have bought this for nothing," Dad would growl, "If your uncles had helped me out." Aunt Esther's son, Arthur, told me that his mother had approached her brothers to help finance the purchase of land at the edge of Bridgeport that would have rewarded her handsomely but had been turned down. The days when Annie had directed her children to cooperate were over. After her death, High, Simon, Jules and Bob broke up their business partnerships and went their separate ways. When Bob died, however, the brothers and sisters all contributed to a fund, its records meticulously kept, according to my cousin Arthur Nishball, by Miriam, then Esther Nishball, so that Bob's son Alan could go to college. My mother was close to all of them. Since her oldest brother, Simon, was in Providence we went there almost every Passover and Thanksgiving, which were our major family holidays. When my father ran for state representative, Simon and his wife came up to lend a hand on election days. My mother never talked about Simon, what kind of a brother he had been, or even what she thought of him. Quiet, reserved, like his wife, my Aunt Ruth, I have no idea who he was or what he thought. I imagine I was just as much a puzzle to him. Once, when they came up to visit my parents I was given a choice, a pair of new roller skates, or tickets to Gilbert and Sullivan's *Iolanthe*. They expected me to embrace the roller skates but an operetta was more desirable to a boy who lived in dreams of the theater. Shaking their heads at me, my aunt and uncle surrendered the skates and I got to see *Iolanthe* as well. My mother often "dumped" me at their house for a week when she went off with my father for a vacation. My older cousin Cissy, their middle daughter, could sometimes be cajoled to take me along in her adventures, but apart from a tricycle there was little for a boy to play with. Now I understand how generous Simon and his wife were to his younger sister, my mother, as well as to my sister and me. At the time I could only feel the boredom of a boy in a house of girls. Criticism of our manners seemed to radiate from the Lesslers towards me, and Mother often seemed to be in league with their head shaking.

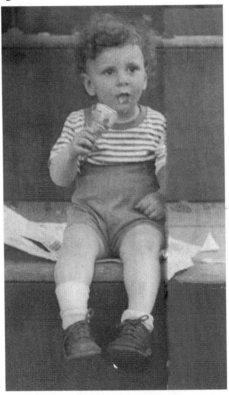

"His drawings are pretty unintelligible." Mother's observation in my baby book has just the note of sarcasm in it that I well recall. Was she hoping for a genius like my father? Her remark about an IQ of 200, while I was still just a few months old but wildly waving my arms around in the crib would suggest it. I appear above, April 1941, at twenty months, with Einstein's curls, but already fading as a possible prodigy.

It strikes me now that in the first image I have of my mother, that profile of her in a newspaper clipping in a play at Bridgeport High School she is in costume, acting. In many of the images in her album, I sense that she is playing a role, trying on a persona or hiding in one, concealing what she feels. Not in all of them, certainly, but the anger I so often saw on her face in person—the wary, suspicious look—was rarely shown to the camera. Instead, the cultivated cool abstraction of her graduation photograph, or the smiling, competent social worker, the poised wife of the candidate, often faces the public lens. This was a face I knew well at home, where she also felt she had to play a part in front of me and my sister. I always thought I had inherited my love of theater, of living in the characters I played in high school and college, from my father. I never, though, thought Dad "acted," in the sense that he presented to me or others anyone but himself. He was boisterous, loved to tell stories, was a witty speaker in the Massachusetts legislature, but in the hundreds of photographs I have of him, whether he is with the governors of Massachusetts he served under, or holding me or my sister, the face is the same. I never see him there playing a role. I don't recall him evading a question. He volunteered information, particularly of his childhood, of political life, and of what he believed, that he might well have kept quiet about. Asked a question, "Do you believe in God?" or "Did you resent your father leaving when you were five years old?" he answered immediately and was straightforward.

In her family, my mother learned to act, and yet I also see her in many of these photographs, naked, vulnerable, and joyous. She is a riddle. Telling my father's story, in the main, is to go through the drama of what he lived through and what he accomplished. I listened to him as he thought about himself—and allowed me to share his introspection. Only at the end did my mother put aside her role, public and private, to look at me and allow me a glance at her.

To be truthful about my mother I have to share painful truths about myself. Take that young woman who was not Jewish that I dated for the four years before my mother's death. My mother's godson, Michael Pozen, who was Miriam's son and one of my mother's favorite nephews, had married a young woman, Janet, who converted to Judaism. In a way that marriage broke the ice for my mother, who was keenly aware of her family's judgments. My father told me after my mother's death that my mother was afraid that my girlfriend was not strong enough for me, but Mother never mentioned that to me. I promised my sister long ago not to talk about her in my writing, but my sister's marriage to her husband, who would convert to Judaism but only after they divorced many years later, shook my mother. They were married, however, by a reform rabbi under the traditional Jewish wedding canopy in a ceremony at the Signet Club, a society at Harvard to which both my brother-in-law and I belonged. My mother was a meticulous driver but she evidently crashed our car a few days before the wedding. After my mother's death, and the period of mourning, I split up with the girl I had been dating by then for six years. We both needed different partners. Looking back, I think I wanted a person who might more closely resemble my mother.

I met my wife some months after I left the young woman I have just spoken about. We spent a long time getting to know each other before we married—almost nine years. She also came from another world, born in a small fishing town off the coast of Norway, and then spending her childhood and young adulthood in a slightly larger town two hundred miles north of the Arctic Circle. She would convert before our marriage and with me live a life of Sabbath observance, adhering to a form of Modern Orthodoxy. I have often tried to explain my sense of religion to my daughter, who we sent to a traditional Jewish school with a double curriculum in Hebrew and English. She is still smarting from what she felt was the hypocrisy she witnessed there while growing up within its walls. I thought of my Judaism as inherited from my father and grandfather, but now as I reflect back upon it all, I think it was my mother more than anyone who made me religious. Her influence, however, spoke without words.

Her silence enforced the sense that some invisible border would be crossed if I did not marry within the tribe—not that she would turn her back on me. She drew my sister's husband into the care and concern that she showed to her own children and tried to keep her new son-in-law happy, delighting as well in her new grandchildren without the shadow of a reservation. Only she indicated to me, not by saying anything but by *not* saying certain things I might have hoped for, *not* smiling, keeping her reserve when we were together, that if I went ahead and married someone who was not Jewish, I would be leaving something of her behind. I didn't feel that from my father—despite his very deep and specific knowledge of the details of Orthodox Judaism. He was fascinated by the new worlds in America that he encountered as an immigrant, although he was a proud and loyal Jew. It was from my mother that I felt the long line of ancestors to whom I was anchored through her, and whom I would lose if I cut those ties for myself and my children.

There is a further twist to this riddle. Going back to the documents of my mother's life, over and over, each time I discover new secrets. I wrote to one of my students, that since her family for the most part is still alive, documents couldn't possess this uncanny dimension since the principals can speak for themselves. Once they are no longer with us, what they have written, the images they have left behind, become the sole custodians, apart from our memories or the memories of those who knew them, of their secrets. Materials of their lives come to life in a way they cannot as long as the living are still here to deny or forbid what they have said.

So the memory of "The Gate" a play my mother wrote that is described in her 1928 Bridgeport High yearbook *The Criterion* comes to mind. I vaguely recall the plot of the play from a copy that I once found as a teenager on my mother's shelves, a copy that has since disappeared. *The Criterion* happily gives some details. A Jewish girl, Esther Jaffe, becomes involved with a gentile sister and brother, Maria and Josef, who live outside an eighteenth-century ghetto in the Austrian Empire. Inevitably in her friendship or romance, Esther finds herself locked out of the ghetto where she lives with her father, Abraham. These are the only characters mentioned in the program of the play's production at the high school, apart from two guards and peasants. The stage in *The Criterion's* photograph is a representation of a ghetto gate in a city in Austria, a handsome merchant's stone house just outside, guards in colorful military costumes, and a Jewish girl in the mid-eighteenth-century costume of Marie Theresa's reign, kneeling outside the locked gate. It awoke no curiosity in me since I was reading it without understanding my mother, Ruth Lessler. After weighing the effect on Ruth of her mother's death just three years earlier, it strikes me first of all that there is no mother present among its characters. Nor was the religious intolerance of the Hapsburg empress of Austria and its reflection in the social life of the countries the Austrian empress ruled what drew my mother to the plot or her characters. My mother was wondering whether a life outside the Jewish world she was born into was possible, outside the "gate." Daring herself to dream it! I found the plot described in a newspaper clipping from the Bridgeport papers. "Esther, being a Jew, must remain within a prescribed area of the city, and wears a yellow badge as a token of her degradation. Joseph pities her and plans to flee with her rather than have her endure any longer the unjust persecution.

"He bribes the guards at the gate to let Esther out when he returns. The guards agree to the proposal but are later bribed by Joseph's sister, who hates Esther. The guards are told to arrest the Jewess when she attempts to escape. Joseph returns and as Esther goes up to meet him, the guards arrest her. Rather than go back to the old life, Esther dies." It seems as if Ruth, at sixteen, sadly concluded that her answer to the question of whether she could escape her life within a Jewish world was no, but until Mother married I suspect that it kept recurring in her head. (Very much under the thumb of her older sisters, at this point in Mother's life, the fact that it is Joseph's sister who betrays her has a certain sting to it as well.)

"THE GATE." BY RUTH LESSLER

In the years after my mother passed away, the Lessler family of twelve brothers and sisters not only spread out across the United States, but their children dispersed across the world, married not only into the American religious mainstream white Protestant and Catholic, but also into Japanese, Greek, and African American worlds. Some of her nephews and their children went to jail (though not for violent crimes), while others became doctors, scientists, journalists. One has risen to the high circles of finance and the American government, advising a President of the United States. Whatever frustrations Mother had with her older sisters, their children were like brothers and sisters to her. I can feel her joy in them brimming from this photograph taken somewhere at the beginning of the 1930s with Muriel, Betty's second oldest.

Look how radiant she is with her niece—I saw that Ruth Sylvia too and the smile I directed to her from my sandbox, reflects it.

"Who am I, what am I, where am I?"

I wake up in bed at seventy-three, reciting this mantra, then thinking, I hurt her.

How many times did I wipe the smile that she has in the photograph above from her face. Whatever she felt as a little girl in her older sister's house, as she grew older she regarded her nieces as a nest of younger sisters. She wanted to see me happily married in the midst of a large family like the one she had grown up in. She wanted grandchildren. My sister gave her two, but I waited and waited. My father would live to see my son, named after his grandfather. Why Mother's name in English diverged from her name in Hebrew is one of the mysteries that my search has not revealed. How did my father know that she should be mourned as "Rochel" or Rachel? Had he learned it from her or from another member of her family? Who first called the baby "Ruth" that her birth certificate named only "Sylvia"? Had my mother renamed herself? Who chose the persona of Ruth?

"You will miss her more than me," my father told me a few weeks after her death. He quickly fell in love with his twenty-three-year-old secretary, though that lasted only a year or so. My father never recovered from my mother's death. Through the succession of widows more appropriate, perhaps, to his age, that Dad dated until he passed away thirteen and a half years later, he never found anyone who could remotely return the loyalty she showed. Neither I nor my sister resented any of them. We wanted him to have a good life and the memory of the love my mother had given all of us, the sense of them as a couple, was so strong that I think we knew she could not be replaced.

After she died, I realized how little I had known her, and I began to search for her among her remaining sisters and my older cousins.

Aunt Dorothy and Aunt Miriam both welcomed my questions and talked to me at length about their younger sister and the family. Without them I could not have reconstructed much outside of the albums Mother left and the census and birth records.

When I began to circulate at family weddings, or visit my aunts and cousins, with a notebook or a tape recorder, Aunt Esther, the family censor, who let me know that she disapproved of the language in my books, scolded me publicly, issuing the dictum, "Don't talk to Mark Mirsky." Dorothy and Miriam were still apt to remark, "Don't tell Esther," as the lifelong habit of looking over their shoulders for their elder sister's approval never changed. I am sure that my mother felt the same way, and Esther's headshaking over my first book, which was published while Mother was alive, must have hurt her. It didn't stop my mother from talking about the book in the corridors of the Shattuck Hospital through the very last months and trying to promote it to nurses, doctors and patients, but it must have robbed her of some of the satisfaction she felt in seeing her son's name on its cover. Many things about me must have brought that sour shake of the head from Esther, whose opinion meant so much to Mother.

After my marriage, however, the birth of my son, something changed. I would always stop in Bridgeport on the way up to Boston to see Aunt Miriam. My mother had been the godmother of her oldest son, Michael, and though Miriam was much more reserved than my mother, I felt under the impassive face, an unmistakable sweetness for me. I could show up on my motorcycle, my hair tumbling from under my helmet in my early twenties, and she would open the freezer, pull out a steak and insist that I sit down and have a good meal before I rode on. With the baby in tow, I thought I would try Esther as well, and to my surprise, I saw a smile spread across her face at the front door.

Esther took the baby, my son Israel, from my wife's arms and hugged him. She beamed and I felt that my mother was smiling too and that I had won at least a measure of forgiveness.

When my father died, in the coldest Massachusetts winter of twenty years, it was Esther, alone of my mother's family who would make the trip up for the funeral and stand in the freezing graveyard, to see him buried. Then too, I felt the bond between my mother and Esther, and that the anger and reserve concealed a well of affection too deep for easy words. The family secrets for both of them were too painful to want to recall, shameful and even dangerous, best left unsaid.

If I hurt my mother, so did my father.

After I was born, my mother did not end her career as a social worker as she wryly implied in her album above the newspaper clipping about her position as a professional in Boston. It was my sister's birth, I imagine, followed by the sudden death of my grandfather, who was always delighted to have me about, that probably anchored her to our house. Every two years, from 1946 on, as my father's unofficial campaign manager from the Democratic primary until Election Day, she spent hours calling every registered voter in Ward Fourteen, filling envelopes, and entertaining the volunteers. In the late forties, as the photograph with Governor Dever, shows, she was still looking young and radiant, her energy intact. Eleven years later, my father, disappointed that the sitting governor's promise of a judgeship if Dad did not run for re-election would not be fulfilled, asked my mother to take what he had been offered—a position on the Industrial Accident Board. It came with the title of "Commissioner." My mother did not want to take the post, but my mother and father understood that once out of the House of Representatives, his law business would suffer. I was in college and my sister was soon to go; our family needed the income. "I don't know law," my mother protested.

"You were a professional social worker," my father countered. "That's even more valuable as a commissioner of industrial accidents. I'll teach you all the law you need." On the occasional long ride that I took with my mother and father, as she took up that position, I remember my father tutoring her. Her decisions on appeal went directly to the Massachusetts Supreme Court so that the commissioner's legal standing was equivalent to a justice of the Superior Court. "She never had a single decision overturned," my father would boast. Still, one can't help contrasting her photograph with Governor Dever and my father, ten years before, where she exudes glamour as an unpaid commissioner, and this one below of her being sworn into her seat on the Industrial Accident Board, in 1968 but not by the governor. I can read the careworn lines of her face, and observe that her clothes are almost dowdy. It is my father who is beaming.

It was true though that she mastered what she needed to know almost overnight and her work won her the respect of almost everyone

who had to deal with her. Unfortunately, while my father had agreed to give up his seat in the Massachusetts legislature in return for the appointment, since he was known as a thorn in the side of his colleagues, he still dreamed of a political career. My mother, my sister, and I all knew that it was hopeless. The middle-class voters who had sent him into office were streaming out of the streets of Mattapan, Dorchester, and Roxbury for wealthier suburbs. His students from Hebrew school had all moved away, no longer available as volunteers. He didn't have the campaign funds to mount a proper battle for the state senator's seat, or the governor's council, the two spots that a Jewish candidate in the ethnic geography of Boston in the 1960s could win. There was no chance that as a Jew he could win enough votes to get on the Boston City Council since the elections were citywide. At that moment in time, even the large Italian population barely put one of their own on the council. My mother became not just his campaign manager while she had the responsibilities on the Industrial Accident Board, she also found herself as one of the few workers participating in these futile attempts at getting elected. At the same time, the income from my father's law practice was disappearing. My father had always been eccentric, but when we tried to talk to him about it, he became irrational. I was happy to flee the house, and go to Manhattan, looking for a life out of the shadows of my family's problems.

I don't blame my father, but I can't discount the toll that all of this took on my mother. My sister told me that when my mother's term of office was over at the Industrial Accident Board, she was offered positions with several of the insurance firms who had appeared before her as a commissioner. She refused because she felt that her empathy would always be with the workers who were injured, not with the companies trying to scale down payments. She never spoke of it to me. My father never mentioned it, which means that he must have accepted it, despite their financially tightened circumstances.

I cared about what she thought, but except in that one moment at my aunt Hilda's, where Mother's shocked face revealed how hurt she was not just by the rudeness of Hilda's calling her "obtuse" when my father and I didn't rise to defend her, I don't think I was ever aware of how she might "feel" as a person. I tended to say whatever came to mind and never look back. She was my mother, someone I simply could "take for granted" or "depend on," even though I trembled at the judgment in her voice.

During her illness, we would finally put aside our differences and try to get to know one another, to let each other feel how much we did love each other in the final months when we both knew our time together was rushing toward an end. Thinking back, even before then I felt tremors. I remember when I first came to Manhattan, going together with my parents to a Lessler affair out on Long Island, one that had taken up most of the morning and early afternoon. We left at about three or four. It was the summertime, and the light was still bright. My father decided, since we were near the Rockaways, to visit his mother's cousin Etta, who was still alive in her nineties. We drove into a charming street of beach bungalows and wooden sidewalks hovering over sand. I wish I could find that world again (hurricanes and urban renewal have washed it away), just a few yards from the waves of the Atlantic. It had the magic of a lost ocean-side world. It was the perfect place for a writer to lose himself. Etta, a tall, white-haired woman, remarkably poised, remembered my grandfather Israel and talked about his beautiful voice, how elegantly he recited the *kid-dush* over wine. My father decided, since he was already in Brooklyn, to visit his mother's grave. My mother was tired, angry that her day with her sisters, nieces and nephews was being turned at this late hour into my father's day with the living and dead of his family. More than that, I sensed for the first time that she resented my constant curiosity about my father's family. Again though, rather than speaking about her own, she just let her irritation register. I ought to have sensed that she wanted attention, needed it, known how to ask about her family and drawn her out. I didn't, and now only the sadness of that trip remains. I had, again, hurt her.

If the smile vanished for me through any stretch of years, it would have been my adolescence. At first she tried to help, realizing that I was awkward, scratching at my face, becoming desperate. I was becoming an angry creature in a novel of Dostoyevsky. My mother couldn't follow me there. The last book that we shared was Thomas Wolfe's *Look Homeward, Angel,* but after that nothing on her shelf touched me—Somerset Maugham's *Of Human Bondage*, or Wallace Stegner's *The Big Rock Candy Mountain*. Increasingly, Mother realized that she had a dangerous boy on her hands, self-destructive, ready to experiment with girls, which offended her straight-and-narrow sense of sexual experience. She was an apt detective and could follow the clues I left behind and come up with the story of what had happened. This sense of distance intensified in college. I took a girl out to our beach house without asking permission, lost the car keys and my parents had to come and retrieve us. Her icy stare left the girl in a state of shock and I was too embarrassed to apologize properly. She opened my bedroom door, inopportunely for me, one day and discovered me naked with the young woman I was courting at the time. A tempestuous love affair with another young woman with whom I was trying to maintain a connection, while she was still in school at Radcliffe in Cambridge, while I was at Stanford in graduate school, meant phone bills of hundreds of dollars that I had to ask my parents to pay. Adding insult to injury, when I twice flew back to Boston that year, I bypassed my parents' house to see the young woman, spending only a day with my mother and father. They had paid for the tickets. I could feel how hurt they were but self-obsessed I brushed remorse aside. My mother wanted to talk to me but neither of us knew how to initiate that conversation. I could listen appreciatively to my father's stories of his childhood, of his time in the legislature, his political opinions …

But Mother's stories …? Aunt Dorothy was the storyteller and she had lots of sharp anecdotes. "Esther used to have her clothes made by a tailor … she had a gorgeous coat with a beaver collar, and a light-tan fabric, a winter coat. My mother said, 'That's nice. Would you like one? Dotty?'

" 'Sure.'

"So my mother took her coat with us and we owned a house on Penn Street where there was a tailor. She said, 'Copy this coat.' She made the same coat for me. Well, was my sister furious."

"Were you religious in your family?" I asked.

"I used to go the *shul* with my mother every Saturday morning."

"Did all the children go?"

" ... No, they didn't go. Nobody else! Esther said she was an atheist. Esther used to be fresh at times with my mother. My mother said, 'Wait, when you have children, you won't be so fresh.' Esther was an accountant for a big dry goods firm. Even when we moved to Bridgeport, she still used to come to New York. My mother kept saying she would marry ... Dorothy Levy, because that was her best friend. She never went out with any men ..."

And again, Annie's skill rose to her lips. "My mother sewed beautifully. She used to come home at night from business and make draperies, sew shirts for the boys, and slips, petticoats for us, and dresses. She used to be able to walk on Fifth Avenue, take a copy of a dress in the window, and come home and take newspapers, and cut out the patterns and make the same dress."

Celia's daughter, my cousin Shirley, another storyteller, recalls Annie's skill. "My mother in those days had migraines—all the time ... She would call and say I'm sick and my grandma would come over to watch me while she lay down ... And while my mother was sleeping, my grandma Annie would take a newspaper, and put it over my head and measure it, and mark it out. [She] had some fabric with her. And by the time my mother got up, I had a new dress." Aunt Dorothy's tale of her grandmother's kitchen takes me back to the family at the beginning of the last century. "The two sets of grandparents were called the *geller zaider* [blond grandfather] and *shvartzer zeider* [black grandfather] ... the other grandmother [Sarah] had black hair but her husband Michael Aaron had blond hair and blue eyes... Betty and Esther tell this story, how they went to visit the grandmother in Manhattan, when they were living in Manhattan. And the grandma wasn't home. And they saw a big pot, a tub of borscht on the fire. And somehow, accidently, they went to look at the borscht, and they turned the whole borscht over on the floor. So Betty and Esther, or Betty and Celia, whoever it was, took rags and they mopped it and they put it back into the pot. [Laughter] They put the borscht, as much as they could, back in the pot. And when the grandma came home, she said, '*Kindelach, Kindelach*, I have some delicious borscht for you.' She knew they loved borscht. She peeled potatoes to make it. And she couldn't understand why didn't eat the borscht." Dotty had a treasury of tales; Annie's gradual acceptance of Willy Cohen, the darker moments of his family—it still surprises me that she would have entrusted such stories to my keeping. She was, however, a formidable aunt. In my early thirties she kept asking whether I was or was not coming to one of grandchildren's bar mitzvahs on Long Island. Despite persistent telephone calls from early March to late May, I put her off. "Mark, the plates cost fifty dollars a setting; are you coming or not?" "I don't know yet, Aunt …"

At the beginning of June she announced sternly, "Right now, yes or no."

"Okay, I guess then, it has to be 'no.' "

A long shocked pause. "No?"

"No," I repeated sadly. I would be up in Massachusetts.

Another pause, and then a furious cry, "You no good son of a … You wrote those disgusting things about our family …"

"Aunt Dotty, you read my book?" [*My Search for the Messiah.*]

"You …"

"Aunt Dotty, I'm coming."

And I did, arriving with my girlfriend on a motorcycle to an enthusiastic welcome.

I have only a small legacy of stories from Dorothy about her sister Ruth. I also have Mother's letters; the way she signs several of them, love, love, love—leans over a letter of my father's to add it as well, as if she cannot hold back a rush of affection, and after dealing with that health crisis brought on by my sexual life, the generous remarks about sending out an SOS; these give me a glimpse of who she was. There are sentences that brought me satisfaction at the time, but whose deeper significance escaped me. In particular when Mother thanked me for sharing details of my life with her, and in one note, offered a critical response to a story of I. B. Singer's, as if to say that she did want to share something of my literary imagination … It is painful to read over these letters, to see the opportunities for intimacy I missed.

June 18, 1960 postmark Mark Jay Mirsky c/o Provincetown Playhouse:

Perhaps thru writing we can communicate and share your joys and problems without such feelings of annoyance when we are face to face ...

September 1, 1960

It was good to hear from you. Reading between the lines –I realize you are steadily, more & more, on your own—in a way we miss the old S.O.S. calls ... "

Long live your shaven face and short hair cut!! I'll weep no more!!

Love Love Love

Early spring of 1962, she writes to me at Stanford University, Palo Alto, CA

Dear Son:—

Your letters sound suspiciously lonely—or have you mellowed so that your bellows have become soft chidings. I suppose with so many miles apart, it[']s hard to rant in your old way—for C—sake. I'll visit whom I please—& stop being so petty about duplicate books!! Anyway, it's a new role, and I like it—particularly after I had scolded Didi for not writing home ... The warmth of your letters, your allowing us to share in some of your activities & your problems, really makes the day a happy one for us—I don't want to sound maudlin—but just to let you know we appreciate your loving letters ...

Now that I'm back to the grind again, my reading has been curtailed. I was half through The Power and the Glory by G. Greene and had finished Singer's book, The Magician of Lublin. Dad has also read the book. I think the author has a good insight into the local customs and feelings of his characters, his style was simple and interest building and the plot of the story realistic and humanistic—all is not gold that glitters—so far as awe of people's possessions & status in life. Yet despite the feeling that the magician has of muddling up people's lives about him by his role in their lives, these people would have come to some such ends in any event by their natures. And by nature the magician was really a philosopher & student and so eventually turned for that advice to religion!

Well it's now 2 A M Boston time Sunday nite [sic] and time to retire.

She was trying to catch up now, and read texts that interested me. She was asking a serious question that Singer had left unresolved—did my father's and the novelist's fascination with Spinoza, with philosophy, in fact have answers to the practical questions of life and death? Did they lie instead, as she suspected, in the realm of religion? How did I respond? I am afraid to look in those letters of mine that she carefully arranged, predicting an important career. She wrote on March of 1965 when her term as commissioner was over and my father's law practice was producing little income. At the end of the letter her anxiety shows. "One never knows when a big case can come his way. However for the first time we have to draw from savings to pay our income tax."

Mother began this letter (a piece of which I quoted before) like a novelist, the cold Boston winter lingering: "*The day is damp and a wet snow is falling.*" My father has not returned from court where he was "*defending a Russian whose Ukrainian wife left his bed & board & wants $60 a wk when the man only earns $67. Dad is not expected back until 2 so I am amusing myself by chronologically assorting your letters from California to your service days—thru Woodstock [N.Y. at the Playhouse] & N.Y. The story of your life—and your changing attitudes toward the world & women—. When you are ready to write an autobiography—or become that famous that some other writer wants to know of your life & background, these letters will serve to help the world know you. Some of your sentiments, you would hardly recognize yourself.*"

Only in these letters did we seem to go back and forth outside the framework of disapproval. In her albums, a photograph catches my attention underneath which her neat handwriting has inscribed my age. I suspect it was snapped on a bench in Franklin Park, just a few minutes after the one that began this chapter. The park was a brief ten-minute walk up from our front door in Dorchester. A small paradise for a child, despite the challenge of climbing the incline of Glenway, the steep street that led to its gates from our doorstep, the park housed a zoo, and acres of lawn, puddingstone caves, a small pond, a refectory with a cafeteria, abandoned, ghost-ridden buildings. A masterpiece of landscape architecture by Fredrick Law Olmsted, for most Bostonians Franklin Park remains to this day a misunderstood puzzle, just a zoo and a golf course. I've written a cover story in the *Boston Sunday Globe* about the park, set several stories in it, and a novel *Puddingstone* whose title was meant to have *Franklin Park.* before it. To find myself as a child in a place that still holds the charm of the biblical Eden, held tight by my mother seemed to roll back time. I see that in this second photograph my mother has come forward from her abstracted mood a moment before and flashed that smile, which always overwhelmed me in its sunny joy. The smile, however, is for the camera (wielded probably by my father's Harvard classmate and friend, Bill Sharp) not for me. My inquisitive look has faded and I have retreated into my own thoughts, possibly angry that I am being posed. We have missed each other's mood.

I had so many questions to ask of her, questions that only she had the answer to. Above all there is one that I find often on my lips, "What do you see of you in me?"

MARK JAY MIRSKY'S REVIEWS

"A joy bringer. Mirsky writes his head off ... An authentic inventor ..."
The New York Times, Sunday Book Review

Recent Publications

Puddingstone, Golem Books (2014)

But here is joy, and its name is *Puddingstone,* and its miraculous-mercurial voice is Mirsky, pure dervish-dancing antic exuberant erudite Mirsky! Mirsky who can take on a Boston Irish (hooligan-kid) idiom, or burst into a lyrical force, or an acrobatic comic tumble—and suddenly out flies a great flowing, flaming, breathing, kabbalistically panting poem! Viz.: "In a night crisscrossed with falling stars, of girls, trembling in the cups of their undergarments, sitting and rising and sitting again, I heard of the captivation of the Holy One, in the guise of a female, through a flaw, a crack, a holy infinitesimal spirit that widened out from its hair's breadth at the moment of creation until it assumed the dimensions of a flaw, an independent existence ..." (Ah, what would I give to have been the author of "girls, trembling in the cups of their undergarments"! Not even *shir hashirim* can do better than that.)

Thank you, holy-unholy Maishe, for putting me in possession of this book-like-no-other.
Cynthia Ozick

The energy of the language alone should be enough to carry any reader—then beyond that the marvelous intelligence and imagination, the very acute ear for dialogue, the medley of voices and range of characterization, the wildly inventive episodes, plus the breadth of learning you bring to bear on each of the narrative movements—all amounts to a great rich smorgasbord of a novel. Really, what's not to like? It's a distinguished book ... and a scandal that it wasn't picked up by Knopf et al.

Steve Stern

Framed by, I believe, a faith and haunted by some imminence or chance of a Jewish Messiah, the melee of Mark Mirsky's multi-ethnic Boston made up out of what he knows inimitably well explodes at us in *Puddingstone*. Named after layers of geologic past and present. Rabelaisian in its collision of intellect and bodily function and American in its freedom of vivid population and language, its anarchy is original, tightly plotted, and alive. In fact, has there ever been such a novel about the other Boston? Particular in its neighborhoods, real and in relentless motion, an un-genteel Boston that has been there a while emerges novel and surprising. The voice seems to expand, to reach into other identities contained by visions sometimes esoteric in intricacy, poignant in passion, telling a crowded tale too dangerous and disconsolate to be only comic ...

Mirsky's mob roams our fantasies and settles along the arc and flare of his art, which is not only of words but draws richly taut between theater and thought, the dross and the angelic, fragments and their embrace at times suggesting our tipping national disorder, and somewhere also a "hidden universe" believed in as if God said, You would not seek me if you had not found me.

Joseph McElroy

Other Fiction Reviews

Thou Worm Jacob, Macmillan (1967)

One of the old, rude, joyous storytellers come newly to life. In *Thou Worm Jacob*, his Jews—the ten saddest Jews in the environs of Boston—are created with humor, pride, despair, and a kind of ancient love. To me, the book is amazing.
   John Hawkes

Your strange eloquence is beautifully sustained through one weird history after another, your humor seems to me uniquely right, you never make a false move as far as I can see; and the greatest impression the whole thing makes on my mind is of piety—piety about the past, and about the passing of things, that is unsentimental and poetically just.
   Howard Nemerov

Mark Mirsky is a miracle worker. He has the tears of comedy, the laughter of tragedy, and the speaking voice of life—all in a stylization that lets us know instantly we are in the presence of a great teller of tales. I hope never to miss a word he writes.
   John Ciardi

Here is a book above the ephemera of best sellers. I say, long may it be read!
   Francis Russell, *Christian Science Monitor*

Thou Worm Jacob is a pure comic novel with a serious communiqué from the author, in which he laments the passing of the old-world, and other-worldly, Jew. Not other-worldly in the sense of despising money and what it can buy and do for you, but in the sense of a timeless and spaceless cultural inheritance whose last shards huddle together—ringed about by the Shvartza (Negro) and Irish Goyim (Christians)—on Blue Hill Avenue …
   Anne Bernays, *Boston Sunday Globe*

This first novel is an exploding star of talent, nostalgia and comedy.
Los Angeles Times

Proceedings of the Rabble, Bobbs-Merrill (1971)

Mirsky piles public outrage on private injustice; satirizes America as a gathering of vermin and takes his title from the Olympian rat, Jonathan Swift, the man who was "so enormously satisfied with the procedure of human things," that he thought of preparing "A Modest Defense of the Proceedings of the Rabble in All Ages." Mirsky's defense is a cheer for politics, our national psychodrama where everyone has fun being the rat he is. And for every ton of spleen in this novel, there's an ounce of truth that makes it grimly, stinkingly good.

What breaks through Mirsky's satire is a terrible sense of people as grotesque, doomed to weakness or rage and fighting to get away from themselves, from that awful truth so gently put by Pogo: "We have met the enemy and they are us."
Josephine Hendin, *The New York Times, Sunday Book Review*

America in ruins. Minds shattered. Pigs, rats and vultures picking over the mountains of garbage in the streets of New York. A powerful political movement, dressed in black shirts controls limp minds without ever defining its stands, left or right. Madness in subways and television ... And through it all, unlikely and hazardous as it sounds, Mark Mirsky shines through his wicked laughter, blazes in his jagged, sensuous nightmare prose ...

Mirsky's writing is some dream process for both writer and reader, it is also extremely well-made, reading often like a prose poem. His flashing montages fit with one another if you take your time in the labyrinth ... Mark Mirsky is a scary new writer, capable of jolts and flights to turn both the head and the stomach. He is Swiftian in his twisted prophecy.
William Gallo, *The Rocky Mountain News*

This compelling novel about private and public madness pulls the reader into a whirlpool of insanity and a bestial vision of horror and doom ... It reads like a nightmare delivered intact.

Publisher's Weekly

Blue Hill Avenue, Bobbs-Merrill (1972)

New and Recommended in *The New York Sunday Times,* November 19, 1972

Mark Mirsky's new book is many things but it is primarily literature. To me the Jewish experience is, when it is not in a book, a closed book. Mr. Mirsky makes it universal, but first one is aware of the medium, the rich graceful strong language, the awareness of the need to make reality real through coaxing a pattern out of it. This is words magnificently employed. This is literature.

Anthony Burgess author of *Clockwork Orange*

The Secret Table, Fiction Collective (1975)

The two novellas and three stories of Mark Mirsky's *The Secret Table* are hermetic: some magical, some merely private ... what John Barth did for Greek heroes in *Chimera*, Mirsky does for Onan, makes him into a bodied person and a persona for hermetic interests. Mirsky's Onan is the heir of a lost or concealed mystic tradition. He alone of Jacob's progeny rebels against the natural circle of breeding and death. With his spilled seed and sand Onan creates an artifact that regenerates him. Onan is Onan's child, the artist created by his art. Filled out with quotations from scholarly texts, flashbacks to Cain and Noah, a slangy Leah, trickster Jacob and stupid shepherds, the novella becomes its own apocryphal text which threatens to displace the few lines in *Genesis* that are its source.

Thomas LeClair, *The New York Times, Sunday Book Review*

Origins, ancestors, and seed. These primal tokens are explored and embroidered upon by Mark Jay Mirsky in *The Secret Table*. Considered separately, the two novellas, which complete the book, are as different as New England and the Middle East. "Dorchester, Home and Garden" begins and continues in a state of modern urban siege with the hunter Maishe, stalking his childhood, hunted by a succession of anti-Semitic gangs. The spaced-out narrative is interspersed with nightmare and fantasy humor and erudition. The Dorchester homes and gardens, with their dogs and alleys and picket fences are reminiscent of *The Brothers Karmazov*, as is the brooding, introspective tone ...

"Onan's Child" is rich, absorbing, and most of all sensual ... the reader is carried along by Mirsky's passion, and by the sheer imagination with which he fleshes out the skeleton of an old, old tale. Onan's agony becomes real.

The two novellas, disparate as they are in tone and in setting are united, not only by the single theme of genesis, but also what could be a single protagonist; the Maishe in search of a past could be the Onan in search of a future ... *The Secret Table* stuns, occasionally overwhelms. But partly because of the richness of its language, it also eventually captivates and seduces.

Susan G. Carlisle, *Fiction International*

Mirsky's book is about the magical, private sources of the imagination attempting to confront a drab, frightening or mysterious world. The novellas "Dorchester, Home and Garden" and "Onan's Child" are related tales in which the Jewish experiences of fear, loss, and paranoia are transformed into vibrant sensuous language. "Onan's Child" is similar to some of the fiction of Coover and Barth in that it reinvents a mythic character and provides the modern reader with a new perspective on familiar events... . Mirsky's talent lies ... in creating a highly expressive—one is almost tempted to call it "erotic"—prose that captures the power and poetry of Jewish speech as effectively as any of the now-famous Jewish writers of the '50s and '60s ... Mirsky's sentences are themselves sensuous objects which are able to illuminate his scenes with a radiance of language.

Contemporary Literature

The Red Adam, Sun & Moon (1990)

A densely plotted, magically written novel that reminds one of how tied love, sex and mortality in fact are. Few contemporary Jewish American fictions are so thoroughly haunted by the divine, so energized by the juxtaposition of the evil and the divine, and so utterly committed to the creative act in both its reverence and its comedy.

Sanford Pinsker, *The Jewish Post and Opinion*

In a section of Mark Mirsky's *The Red Adam*, we read of a golem—Jewish mystical tradition's artificial man—created when a violent storm, blowing through the broken window of a New England study, blows hundreds of documents together from the Talmud and the Kabbalah along with a powerful dose of Jonathan Edwards, the great Puritan divine. This paper golem, its function more metaphorical than actual, is not, as it happens, the clay monster that spells havoc for a small New England town: that we read of a little later. Nevertheless, the range of quotations with which its genesis is interleaved takes the measure of Mr. Mirsky's creation ... Mr. Mirsky, transplanting Jewish legend to the New World, has indeed been mindful of the medieval formulae: he has made his golem from virgin soil, creating with *The Red Adam* a new genre—Jewish American gothic.

Saul Rosenberg, *The Jewish Forward*

Non-Fiction Reviews

My Search for the Messiah, Macmillan (1977)

Mark Mirsky's book is cut in a very modern style but the fabric out of which it is made is the *taliss*, the Jewish prayer shawl ... the book is a well-written autobiographical account of his search for his self, his

Jewish self. That personal search becomes linked with his rediscovered Jewish family" of the extended past and present and their 4,000 year quest for meaning and transcendence ... It is both fascinating and instructive to follow the author's spiritual trajectory from his childhood exposure to juvenile Judaism in a Dorchester, Massachusetts Hebrew school ("The American Hebrew school often seemed a conspiracy against it.") to his mature appreciation of the genuine liberating power and relevance of Jewish ideas and values encountered in their highest expression. Mirsky truly understands how radical a breakthrough in human consciousness have been the central biblical and rabbinic affirmations about God.

Marc H. Tanenbaum, *The Washington Post, Book World*

Rabbinic Fantasies, Jewish Publication Society (1990). Paperback, Yale University Press (1998). Edited by David Stern and Mark Jay Mirsky

A concluding essay, "In a Turn of the Scroll: An Afterword," written by Mark Jay Mirsky, reaches quite beyond the objective tone and character of the volume by including a moving personal statement of that editor's romance with the Talmudic story. The Afterword also includes an impressive insight into the *Alphabet of Ben Sira* ... [which] in itself makes the book worth reading and acquiring. Mirsky traces his growing fascination with the Talmudic story, embedded within a legal discussion, and with its qualities that inhabit "that extreme territory of speech where the irrational, the inexplicable and human emotion touch each other" ... A somewhat indefinable kinship of the Talmudic story, as well as of the later Jewish story with Kafka, is heard here ... Mirsky has voiced something felt by others who have lived with what might be described as an existential fascination with the Jewish story down the ages.

Aryeh Wineman, *Menorah Review*

Stern and Mirsky isolate sixteen stories that otherwise defy usually generic classification and are unaware of their own fictionality, claiming instead to present parts of the historical record. Their gathering here fills an important gap in our understanding of the diversity of Hebrew literary expression ... Stern's introduction and Mirsky's "afterword" on the significance of this new way of organizing old scrolls, are important texts in their own right. The book will be enjoyed by readers of rabbinic literature and it is a useful addition to syllabi on the Jewish textual tradition.

Leonard Gardner, *Religious Studies Review*

Diaries 1899-1942 by Robert Musil, Basic Books (1998). Edited and with an introduction by Mark Mirsky. Translation and Preface by Philip Payne

Los Angeles Times, "The Best Nonfiction of 1998,"

The unprecedented diversity and intellectual range of Musil's preoccupations is most nakedly evident in his *Diaries*, and their American publication is an important cultural event for which everyone involved with the project deserves our gratitude. Mark Mirsky and Philip Payne's edition of the *Diaries* can now take its place alongside the English version of Musil's major writings.

Michael Andre Bernstein, *Los Angeles Times*

Philip Payne's able translation, and Mark Mirsky's exuberant introduction, invite new readers into Musil's imaginative world. It is as if a private library has been now opened to public use and benefit.

Steven Dowden, *The Washington Post*

Dante, Eros and Kabbalah, Syracuse University Press (2003)

Mirsky on Dante is like Charles Olson on Melville. He's written a brilliant enjambment, a work of speculative, imaginative scholarship that is literature itself.

Russell Banks

A masterpiece. A long intoxicating prose-poem, a saga … It is stunning and it "is" poetry. And the language is, in every syllable, as flawless as it is intoxicating.

Cynthia Ozick

The work is altogether original, yet its author seems to belong in the company of Nabokov, Butor, Barth, Barthelme, Garcia Marquez … Some Dante scholars of the imaginative case will applaud; the most conservative ones will doubtless be shocked. But it is hardly a book to be ignored.

Albert Guerard

The Jews of Pinsk, Volume 1: 1506–1880 & Volume 2: 1881–1941, Stanford University Press,(2008, 2012). Edited by Mark Jay Mirsky and Moshe Rosman

The Jews of Pinsk is a treasury of the four-hundred year history and culture of one of Eastern Europe's most important Jewish communities. Here is everything: communal organization, economics, legal status, religion and education, geography and topography, taxation and expenditures, hospitals, synagogues, and benevolent societies as well as individual leaders and rabbis. It is also a smoothly readable book, reflecting the novelist's hand that went into the editing. The novelist's hand is also present in the unusual foreword that reflects on [a] personal connection with the town through the story of [a] father, a son of Pinsk, and [the] efforts to recover the memory of Pinsk from the few who remain to tell the tale.

Raymond Scheindlin, Professor of Medieval Hebrew Literature, Jewish Theological Seminary of America

This year [2008] saw the publication of a vital work: the English translation of Mordechai Nadav's 1973 classic of Jewish communal history, *The Jews of Pinsk: 1506–1880*. Nadav's book—a scholarly companion to Pinsk's massive 1966 Yizkor book—opens a wide window onto a remarkable place, a centuries-old citadel of rabbinical learning, Hasidic piety, Hebrew and Yiddish literature, theater, journalism, grand cantorial music, Zionism, and Jewish Socialism. It is a reminder that Pinsk deserves to be known as much more than the shopworn punch line for "Minsk and Pinsk" gags ... Nadav's book is actually one of two compendium tomes, the second of which, Azriel Shochat's even more massive *The Jews of Pinsk: 1881–1941*—is set to released in translation shortly ...

The story of the latest Pinsk scholarship begins with the editor of its English translation, Mark Mirsky, the Boston-born son of a proud Pinsker father who regaled his child with tales of the old country. In his preface, Mirsky describes the impact of discovering Pinsk's multiple Yizkor volumes: "In these books I found a lost family that was mine, its joys, its sadness, its memories."

When Mirsky shared his "discovery" of these books with Harvard University's campus rabbi, Ben Zion Gold, his friend and mentor, Gold told him: "You have a duty to perform. You must bring these books into English. They show what was lost in the Holocaust. Not one generation of Jews, but a whole world, four and a half centuries of Jewish culture torn out of the heart of Europe."

Alan Nadler, Director of Jewish Studies, Drew University

About the Author

Mark Jay Mirsky was born in Boston and grew up in the Dorchester, Mattapan, Roxbury districts, which border Franklin Park to the east, north and south. Attending Boston Public Latin, Harvard College and Stanford University, Mr. Mirsky has previously published five novels, *Thou Worm Jacob, Proceedings of the Rabble, Blue Hill Avenue, The Red Adam*, a collection of short stories called *The Secret Table*, and his latest novel, *Puddingstone*. Among his books of criticism are: *My Search for the Messiah; Dante, Eros, and Kabbalah; The Absent Shakespeare*; and *The Drama in Shakespeare's Sonnets: A Satire to Decay*. He is the coeditor of *Rabbinic Fantasies* (Jewish Publication Society, reprinted by Yale University Press) *The Jews of Pinsk, Volumes 1 & 2* (Stanford University Press), and the editor of Robert Musil's *Diaries* in English (Basic Books). He founded the journal *FICTION* in 1972 with Donald Barthelme, Jane DeLynn, and Max and Marianne Frisch and has been its editor-in-chief up to the present. A professor of English at The City College of New York, he has served as its chairperson and director of Jewish Studies. His reviews and articles on architecture and literature have appeared in *The New York Sunday Times, The Washington Post, The International Herald Tribune, The Massachusetts Review, Partisan Review, The Progressive, Haaretz*, and numerous other publications. His play *Mother Hubbard's Cupboard* was performed at the Fringe Festival in 2007 and is available at www.indietheaternow.com

An autobiographical essay published in 1999 on Mark Jay Mirsky can be found in Volume 30 of Gale's *Contemporary Authors,* and a chapter is dedicated to him in Jules Chametzky's collection *Out of*

Brownsville. Both his latest novel about a Boston lost in the 1960s, *Puddingstone, and A Mother's Steps are available in print and e-book versions.*

His articles appear on the FICTION website, www.fictioninc.com, and his blog www.markmirsky.com